Boring Records?

of related interest

Competence in Social Work Practice
A Practical Guide for Professionals
Edited by Kieran O'Hagan
ISBN 1 85302 332 9

Good Practice in Risk Assessment and Risk Management
Edited by Jacki Pritchard and Hazel Kemshall
ISBN 1 85302 338 8

Good Practice in Supervision
Statutory and Voluntary Organisations
Edited by Jacki Pritchard
ISBN 1 85302 279 9

Handbook of Theory for Practice Teachers in Social Work
Edited by Joyce Lishman
ISBN 1 85302 098 2

Communication Skills in Practice
A Practical Guide for Health Professionals
Diana Williams
ISBN 1 85302 232 2

Boring Records?
Communication, Speech and Writing in Social Work

Katie Prince

Jessica Kingsley Publishers
London and Bristol, Pennsylvania

A Mind to Murder (1984) by P.D. James quoted with the kind permission of Faber and Faber Ltd

First published in the United Kingdom in 1996 by
Jessica Kingsley Publishers Ltd
116 Pentonville Road
London N1 9JB, England
and
1900 Frost Road, Suite 101
Bristol, PA 19007, U S A

Library of Congress Cataloging in Publication Data
Prince, Katie, 1942–
Boring records : communication, speech, and writing in social work
/ Katie Prince.
p.   cm.
Includes bibliographical references and index.
ISBN 1-85302-325-6 (alk. paper)
1. Social case work reporting. 2. Confidential communications-
-Social case work. 3. Social service--Records and correspondence.
4. Communications in social work. I. Title.
HV43.P8 1996
361.3'2'014--dc20   95-41381
                                                      CIP

British Library Cataloguing in Publication Data
Prince, Katie
Boring Records: Communication, Speech and
Writing in Social Work
I. Title
361.3

ISBN 1-85302-325-6

Printed and Bound in Great Britain by
Biddles Ltd., Guildford and King's Lynn

Contents

To Julia, James and Jessica

Acknowledgements

Boring Records? grew slowly from research which was successfully submitted to the University of East London for a PhD and which was enriched by a blending of sociological ideology from that university with the psychotherapeutic approach to work with children and families at the Tavistock Clinic. Staff from both institutions have therefore contributed much to this book and I thank them for their patience, practical support, ideas and resources. I am particularly grateful to Dr Carol Satyamurti for her skilful supervision of the research and guidance in writing the book; to Professor Michael Rustin for his continuing interest in the topic as well as an apparently endless supply of theoretical frameworks; to Professor Jane Aldgate for her helpful suggestions; to Elizabeth Oliver-Bellasis, Alan Shuttleworth and Brian Truckle for insights into communication between children, carers and workers.

I am grateful to the clinic team who helped me to carry out the action style research, especially my then line manager. Colleagues, friends and family have been very patient and I am grateful to Dr Brynna Kroll and Barbara Prynn for their sympathetic support, to Angela and Michael Simmons for their friendship, encouragement and advice, and to my husband Chris for his unfailing assistance with word processing and literature. Heartfelt thanks also to my publisher Jessica Kingsley and her staff who have been consistently encouraging and positive in their suggestions.

However, much material in this book belongs to the social workers, parents and children who gave so generously of their time to explain how they felt about spoken and written communication. Special thanks are due to them for their help and interest, and in particular to Joe for his drawings of fears, Heather for her chart and Jo for her diary.

Author's Note

In the last decade people using social work services have been called 'clients', then 'customers' and latterly 'service users'. Children and their parents attending child guidance clinics have commonly been known as 'patients'. In addition to 'parents' and 'children' the word 'client' has been used throughout *Boring Records?* to denote family members who were receiving help from the clinic social worker.

For the sake only of consistency in the use of pronouns, clients and child psychiatrists have been referred to as 'he' and social workers as 'she'.

In recent years multi-agency services for children with emotional and behavioural difficulties have developed under many different titles. 'Child and Family Therapy Service', 'Child and Adolescent Psychiatric Service', and 'Child and Adolescent Consultation Service' are some examples. To prevent confusion the original term 'Child Guidance Clinic' has been used throughout the book, although I acknowledge that many teams do not now use this title.

Preface

The title *Boring Records?* should not mislead the reader into hoping that this book will give guidance about writing social work records which are easy and interesting to decipher. Little detail will be given about the format and content of different types of record and the book is not intended as an instruction manual on how to write social work records but rather as a unique and serious attempt to consider the processes which are at work when social workers, colleagues and clients talk one with the other and records made of these conversations are accumulated into agency files. During the research on which this book is based, samples of both clients and social workers involved with child and family guidance clinics were invited to share their views about the practice of keeping such files of records and to try to put into words what the activity meant to them, what they thought it was for and to consider whether greater client participation in the process would have, however indirectly, added benefit for the children. As the research interviews progressed a pattern emerged in which both clients and social workers began by saying they had little to contribute to the researcher, the topic was *boring*, record keeping was a *boring* low status, routine chore which was fitted in only when the real *non-boring* face to face work had taken place. However, once relaxed and allowing themselves to take up a unique opportunity to consider what social work records meant to them, both clients and social workers talked in a flood, with emotions of anger, fear, cynicism, confusion and anxiety expressed freely. Thus dismissing record keeping as *boring* seemed to have become the usual way of pushing all its inherent difficulties, complexities and conflicts well away from painful scrutiny and examination. Yet it is these particular conflicts and complexities which are of interest: they convey such rich information about the way clinic social workers communicate with their clients and colleagues. Social work records constitute a complex web of communicated words and meaning, first spoken, then interpreted and lastly converted into written language to be read and re-interpreted at various times, by various others. Whatever it is, this activity has enormous consequences for both workers, clients and agencies – it is not *boring*.

In the course of their careers social work practitioners will produce thousands of written reports on their work. The activity is likely to take up one fifth of their professional time. They will record accounts of interviews with parents and children, of discussions with other professionals and will prepare summaries, contact sheets, memoranda, court reports and a myriad of application forms requesting resources to assist clients. They may have some departmental guidelines about the agency's expectations as to format, content, confidentiality and access in social work records, but it is unlikely that they will have received comprehensive training about the meaning of these files of information, how they function in terms of power, surveillance, communication and negotiation. It is hoped that this book will encourage the reader to take time out from thinking about record keeping as a concrete activity (Dictate, draft by hand or word process? What kind of a report to write? Who should have copies? Is the information correct?) and allow themselves to consider what the record actually is, what it does and what it means in terms of the communication process between worker, client and agency. Keeping records is an apparently mundane, 'taken for granted' activity but the research generating this book demonstrates that we ignore its complexities only at our peril and that clients do not share the social worker's view of the purposes for which conversation is turned into files of writing.

The research focused upon social work recording activity in child and family psychiatric clinics (hereafter called child guidance clinics). Such multi-disciplinary agencies allow close scrutiny of working practice between clinic social workers, consultant child psychiatrists, therapists and psychologists as these professionals commonly share work with the same child and family. The social workers' records occupied a pivotal position in these clinics and were often the cause of much controversy and disagreement once the 1987 Access to Personal Files Act required them to be 'open' to their subjects. It quickly became apparent that the initial plan to study the effect of this 'openness' would reveal only the tip of an iceberg and that greater interest lay in interviewing samples of clinic social workers and clinic clients to gather and examine their perceptions of the social work recording task. The 'taken for granted' definition of 'record' was immediately challenged and re-drawn to include childrens' art work, diaries, charts, videos, messages, genograms and work on whiteboards and flip charts – this broader framework stimulated thinking about ownership, and inherent and contextual meaning. As mentioned above, both social workers and clients feared that they would have 'nothing to say' but the very opposite proved to be the case. Their lengthy, and often emotional, contributions were thoughtful with words chosen carefully as they tried to express 'exactly what they really meant'. The poignancy and nuances of meaning are best preserved and presented by quotation – thus much of the book allows the reader to share the interviewee's perception and belief with the minimum of editorial interference.

Chapter Three surveys the material arising from semi-structured interviews with twenty-eight clinic social workers whose perceptions about social work record keeping in child guidance clinics were tape-recorded and then fully transcribed. In general they saw the task as surrounded by many personal, professional and organisational dilemmas. The conflicting demands of their recording mirrored those of their professional role, at a time when they felt particularly under-valued by their social services departmental managers. Interesting findings were highlighted concerning the records kept during family therapy work and the problems of ownership of 'work' produced in sessions co-worked by more than one discipline. Clinic social workers seemed confused about the purpose(s) for which they recorded and further exploration of these reasons showed great inconsistency. They had much to say about jargon! In discussing the likely effects of the Access to Personal Files Act, it was clear that on the whole client access to social work records was seen as a hazardous process which relationships between clinic professionals were too fragile to bear, given the changes to practice which would be required.

Chapter Four presents the client's view. Semi-structured interviews with twenty ex-clients were designed to discover how parents saw social work records in the context of the service provided to them and their children, how much they knew, or had thought, about what was written concerning their children, who could see it, where it was stored and what it represented for all parties. Clients were often confused about the role and identity of the clinic social worker – making explicit the existence of social work records also makes it clear that the client is in contact with a social services professional, not a nurse, secretary or medical assistant. In general, parents did not share the social workers' views as to the purpose of recording: for example, a surprising number believed the social worker kept records to keep track of hereditary conditions. Parents worried that they were inarticulate, feared their communication might be misinterpreted and that as a result their child would be given inappropriate treatment. They relied upon the social worker to be a good communicator and to help them find the 'right' words. Clients considered the exchange of information was unequal: they felt disadvantaged by record keeping but regarded it as a price to be paid for help with their children. Material concerning assessment and statementing of children with special educational needs exposed issues of communication for both parents and professionals. These long interviews ended with thinking about how far parents wanted to be 'partners' with the social worker in compiling the record of their interaction; how far had they been informed about recording, access and confidentiality; would they have liked to have read the record or joined with the social worker in writing it.

The final chapters are concerned with empirically examining the process whereby conversation and communication becomes recorded. The author describes an 'action style' project which she undertook while working in a small child guidance clinic. Eighteen families were offered access and participation in the record keeping process and detailed accounts of the changed recording practice were examined. Factors which assisted or hindered participation were identified and broader themes (such as power, language, negotiation) were linked with some selected theoretical perspectives in order to suggest ways of thinking about the mass of complicated material which the project generated. Many practice related issues are illustrated by vivid case material which will be of particular interest to workers in multi-agency settings. Who is the index client/patient – parent or child? How can the confidentiality of third party information be preserved if recording is shared with clients? Where should we file the child's 'work' produced with the social worker in the clinic? How do we process sensitive information between the multi-agency clinic and other professionals and agencies, especially schools? What is the best way to reach a common understanding whilst struggling with meaning in the language used by parents, children and other agencies? Overall, despite the many practical difficulties experienced by the researcher, it proved possible to identify some positive benefits for clients who participate in recording their own case notes.

The concluding chapter draws together what has been demonstrated by the research. This task is not easy. Roughly speaking, social work recording can be described as being 'about' power, symbolic interaction, communication, meaning, and, to borrow Poster's (1990) phrase, 'the mode of information'. Many social workers and their clients viewed it primarily in terms of one or other of the above. Yet the thrust of the book is that it is, at least, about all of these things, and the significance of this multi-faceted task can only be understood if examined from a variety of theoretical perspectives. The latter are introduced in the first chapter which, of necessity, gives very sparse treatment to what are very complex philosophical and sociological ideas. Nevertheless, recognising that some of this material may be unfamiliar to social work practitioners, it seems useful to introduce these themes at the beginning of the book, to be illuminated later in reference to case material. Chapter Two reviews the (sparse) literature concerning record keeping in child care social work and describes practice and legal developments which have influenced the way these records are kept in the present contract culture of 'customer care' social services departments.

The research raises more questions than it answers. In the interviews with clinic social workers and clients, each frequently made statements which they then contradicted, saying, 'but then again, now you ask me, I also think…'. Rather than viewing this as an irritant, it is, like the huge volume of research material, evidence of the complexity of an apparently routine social work activity which is required and shaped by the local authority bureaucratic process. It is this, often contradictory, multi-faceted complexity of social work record keeping which the book seeks to draw to the attention of practitioners whose work involves written accounts of communication with 'clients'. Consideration of this topic is overdue: it is eight years since the Access to Personal

Files Act was implemented. Social work is, more and more, performed and managed by procedural dictate, and it must be of concern that 'social workers spend more and more time writing records and reports to the point where the written word may be assuming more social significance than the events described' (Davies 1991 p11).

CHAPTER ONE

Spoken and Written Language
A Theoretical Framework

The apparently unpopular, time consuming practice of social work case recording seems to have inter-related layers of significance for clients, practitioners and their colleagues. The task is perceived quite differently by writers, speakers, listeners and readers, whilst managers and medical consultants insist that recording systems meet their own purpose and strategies. It is important to consider how the task of record keeping is located within the functions, relationships and ideology of the multi-disciplinary team, and to appreciate that its meaning is different for consultant child psychiatrist, social worker and client, according to the relationship and role each adopts toward the other. Clinic social workers are evidently concerned not only about ownership of their recorded work but also about the extent to which their records adequately reflect the content and quality of their communication with clients. The status of such 'records' is extremely difficult to be sure of and can be variously described as ephemeral, incomplete, exaggerated, controlling, therapeutic, injurious, protective, important, obligatory, useful...i.e. what it actually *is* is 'in the eye of the beholder'. The purpose of this chapter is to focus upon some selected themes and theoretical ideas which, taken together, might further our ability to think in some depth about the nature of communication in case recording, what the activity means to those involved, what it stands for and how it functions as deeds, weapons, diversions and status markers.

The concept of 'negotiated order'

The research interviews with clinic social workers concentrated on putting, as it were, a particular slice of their professional activity under the microscope in terms of its legal, agency, clinical and therapeutic aspects. The 'specimen' reliably reflects issues and conflicts within the clinic team, rather in the style of litmus paper indicator testing. It seems that a mycelium of complicated negotiation underpins the working relationships of clinic personnel without which the social workers could not accommodate conflicting instructions (particularly in respect of computerisation, filing and client access). Thus there is real interest in the capacity of the recording task to act as an index of relationships, negotiation and conflict in the work of multi-agency child guidance teams. Support for such an idea is most obviously found in the work of Anselm Strauss on negotiation, applied widely to individuals, organisations and entire societies (1978), and in the concept of 'negotiated order'. The well-known work *The Hospital and its Negotiated Order* (1963) considered ways in which professional staff, lay workers and patients were 'enmeshed in a complex negotiative process in order both to accomplish their individual purposes and to work, in an established division of labour, toward clearly, as well as vaguely, phrased institutional objectives' (Strauss *et al.* 1963 p318). Strauss stresses the inter-play of professionals and non-professionals, the transactions between professionals, and the effect of external pressures upon negotiations between personnel. He suggests that if organisations possess certain characteristics (personnel trained in different occupations and traditions; some personnel mobile and working in and out of the organisation) they can appropriately be viewed in terms of a 'negotiated order'. Child guidance clinics meet these criteria and the paradigm offered by Strauss has clear relevance to the paperwork transactions negotiated by social workers, their managers and medical colleagues. The concept of 'negotiation' has to be understood meta-phorically. Strauss is not suggesting that personnel are always immersed in explicit negotiation of their relative positions as would be apparent in, for example, the making of business deals. It is rather the unexpressed, implicit mutual re-alignment of attitude, concern, performance and emotion which can be regarded *as if* it were a process of bargaining and negotiation.

The work of Anselm Strauss is located within the tradition of American sociology generally termed 'symbolic interactionism' which emphasises a focus upon the acting individual rather than upon larger social systems. Some individual contributions to this approach are usefully applied when thinking about the behaviour and communication of individual participants in the client/worker/agency triad as they 'performed' the apparently mundane task of recording social 'work'.

Symbolic interactionism as a perspective

The symbolic interactionist approach does not accept that forms of social organisation are determined by external factors (such as geography or econom-ics) but considers that the organisation of social life emerges from the processes of interaction between members of the society. Interactionist theories therefore tend to commence with a study of individual activity from which theory might arise to illuminate the relationships of individuals with social groups, organisations, institutions and wider society. Recording behaviour can be examined in this framework, the clinic clients and personnel being seen as social actors, interacting as a 'cast' upon the 'stage' of the wider child guidance clinic network.

Clients as well as social workers are consistently concerned with 'what is meant'. Both fear their communication is unclear and that in misunderstanding their situation the client/worker/colleague might 'make something else' of their interaction. How damaging might the resulting written accounts be to their reputations and what might others 'make' of these records in the future? Such concerns are well founded. Individuals who fail to understand the meanings most people attribute to objects, who cannot predict the actions of others or fail to appreciate that 'if men define situations as real, they are real in their consequences' (Thomas 1966), are considered out of touch with our society and risk being labelled as mentally ill (Thomas 1928). Acquisition of meaning is a basic element in interactionist theory and is highly relevant to the interpretation of this material. Meaning can be seen as derived from the actions of social actors towards physical and abstract objects with perceived characteristics varying between individuals, between contexts and over time. This concept of 'mutual actuality' requires researchers to be principally concerned with the way subjects view their world, objects and experiences.

Interaction depends upon the use of shared symbols: language provides one common system of shared symbols by which people indicate to each other and to the self (selves) whilst constantly observing the reactions and actions of other(s) in order to predict response and accordingly alter their own output. Such 'taking the role of the other' also involves reception of cues from non-human objects so as to check out accuracy and the need for change. This continuous and simultaneous process is neatly distilled in the definition of symbolic interactionism as an active series of social processes which involves 'the fitting together of lines of behaviour of the separate participants' (Blumer 1969 p70). The clinic social worker's predicament is interesting in the very complexity of its confusing, paradoxical, overlapping network of factors which the social worker, minute by minute, has to take into account when recording her work with different clients, for different reasons, in different situations, with varying degrees of client participation, and using different media. Blumer's work appears highly relevant to the process of mutual adjustment between client and worker in participative case recording as words are sought, offered, agreed and written.

The process of writing down interaction between social worker and clinic client is only meaningful in the context of a complex network of interaction between colleagues, agencies and elected governments. Such multiple aspects of client 'self' and worker 'self' emerge repeatedly as the context of the social work task changes in response to pressure from agency, colleagues, legislation, and the impact of the social 'self' of the client. It is useful to view the worker's changing interpretation of her role as an interactive process between her 'self' and the social context.

The clinic social worker's performance of the recording task appears to be so highly dependent upon the expectations of others that she seems to be 'acting a part'. The earlier work of Erving Goffman offers vivid models to describe such processes of interactive social life. The dramaturgical model likens social actors to actors in theatrical performances, presenting their roles (selves) in ways which successfully accord with their situation (Goffman 1961). The game model conceives of the social actor as a strategist working within a framework of rules so that social order results from the strategies adopted (Goffman 1963, Harre and Secord 1972). People (actors) are seen to be following what is 'done as a rule', i.e. operating within a defined framework of meaning. A well known example is that of conjurors displaying behaviour which in other situations would meet with incredulity (Goffman 1975). This highlights the importance of convincing performances in reaching agreement as to a framework of rules. These ritualised aspects of daily life are important clues, which, collated, give an account of the creation of social order through rule following (Goffman 1963). It is easy to relate Goffman's actors, theatres, games and rules to the 'convincing performances' given by child psychiatrists, social workers and clients upon the clinic stage, ably supported in the wings by a cast of managers, educationalists and secretaries.

Ethnomethodology and the work of Harold Garfinkel

An ethnomethodological stance is also 'interactionist' in its concern with people, language and social intercourse. However, this approach focuses upon what is usually taken for granted or ignored by other writers and involves close examination of the common sense activities by which we all interpret our social environment. The value of detailed consideration of mundane activity is explored by *Studies in Ethnomethodology* (Garfinkel 1967) in which a variety of everyday activities were studied so that their 'taken for granted' aspects emerged. This approach is helpful in considering the apparently trivial dilemmas expressed with such emotion by the clinic social workers when they were describing their efforts to communicate *exactly* what they wished to convey, both orally, and in writing. Thinking about social work recording from an ethnomethodological perspective is particularly valuable as the approach supports the idea that the 'ordinariness' of the activity is not sufficient reason to deny it close attention.

It is interesting that one of Garfinkel's best known studies, *Good Organisational Reasons for Bad Clinic Records*, is concerned with what the case recording by clinical teams really 'amounts to'. From his complex findings, two are particularly striking in the context of this book: case files can be read as either an *actuarial* record or as a record of *therapeutic contract* between the clinic and patient; and the need for written representation to 'construct the patient as a case from a mosaic of documents within a case folder' (Garfinkel 1967 pp198–203)

Further work by Garfinkel, Sacks and others on language in relation to social reality has been reviewed (e.g. Heritage 1984). Of particular note are: the concept of 'indexicality' (the sense of actions and utterances is a feature of, that is 'indexical' to, the situations in which they arise and are recognised); the description of social activity so as to make it 'account-able'; the importance of natural language (the speaker/hearer's capacity to use common sense knowledge so as to make a 'for all practical purposes' determination of the sense of the description – to 'make out' what it 'amounts to'). Close study of people in conversation led to the approach known as conversation analysis (Sacks 1974). This is based upon empirical study, second by second, of mundane conversations and gives valuable insight into the patterns, assumptions and routines governing such apparently 'ordinary' interaction as people 'speaking' to each other.

Speech, writing and text

Social workers aspire to 'effective' communication with their clients, are aware of the difficulties imposed by translation into other languages, and in general, know something of Bernstein's work on 'public' and 'formal' language (Bernstein 1959). However, both clients and workers in the research sample expressed their desire to grapple with 'effective communication' in a more comprehensive way. They were concerned with being understood, misinterpreted and with using the 'wrong' words. Clients referred to distance between hearer and speaker in terms of metaphor: 'get things across'; 'on the same wave length'; 'put matters on the table'; 'expressing the depths'; 'getting hold of the right/wrong end of the stick'. Clearly what is transacted between client and worker (whether orally or in written form) is part of a more fundamental linguistic process, needing reference to work on the nature and interpretation of language itself. Space allows only brief identification of some thinking in the field of language and linguistics which relates to communication between worker and client as conversation is converted into written record.

What does the clinic social worker understand of the statements made to her by clients, statements which she then invests with her own linguistic foibles as she creates a permanent record of their interaction? What do clients understand when they gain access to these writings? Hermeneutics, the discipline of interpretation of language, provides one theoretical frame in which to view conversations and writing in multi-agency settings, taking understanding as the central focus. The art of understanding can be portrayed as a 'hermeneutic circle'; the interplay between two people in conversation thought of as a dance, one wishing to communicate and the other to understand (Schleiermacher 1977). The distance between the two players is 'mitigated by a shared language and a common humanity; secured upon these two rocks, hermeneutics bridges the distance between partners in conversations'.

An alternative model for understanding speech situations involving a speaker, a hearer and an utterance is that of 'speech acts' (Searle 1971 p39). Speech act theory draws attention to the way language is actively 'doing things' rather than merely representing events or transactions, and such 'acts' are characteristically performed in the utterance of sounds or making of marks. For example, 'the man promised he would buy food' is an 'act' of 'promising'. Searle writes of 'illocutionary' acts which are performed with particular intentions and governed by rules. Thus speaker/writers and hearer/readers are engaged in an activity as they, for example, question, assert, predict, wish, promise. Speech acts are more meaningfully discussed in the context of research material emerging from the action-style research presented in Chapter Six.

It would be difficult to dislodge two popular images of the social worker at work: engaged in earnest conversation and writing in large files. Close attention is needed to the connection between these two activities but, in the complex field of structuralist and post-modernist thinking about language, it is particularly difficult to select, and so briefly describe, the most relevant contributions. *Course in General Linguistics* (Saussure 1916) is seminal to discussion of meaning moulded by language. Saussure saw the world as shaped by human sign systems; nature imitating language. He argued that language was only one of many codes, a network of structural relations existing at a given point in time which allowed of meaning only in accordance with its ground rules. Speech acts (la parole) are distinguished from a general system of articulated relationships from which language is derived (la langue). Language is seen as based upon a tariff of differences providing a small group of linguistic elements able to signify a vast repertoire of negotiable meanings. Saussure's framework 'requires us to view social work as a linguistically grounded enterprise. Language, not man, is at the centre of things' (Rojek, Peacock and Collins 1988 p120).

Saussure considered writing to be a secondary form of linguistic notation, dependent upon the primary reality of speech and a sense of the speaker's presence behind his words. This 'privileged status for speech' is discussed by Norris (1982) who quotes Barthes describing language and speech imitating processes of thought which 'shuttle' from one to the other:

> A language does not exist properly except in the speaking mass; one cannot handle speech except by drawing on language. But conversely, a

language is possible only starting from speech; historically speech phenomena always precede language phenomena (it is speech which makes language evolve) and genetically, a language is constituted in the individual through his learning from environmental speech. (Barthes 1967 p16)

Rousseau, in his *Essay on the Origin of Languages* (1967), also regarded writing as the supplement of spoken language, just as speech itself is at one remove from whatever it depicts (Norris 1982). Levi-Strauss considered it was possible to find the underlying codes and patterns of signifying systems which cut across cultures and nationalities. His structural, anthropological stance 'longed for' speech before writing and viewed the latter as an instrument of oppression, violence and exploitation (Levi-Strauss 1961).

The research interviews contain very interesting perceptions of clinic clients about the differences between spoken and written communication. They held widely polarised views on what 'happened' to their conversations when these were recorded in social work case notes. Rousseau viewed writing as a 'necessary evil' (Norris 1987 pp97–141) and the following two quotations from clinic clients illustrate the relevance of such literature in exploring the intrinsic qualities of writing and speaking:

'I can't explain myself very good. I get all nervous. I can say things but they come out wrong or I go back on what I've said. I can write down better than I can say it. Things are down there then, down there in words.'

'If somebody sort of sees you and writes it down and then somebody else asks you the same thing and you say it differently it all ends up written, like...wrongly. You feel...like they are looking at you as summat that they heard.'

Social workers and their clients are both concerned with how others might interpret records written about them – what others might 'see in them', 'see behind the words' or attribute to omissions. Thus it seems the controversial and complicated 'deconstructionist' approach, associated with Jacques Derrida (1977), can apply to the close reading of case records, as to other texts. In the original sense, deconstruction of the text implies a 'taking apart' in order to de-stabilise underlying intellectual foundations, but the practice is commonly regarded as one of de-coding until no further meaning can be uncovered. Derrida emphasises the importance of writing: 'Writing emerges both within the very theme of speech and within the text which strives to realise and authenticate the theme'. His famous phrase 'there is nothing outside the text' underlines this point (Norris 1982). De Man, Derrida's American counterpart, supports the value of deconstruction but considers that what the text performs, is, in the last analysis, the part of it which is 'immune from further sceptical attack'. When reading, 'we are only trying to come closer to being as rigorous a reader as the author had to be in order to write the sentence in the first place' (De Man 1979). The concept of *differance* is also associated with Derrida (1978) and suggests that the meaning of a word does not reside in the word itself but in its difference from all other words – it contains traces of the different. Derrida's approach is not universally admired and it is not easy to understand its precise application (Lennon 1992). Such ideas seem to have more in common with literary criticism than with writing and talking in child guidance clinics but the text of records is open to interpretation in the same way as contemporary literature. The latter has been subject to an important tradition in literary theory stemming from the work of Mikhail Bakhtin and a useful article (Selden 1991) describes Bakhtin's discourse of language as follows:

> Instead of seeing language as a system for picturing the world, he insisted that languages had to be considered in a social context. Every utterance is potentially the site of a struggle for meaning: every word that is launched into social space implies a dialogue and therefore a contested interpretation. Language cannot be neatly dissociated from social living: it is always contaminated, inter-leaved, opaquely coloured by layers of semantic deposits resulting from the continuing processes of human struggle and interaction. Words are therefore inevitably marked by ideological struggle: they are multi-accentual not univocal. (p98)

Such an account echoes the descriptions of clinic social worker and client struggling together to find and agree upon words which convey the meanings they intended and which, when written down, are not ambiguous, inaccurate, critical or unprofessional.

Power, social control and the philosophy of Michel Foucault

Parents and children attending child guidance clinics lack sufficient resources to solve problems of parenting and growing up, and in seeking help, enter an unequal bargaining situation where the balance of resource power favours the agency and its workers. In the last decade *empowerment* has become firmly woven into the vocabulary of the caring professions and both clients and workers appear to regard case recording as an activity which, in powerful ways, divides, labels and assesses. Evidence of concern about unequal power relationships emerges in the literature and in action research into social work recording (BASW 1986). Goffman's later work describing the stigmatising process of 'having a file' and 'being known' is as obviously relevant as his concern that 'the dossier was a too powerful influence, moulding lives' (Goffman 1968).

Such one-sided information gathering can be regarded as evidence of coercive power (Hillyard and Percy-Smith 1988). The power of language in enforcing conformity can be seen as a form of therapeutic control (Horovitz 1982) and the research interviews show the extent to which case records are also used by the agency to control and evaluate the worker – all of which serve to highlight the significance of the remark 'words, rather than force, are the major mechanisms of social control' (Entrago 1969). Practitioners need to think carefully about, and attempt to reconcile, differing concepts of stigma, coercion and therapeutic control in the context of the multi-disciplinary team, and to consider how far they influence the policies, perceptions and practice of social work record keeping. It is notable that issues surrounding the inequality of status power between medical consultant and social worker emerge repeatedly throughout the research interviews.

In recognising the complex web of power relationships surrounding the compilation and maintenance of records by one member of the client/worker/agency triad about another, the approach of Michel Foucault provides a conceptual framework to think further about the fundamental nature of the 'taken for granted', 'ordinary chore' of report writing. In *Discipline and Punish* (1975) and *Power/Knowledge* (1980) Foucault wrote persuasively not only on the concept of 'discourse' in general (see below), but also on the particular discourse governing power relationships and the 'disciplinary society'. It is this part of his work which expands and informs our thinking about what it is that the clinic social worker is in fact doing when she writes details of the lives of individuals, to be discussed by others, in order to decide their best interests. In the translation of *Discipline and Punish* the 'docile' individual is convincingly presented in relation to specific techniques of power – the so-called disciplinary technology. Foucault conceived of disciplinary power as meticulously detailed techniques, used in subtle arrangements to transform, improve and manage the 'bodies' subjected to it, so as to induce docility and order. His images of observation, surveillance, examination, confession and panopticism have particular relevance to assessment, record keeping and accountability in social work. The importance of hierarchised, continuous, functional surveillance lies in the unequal power which it bestows:

> In the form of a network of relations from top to bottom, but also to a certain extent from bottom to top and laterally…this network holds the whole together and traverses it in its entirety with effects of power that derive one from the other; supervisors perpetually supervised. (Foucault 1975 p176)

The quotation conjures up clear pictures…the clinic social worker supervising the capacities of parents attempting to control wayward adolescents; managers supervising the work of social workers, themselves scrutinised by senior managers answerable to elected members anxious to secure public credibility.

Categorisation of people is endemic in local government and has great significance for those so 'ordered, ranked or time-tabled'. (Caseload management schemes, child protection registers and statements of special educational need are but three examples.) Foucault's conception of the 'normalising judgement measuring in quantitative terms and hierarchising in terms of value, the abilities, the level, the "nature" of the individual' describes graphically the way in which children and families are 'seen' during clinical and social work assessment. Historically, the idea of the 'examination' pushed study of the individual into the field of knowledge, thereby involving a system of intense registration and documentary accumulation. (Prior to such 'birth of the case' individuality had remained below the threshold of description, for to be the subject of individual regard was seen as a privilege.)

Foucault challenges the idea that language reflects reality. He emphasises that words mean different things to different people, that contexts alter meaning and that what is 'true' and what is 'real', is in principle, indefinable. Foucault stresses the importance of descriptions of areas of knowledge, domains, discourses which are not based upon, and do not refer to, a subject. He uses the word 'genealogy' to describe this way of viewing the network of writing, speech and activity which forms a framework for specific areas of life (separate discourses).The concept of discourse, when applied to social work, raises many issues about the validity of our ideas on, for example, therapy, diagnosis, interpretation, needs, capacities and participation. It offers a compelling, if complex and sophisticated, perspective from which to view record keeping activity which both 'docile individuals' define differently: the clinic social worker as 'keeping a record of the work'; the clinic client as 'them writing a file about us'.

This chapter has briefly referred to thinking from sociological, linguistic and philosophical traditions which is relevant to an area of research found to be conceptually more complex than it might at first appear. Selected theoretical perspectives have been introduced, not primarily to elaborate, test or question the ideas themselves, but as resources to better consider the empirical material. This should extend the context in which these ideas and approaches can be shown to be relevant and illuminating, and will indicate the potential for their application to differing professional child care issues and settings.

Major insights from these perspectives are each *separately* valuable. This important point is best illustrated and expanded by reference to, say, three examples of previously quoted thinking, each of which provides a valid framework for the topic. Symbolic interactionism illuminates the 'negotiated order' of record keeping systems and is a fresh application of a perspective previously found useful in the sociology of the caring professions (as for example Satyamurti 1981). In addition, adopting an ethnomethodological stance focuses upon case recording as a topic rather than simply a resource, and by standing aside from the ordinary routines of clinic practice, reveals this mundane activity to be a fulcrum of conflict and anxiety. This method of reflection is able to follow up the meaning of these conflicts and anxieties so as to connect the micro-analysis of record keeping to larger relations of organisational and professional power. Third, a most valuable Foucauldian insight regards record keeping as a key part of the disciplinary/surveillance system; the material shows clearly that clients perceive it to be so. Using this perspective the scope of the model extends to a new 'discursive process', namely, these kinds of records. A Foucauldian might argue that language, created within societal codes and by macro-institutional practices, is a system imposed upon its members, and that open negotiated records might merely intensify and deepen the process of control. While bearing this in mind, the research is able to identify other potential for creating a new shared space in which clients make their own choices.

Much of the material contained in the later chapters can be taken as extended illustration of these complex arguments about the nature of recorded social work communication. Social work itself continues to undergo rapid change in response to cultural, economic and political change over which the profession, agency or practitioner has little control. However, it is not the pace of current change which so greatly affects the framework and relevance of this book: it is rather that the social work profession currently emphasises particular service developments (e.g. customer care, user participation) which purport to adopt and extend the same ideology as that on which access to personal records is based. The following chapter will discuss open and participative case record keeping as part of such developments and in the context of a somewhat restricted literature on recording child care social work.

CHAPTER TWO

A Context for Record Keeping in Child Care Social Work

It is interesting that against a background of society's accumulating and conflicting expectations social workers continue to compile written accounts of their involvement with clients in more or less the same way as they have done in the past. Notwithstanding a trend towards laptop computers, large files of case notes inevitably accompany a social worker and appear to represent an occupational badge akin to the medical bag or barrister's silk. Social workers portrayed in the media are inevitably surrounded by files and appear to depend heavily upon recorded case notes; they fear their loss and often cradle files possessively when in conference with other professionals. Given the value social workers appear to place upon such recorded material, and the time involved in its compilation, the lack of comprehensive text books devoted to this particular practice skill is somewhat surprising. There are a few notable exceptions (Sheffield 1920, Bristol 1936, Hamilton 1946, Timms 1972, Kagle 1990). Other social work literature concerning recording is widely spread and apart from articles devoted to the merits of a particular issue, style or purpose of recording, is usually found associated with other topics in books on social work theory and practice, or referred to in sociological studies (eg Garfinkel 1967, Satyamurti 1981, Pithouse 1987).

It is not proposed to provide a comprehensive account of the evolution of the present form of record keeping – this is well provided by Kagle in her introduction to *Social Work Records* (1990). However, it is necessary to highlight particularly significant contributions which have shaped the way past and present social workers have recorded their work.

Overview of earlier literature

From the days of the Charity Organisation Society records were kept for information but even in the 1930s Bristol and Sheffield emphasised the connection between recording and good practice. Early writers were primarily concerned with the purpose of recording. Hamilton (1946) identified four purposes (practice, administration, training and research) but also concentrated upon style, developing a case recording format which was widely adopted. Use of records for research had previously been a very contentious issue. A largely critical biography of social work recording (Timms 1972) described the proposals of the sociologist Ernest Burgess. Burgess (1928) thought that research and practice might share the same 'identity of interest' and considered that a complete process record with extensive use of clients' own words would meet the needs of both case worker and future researcher. This met with opposition, particularly from Swift (1928) who felt the ultimate purpose of a case record was treatment.

The connection between purpose and style of work was re-examined twenty years later in a multi-disciplinary context (Kogan and Brown 1954). Part of their research examined why social workers 'made contact' with case files, workers being asked twelve questions about the way they used their files. One interesting finding was that it took an average of 17 minutes to 'consult' the social work file. Eighty-four per cent of the caseworkers' contacts with the file were as preparation before seeing the client and 88 per cent of the 'indirect purpose' contacts involved dictating additional material. Kogan and Brown imply that social work records were used for direct and indirect services to clients and were not required for research, training, public relations or assessment of service priorities.

The need to adjust the format of the social work record according to agency was addressed in the medical arena (Howard 1968–9), in the residential setting (Elliott and Walton 1978) and from an educational perspective (Naidoo 1972). Naidoo presented issues which applied to the development of new record keeping systems in child care, health and education departments and argued for a central intelligence unit in each local authority. (Interestingly, a requirement of the 1989 Children Act is a multi-disciplinary register of children with disabilities, which, if interpreted to include children with developmental delay and emotional/behavioural problems, is clearly in line with Naidoo's thinking twenty years ago.)

By the middle of the 1950s the purpose of case records reflected a professional concern with diagnosis, as social work adopted the medical model of examination, diagnosis, treatment and prognosis. Such 'professionalism' required records to be read by supervisors concerned not only with the accuracy of diagnosis but with the worker's own development as a caseworker. Recording studied in two Chicago family service agencies found that records were most frequently used for the purpose of supervision (Frings, Kratovil and Dolemis 1958). The idea that writing promoted thinking was not new but in considering the record as essentially for the purpose of supervision Frings stated that 'the process of recording has real value for the producer because of the necessity to rethink and reformulate the material in his possession. The end result, once it is done, has minimal use for those producing it' (quoted BASW 1983). The 'diagnostic record' had thus shifted the focus from information to diagnosis and treatment.

Whether spoken or written, communication between social worker and client is inter-woven with issues of language and meaning. Timms' earlier work, *Language of Social Casework* (1968), begins by considering the way in which social workers commonly neglect language: their own and other people's. He asserts:

> Language does not occupy a central place in social work and social workers themselves appear indifferent to its significance. It is worth enquiring why. Two factors can be readily identified; their mistrust of language and their apparent belief that it is somehow indispensable. (p2)

The term 'special language' described language used by groups of individuals placed in special circumstances, there being a common tendency to adapt the language to the functions of a particular group (Hiller 1933). 'Public' was differentiated from 'formal' language (Bernstein 1959) and the use of special language in social work (jargon) was examined (Butler 1962, Coventry 1971). There has continued to be concern with the 'language' of social work. Attention was drawn to issues of social class and educational disadvantage within communication, with work by Horsley showing that probation officers typically used words and grammar which demanded an above average I.Q. (Davies 1981). 'Received' language, thought and ideas could be viewed as forms of power, unintentionally resulting in new forms of dependency, control and domination (Rojek, Peacock and Collins 1988). A humorous newspaper article acknowledged that social workers are poorly portrayed by the press but felt they made matters worse by 'talking in a language which is hard to pin down' (May 1991).

After 1960 interest also lay in the format of records. The presentation of information in schematic form was recommended and social workers urged to draw, with the client, a diagram of his living arrangements – the household plan (Stockbridge 1968). Case recording by code was suggested (Seaberg 1965) and the benefits of pictures and diagrams described (Bywaters 1981). The Problem Orientated Medical Record, initially formulated as an aid to medical education, organised accountability around a list of patients' problems (Weed 1968). Subsequent promoters of problem orientated recording stressed the effectiveness of this process for understanding, and communicating with, clients, especially in multi-disciplinary teams (Martens and Holmstrup 1974, Burrill 1976).

This concern with format and style of recording was exacerbated in the 1970s by the impact of computerised information technology. Content became secondary to the development of the system's ability to handle statistical and personal data. Much literature at that time was devoted to the specific information technology needs of social service departments. However, the assistance of data and word processing was, and largely remains, the preserve of staff concerned with management of information, finance, personnel and organisations (Kagle 1990). Social workers continue to write, type or dictate reported information which is then 'processed' for entry to the computer – their role in producing the record has changed very little.

Recording statutory child care work

The need for accurate client information and good recording practice has been stressed by child care reports (Seebohm 1968, Barclay 1982). Recording in the field of child abuse has been consistently criticised in enquiries into the deaths of children. Between 1974 and 1981 records kept on eight such children (Maria Colwell, John Awkland, Stephen Menhenniott, Lester Chapman, Darren Clarke, Carly Taylor, Paul Brown, Malcolm Page) were considered incomplete, inaccurate, insufficiently detailed and not read by the people involved. There was a failure to separate fact and opinion, to record precise details about the child and, in the cases of Paul Brown and Steven Menhenniott, to reduce the bulk and complexity of the file. Files held in different locations led to an incomplete picture of the case in multi-disciplinary work. In the report into the death of Maria Colwell the fourth area of concern dealt entirely with case recording: 'Inaccuracies and deficiencies in the recording of visits and telephone messages played a part in the tragedy'. The report stressed 'the importance of recording the actual dates of visits and of distinguishing between fact and impression' and 'it is very important to make clear the source of the information' and finally, 'when children are at physical risk, or in any other comparable life and death situation, the style and content of recording may well have to be more detailed and precise than in more routine work'. The report into Kimberley Carlile, *A Child in Mind* (Blom Cooper 1987), stated the lack of adequate supervision was an outstanding feature in that case. Blom Cooper made clear the necessity for the supervisor to 'go through the case notes and consider whether what has been done was absolutely the right thing to do'.

Such use of case notes for supervision has however been criticised as having inherent unreliability (Garfinkel 1974, Kadushin 1976). Kadushin compared written process records with tape recordings of the same interaction and demonstrated that workers failed to perceive and remember important events. Garfinkel wrote of clinic records being read only by personnel inside the organisation who carry assumptions about what they read – assumptions which would not be understood or shared by outsiders. Such mystification helps the worker to show that they are working in accordance with agency rules: 'the contents of clinic folders are assembled with regard to the possibility that the relationship may have to be portrayed as having been in accord with expectations of sanctionable performances by clinicians and patients' (Garfinkel 1974 p199).

Child care practitioners in the 1980s recognised the value of written 'care plans' to combat the tendency for decision making to drift, as had been so firmly indicated by the report *Social Work Decisions in Child Care* (DHSS 1985). Studies on the continuity of care for children in foster homes pointed out that written documents are an important part of good practice – by their gaps and evasions they indicate areas of poor practice (Stein, Gambrill and Wiltse 1978).

Many writers have encouraged the use of written contracts to frame the work in child care cases, especially the purpose of placement and the details of the practice of care. However the 1989 Children Act has developed the thinking about the child's 'links' with family and neighbourhood as part of a shared responsibility by significant adults to participate in the care process. One method by which this may be achieved is the 'written agreement', which will, at all stages of the care process, clarify for all parties the practical arrangements for children to remain in contact with significant people, things and activities. Use of such written agreements is a necessary part of the social worker's training, and skills and literature on this topic are developing (The Family Rights Group 1990, National Foster Care Association 1990, Rowe 1990). The value of putting emotive material into unambiguous written language is stressed, as is the need for interpreters, lack of jargon and regular review of the agreement. *Put it in Writing* (NFCA 1990) identifies six points about the purpose and content of agreements: 'sharing power, defining roles, setting boundaries, commitment, defining the problem, recognising achievement, contributing to process'. Referring to the above NFCA booklet, with respect to process, Jane Rowe (1990) states:

> The written plan is not an end in itself but a lubricant to the smooth running of a placement. It is but one part of the overall social work process of turnings, pitfalls, achievements, perils and havens along the road to rehabilitation or independence. (1990 p26)

Written agreements should also be considered from the perspective of the family and there is a need for genuine negotiation to find practical ways of demonstrating a real wish for partnership. Written agreements must not be full of 'trip wires to provide evidence in court', should be flexible, informal and bring clarity rather than 'fudge' issues (Family Rights Group 1990).

Civil liberties – freedom of information

The spirit of 'negotiation, partnership and participation' required to work successfully with parents on written agreements in the 1990s has its roots in the civil liberties movement of the 1970s, which questioned ownership of material kept on personal files and argued persuasively for clients' moral right of access to aspects of themselves as recorded on paper or otherwise (Cohen 1974). With the advent of computerised banks of personalised data came greater awareness of the role played by records in the unequal power relations between agency and client, and the responsibility to justify such exercise of power (the least restrictive alternative). 'If there is an alternative way of accomplishing the desired end without restricting liberty, then, although it may involve great expense, inconvenience etc, the society must adopt it' (Dworkin 1972 p84).

Both before and after referral the power to offer, maintain or withdraw the service rests largely with the social worker and her agency. However, the exact extent of this power, or indeed what can be expected of the social worker and her service, is not always clear to a large proportion of clients of social services departments. There are vivid descriptions of the confusion and uncertainty felt by clients about the implicit powerfulness of the social worker (Mayer and Timms 1970, Rees 1973, Sainsbury 1975, Satyamurti 1981). An accumulation of personal records must augment this power.

Whether computerised or manual, data banks threatened personal liberty and privacy and, even with safeguards, could be seen to be part of a system of social control operated by the 'coercive state' (Hillyard and Percy-Smith 1988). Categorisation of people was, and is, endemic in local authority settings and has great significance for those so 'ordered, ranked or timetabled' (Foucault 1975). Well known examples include child protection registers and caseload management schemes. Child protection registers record the names of children by category of abuse – a system which is universally accepted. Some caseload management schemes record all previous contacts made by the client with the agency so that a points score indicates how seriously requests for help should be taken. (In effect the 'totting up' procedures for interrogation of child protection registers works in the same way.) The written data kept on social work clients is frequently based upon investigation and scrutiny in the person's home where information gathering is peculiarly one-sided and may include assessments of child care and housekeeping arrangements. The inclusion of home care assistants' notes on social work files is an instance of surveillance of private lives by an agency of the state – a process summed up by Foucault:

> The examination leaves behind it a whole meticulous archive constituted in terms of bodies and days. The examination that places individuals in a field of surveillance also situates them in a network of writing; it

engages them in a whole mass of documents that capture and fix them. (Foucault 1975 p189)

It is now almost two decades since the British Association of Social Workers (BASW) considered that clients had a right of access to their records (*Clients are Fellow Citizens* 1980), and their report for the BASW case recording project group entitled *Effective and Ethical Recording* 1983 rigorously applied issues of both citizenship and ethics in developing its recommendations. The report was a best seller, needing several re-prints, 'like bread to the hungry with its blend of the philosophical and the practical' (Cypher 1984). It reappraised social work case recording at a time when issues of access by client and councillor, computerisation and confidentiality were all of great concern to workers in social services departments and to their colleagues in medical and other agencies. This document remains the most comprehensive account of the issues, values and processes in British social work record keeping. Although it could only anticipate the Data Protection Act 1984 and the Access to Personal Files Act 1987, openness, participation and partnership were its key recommendations.

Confidentiality

Confidentiality is one of the four basic principles of privacy, the other three being abridgement, access, and anonymity (Kagle 1990). In Britain, confidentiality has been seen as a requirement of professional social work activity and was repeatedly addressed by BASW (1972, 1975, 1983, 1986). It has been generally understood that clients, workers and members of other agencies must be satisfied that their confidence will be respected and that normally the information supplied will not be disclosed without their permission and that of the subject. Recognising that subject access to files would raise different but related issues, in 1988 the DHSS issued guidance (section 7 of the Local Authority Social Services Act 1970) to 'formalise long standing conventions governing the handling of this type of information and its interchange between professionals'. Detailed guidance was provided about limitations to disclosure, consent to disclosure, storage, security, and the circumstances in which the subject's consent could be dispensed with.

Confidentiality can be seen as a 'taken for granted' aspect of social work practice and the guidance was clearly necessary to address a whole sphere of concerns about confidentiality in practice. The degree of priority accorded confidentiality at the 'coal face' was questioned in a study of social workers at work in the time of transition from children's departments to local authority social services departments (Satyamurti 1981). The description of unguarded baskets of files left overnight on desks, free exchange of information between agencies, and the informality of neighbourhood grapevines must resonate within the consciences of many practitioners and with the worst suspicions of their clients.

However, in the last decade situations have continued to arise which challenge the guidance given to local authorities about disclosure of information. The problem of access to the file by non-professional, but involved, elected representatives had first emerged in 1978 when a Birmingham city councillor, Mrs Willetts, discovered during a housing sub-committee meeting that a couple being interviewed about rent arrears were acting as foster parents and that the man had a criminal record. Mrs Willetts unsuccessfully requested the case files from the social services department. It was not until 1982, with much legal wrangling, that Lord Denning gave an appeal court ruling that files should be available only to members of the social services committee. This was later over-ruled by the House of Lords who found:

> The general principle must be that a councillor is entitled, by virtue of his office, to have access to all written material in the possession of the local authority of which he is a member, provided that he has good reason for such access...there can be no challenge to that general principle. (Quoted by Harris 1984)

This decision alarmed the British Medical Association who continued to call for laws to restrict councillor access to social work files (Cohen 1989). The issue of councillor access to files arose in Rochdale in 1990 during the wardship proceedings on twenty children involved in allegations of ritual abuse. The High Court backed demands by elected members of the social services committee to see the 'council's own documents'. Mr Justice Brown ordered the release of case conference notes, case work notes, records kept by children's homes and foster parents, affidavits on behalf of the council and reports of clinical psychologists. But he denied their request to see 'every single document' connected with the case (Ogden 1992).

Access to files by accountants arose first in the USA as a result of Medicare and state funded medical assistance programmes. The examination of social workers' records by 'fiscal outsiders who pass judgement on whether the documentation indicates that the help given qualifies the agency to be paid' was chillingly described by Wilczynski (1981) who wrote 'many social workers complain that the purpose of recording has become distorted...originally intended as a professional document, recording for many seems to have become a tool for billing'.

An associated issue is now the role of social work records in claims for compensation by victims of abuse. Such records must be produced as evidence of care, or lack of care, as in the Graham Gaskin case, or to compensate victims whose abusers were their carers, as in the case of regimes such as 'pin down'. In the latter case, records which established the length of time a claimant had been exposed to the regime were missing, due either to carelessness or 'wilful losing' (Hurley 1992). As compensation under criminal injuries legislation must now be considered in child abuse cases, the social work record may increasingly be required by the legal profession to process claims.

The extent to which confidentiality of information on child protection registers can be guaranteed was considered in the High Court before Mr Justice Waite (Regina v Norfolk County Council 1989). A married man, M, had been suspected of indecently assaulting a young girl and, in placing her name on their child protection register, Norfolk County Council included the information that M was the alleged abuser. The police took no action but M's employers came to hear of the registration and he lost his job. M sought judicial review of the conference decision. Mr Justice Waite found the conduct of Norfolk C.C. 'unreasonable' but the judgement included consideration of the status of child protection registers and conferences, stating his view that 'the absolute confidentiality of a child abuse register could not be entirely guaranteed and M's previous good name was now in daily jeopardy through the risk that inquisitive minds or wagging tongues might breach the security of the register' (Herbert 1989).

Particular problems of confidentiality arise where the record applies to more than one person. Such collective records occur in work with families but also in group work, community work and residential care. In this situation the issues of confidentiality and access are closely inter-twined. The right of access by one member may breach the confidentiality of another. In the child guidance clinic setting the subject of the file is the child but the social work reflects, in the main, work with parents and other professionals. The difficulty of managing the twin demands of access and confidentiality in clinic files is explored in the action research.

Client access to personal records

The Data Protection Act 1984 'protected' the contents of council files held on computer but it was the saga of a young man called Graham Gaskin which effectively forced legislative change to allow clients access to their personal files held by local authorities. It took Mr Gaskin ten years to establish his right to see records of his childhood spent in the care of Liverpool City Council, the fight culminating in a successful application to the European Commission of Human Rights under articles 8,10 and 50. (A fuller account of the Gaskin case is given by Murray 1984 and Parsloe 1992.) When Gaskin made his original application in 1979, both the High Court and later the Court of Appeal refused it on the grounds that his interests were less important than the public interest in an efficient child care service with 'full, frank and confidential' records. Liverpool City Council, after much havering, decided that users could see file entries before March 1983 only with the consent of the writer, and at this point the DHSS (1983) issued *Circular LAC(83)14* which set out principles for subject access to records. This guidance was largely adopted in the *Social Work Order* arising under s(29)2 of the *Data Protection Act* (HMSO 1984).

The British Government finally referred the Gaskin case to the European Court of Human Rights in June 1989. This court upheld the findings of the Commission. Gaskin obtained the right, not to unrestricted retrospective access, but to an 'independent balancing of interests'. The Court held the view that an independent authority must balance the rights of the individual under Article 8 with the needs of a child care policy for confidentiality. Although a consultation document entitled *The Response to the Judgement of the European Court of Human Rights in the Graham Gaskin Case* emerged (DoH 1992), no such independent authority has ever been created (Parsloe 1992). This suggests that the responsibility lies with local authorities to balance the need of the subject for access to files written before 1983 with the need of the contributor for confidentiality. Parsloe argues that the balance is actually the needs of the subject as against the needs of an effective child care policy – and whether the public will be less likely to give information to the local authority if the promise of confidentiality to contributors is found to be broken in the interests of subjects' need for information. She suggests an independent panel should consider such requests for retrospective access and balance 'the need of the subject for access, the need of the contributor for confidentiality and the implication of the decision for child care policy'.

The research on which this book is based spanned the years immediately before and after the enactment of the Access to Personal Files Act in 1987. British social workers appeared less than enthusiastic about the challenges offered by this legislation which was frequently the subject of cynical cartoons in social work magazines. Opinion was divided about the impact which 'open' records was likely to have upon social workers' time and practice. Persuasive reference was made to Scandinavian practice where civil rights facilitated client access to personal files. In Norway, the Administrative Procedures Act 1967 (Forvaltningsloven) protects confidentiality but also lays down the procedures for giving advance notice of decisions affecting people's personal affairs, and spelling out their right of appeal (Doel 1989). Study of the 'ideal' open records system in Denmark suggested that open access to social work records was a tenable practice (Payne and Peterson 1985).

As the Act came into effect social services departments had to set up new recording systems alongside new procedures allowing clients to read their files. Authorities varied greatly in both approach and timescales as was reported by a survey of local authority response to provision of access to files (Braye, Corby and Mills 1988). It appeared that 'very few authorities have considered the implications of an access policy for social work practice – many more paid attention to their policies' implication for recording techniques'. Braye *et al.* considered the prevailing approach both bureaucratic and *ad hoc*.

Many articles appeared in social work magazines stressing the difficulties involved. There were problems with the 'optional' £10 fee for access to the file, training for staff, the need for special interpretive counselling to prevent clients being harmed by what they read, and the important exceptions whereby material on file could be withheld (Fielding 1989). The question of children's understanding of a request to read their file was raised as was the necessity for the authority to be satisfied that requests were made in the child's, not parents', interests (Dolan 1989). Client access to records was linked with client participation in case conferences (Froggatt and Shuttleworth 1984), a topic researched some years later in a study of parental participation in case conferences held in Hackney Social Services Department (Shemmings and Thoburn 1990). Recent research undertaken in Essex Social Services sought the opinions of 80 team leaders before the Act was implemented and compared them with those of 334 social workers six months after implementation (Shemmings 1991). The views of the team leaders were found to be very polarised and in general there had been no difference in staff reaction since 1987. Shemmings also comments that surprisingly few studies of recording have sought to analyse the language used by social workers.

Partnership, participation and therapy

Two pieces of research in the late 1980s concentrated upon issues of partnership within an open recording process. In one small scale study a team of Sheffield social workers made their case records available to a selected number of clients (Doel and Lawson 1986). Seven cases were identified which would avoid the complications of third party information. Notwithstanding the very small sample, the study provided considerable material and distilled a seven point programme which it was felt should underpin implementation of client access to records. Overall the study suggested that a focus on shared recording can begin to alter the kind of work done by the social worker, helping to promote a partnership between worker and client.

In May 1985 the British Association of Social Workers and Brunel Institute of Organisation and Social Studies (BASW/BIOSS) set up an action research project investigation into 'live access' case files in eight area teams. John Ovretveit was appointed to act as researcher. From the first the aim had been to improve social workers' recording skills within an increased capacity to practise social work which reflected social work values and principles in the *Code of Ethics* (BASW 1975 and amended 1986). The report on the study was concluded in 1986 and highlighted the main difficulties encountered by social workers attempting to improve their records and involve clients more fully in this part of the social work process. A particular recording format was used throughout which incorporated a contact sheet, short and longer term review forms and a 'restricted client access' section. This record keeping format was, with various modifications, subsequently adopted by most local authority social services departments. The project outlined three areas where future research was needed – training in recording, recording in residential work and 'client-centred participatory recording practice'. In this last area Ovretveit feels 'methods are needed for involving different clients in assessment and planning, and for clarifying the advantages and limits to participation, especially in child and family work' (Ovretveit 1986 p46). The need for research into training in recording was addressed in interesting collaborative work between a university social work department and a social services department, facilitating the introduction of a 'shared recording policy' (Thoburn 1988).

Practitioners may well have been sceptical of the value of sharing the task of record writing with their clients but written testimony to the benefits has appeared from time to time in social work literature. A seminal article explored the issue when open recording was adopted by the Family Service Association of Greater Boston, Massachusetts (Freed 1978). Freed described the initial scepticism and deep concern by agency staff who considered the casework relationship and therapeutic process would be harmed if records were 'rendered innocuous' to avoid law suits. Nevertheless, reading and discussing the record together gave client and worker greater mutual understanding and confidence. For the worker, more usable records required greater clarity, more meaningful words, less jargon, more focus and more precise thinking. Freed concluded that the client's right to see their casework records could be used by the social worker as a valuable tool to increase communication in the casework process.

Since 1978 specific aspects of 'open' records have been identified as particularly helpful. Client recording was felt to provide structure for the interview, continuity between sessions and to be a valid therapeutic tool in the helping process (Wilczynski 1981). Parry observed that the approach dispelled the mystique of the therapist, doubled the time normally spent on recording and saw no way to apply the technique to statutory child care cases (Parry 1985). Neville and Beak reviewed their experience in piloting the implementation of the Act. In addition to producing a staff training package, they examined the response of clients being asked to sign their records, and the role of client recording in crisis work. On the latter topic they quote Mitchell: 'I have found joint work on the actual writing of the social work record to be an invaluable means of ensuring that crisis experience is not lost and that it is put to good use in subsequent work' (Mitchell 1990 quoted by Neville and Beak 1990). A study was made of nine practitioners using client recording in a community mental health centre. Although all the staff groups felt client recording should become policy, it was interesting that social workers expressed the most positive views (Badding 1989). The phrase a 'paper dialogue' was used to support the belief that a shared written framework between worker and client managed conflict and shaped the session (Doel and Lawson 1989). A small piece of consumer research examined client reaction to the experience of sharing records with their social workers as part of the service to twelve clients of Essex Social Services department. Overall, these clients welcomed the opportunity to see their records and they liked being able to correct inaccuracies (Raymond 1989).

A small survey used questionnaires to ask about case recording practised by child care social workers in Yorkshire (Burke 1988). The method of recording assessments was examined and linked with the process of consultation, super-vision and the use of policy guidelines on recording. The study showed that social workers were recording assessments in different ways, did not always consult supervisors and often had no knowledge of agency policy about record keeping. These findings connect well with those of Pithouse (1987) who viewed social workers' written records as a 'negotiable resource within an invisible trade'. His description of records constructed as a gloss to protect workers from the scrutiny of supervisors, and the 'skilfulness' of experienced workers compiling and selecting records to confirm their own viewpoint, constitutes a powerful rationale for client participation in the process.

Some practitioners have described their experiences of sharing records with individual clients. One worker recorded in detail evidence of poor parenting observed on home visits. Subsequent sharing of this material with the mother led to greater honesty, confidence and understanding about the reality of the social worker's role and the reasons why particular items were or were not recorded (Cornwall 1990). Powerful emotions were triggered by memories held within a case file shown for the first time to a mother of three children whose own childhood history was of sexual abuse. The need to provide a warm supportive environment for showing this file had been recognised and provided by a clinical psychologist and senior social worker working closely together (Smith and Schumm 1992). The use of personalised diary keeping has been reported for people with learning difficulties – file, life planner and diary constitute a very effective record which encourages carers and workers to become involved with the resident, prevents jargon, and returns power to the users in their daily lives (Shepherd 1991).

There are many ways in which the form and language of recording affect the balance of power between client and worker. Language is more than the use of jargon – social work language tends to distance the service user from the service provider precisely because the language of case files was intended primarily for professionals. If we are really concerned to involve service users in the process of record keeping, we need to look again at the language in which we think, speak and write. In a multi-racial society the recruitment and training of interpreters must be seen as part of the relationship between staffing and service delivery. Social workers need special skills to use an interpreter in an effective way, especially in controlling their own communication in terms of quantity, complexity of thought and style of delivery, in order to help the interpreter (Baker 1989). Making available files written in the client's first language may seem a luxury, but what use is the right of access to information written in a language not one's own? And how far can transliteration convey what was meant in addition to what was translated?

The principle of participation underlies developments other than sharing the contents of case files with clients. Involving parents and older children in child protection case conferences and case reviews is now accepted as good practice. Often parents' contributions have highlighted gaps in agency communication and recording, and have thrown a different light upon information previously accepted as fact by the conference (Horton and Robson 1992).

Complaints procedures have traditionally been seen as somewhat alien to the world of personal social services but many social services departments now offer a separate complaints service for children and young people in their care. Fuller discussion of the role of complaints procedures within citizen participation and advocacy is given elsewhere (Leslie 1989, Dourado 1991, Cohen 1992).

The concepts of partnership and participation are not easy to distinguish when applied to client recording – clients reading their files may be merely exercising their right to see what has been written about them. It is possible to conceive of a 'ladder' of eight levels of citizen participation which shows that genuine sharing of power requires delegation and partnership (Arnstein 1969).

Arnstein's Typology of Levels of Participation

8 Citizen Control ⎤	
7 Delegated Power ⎬	Degrees of citizen power
6 Partnership ⎦	
5 Placation ⎤	
4 Consultation ⎬	Degrees of tokenism
3 Informing ⎦	
2 Therapy ⎤	Non-Participation
1 Manipulation ⎦	

Material described in the action research illustrates the value of this approach, when it was possible to create a 'ladder' of fourteen levels to describe the range of involvement of clients with record keeping in the child guidance agency.

The multi-agency child guidance clinic setting

The above account of social work recording refers almost entirely to case records in British agencies dedicated to providing social work. There is little in the literature which bears upon the multi-disciplinary process and its effect upon the form and content of the social work record, although the study of client recording in a mental health centre (Badding 1989), and 'good' organisational reasons for 'bad' clinic records (Garfinkel 1967 p186) have already been mentioned. Accounts of sharing records with families have been given by two multi-agency teams. Benefits were noted by Manchester's School Psychological Service when written reports in the form of a letter were sent to families (Mittler *et al.* 1986). The practice was felt to accelerate decision making, improve communication and create a framework for mutual working. Also in Manchester, at the Anson House Project, records (including video) were used with parents of handicapped children to note and reinforce progress (Flanagan 1986). Flanagan considered that three years were needed to build up sufficient confidence and effective communication before it was possible to share all the social work records.

In order to understand the differing attitudes of professional groups to record keeping within Child Guidance Clinics, it is necessary to say something about the development of the clinics themselves and, in particular, the changing role of the clinic social worker.

November 1927 marked the beginning of clinical child guidance in its own right in Britain (Burke and Miller 1929). Three major influences drove this initiative: the child study movement, the early psychologists who emphasised measurement (for example Cyril Burt), and a growing public concern for delinquent and 'feeble-minded' children. Clinics were established on an *ad hoc* basis as the so-called child guidance 'movement' responded to increased and diverse demands. Olive Sampson (1980) gives a comprehensive account of the complex origins and development of this 'movement' and details the ways in which, over several decades, medical, educational and psychiatric social work personnel built reputations, both as individuals and as clinic teams.

In 1950 child guidance services were investigated by the Underwood Committee, set up by the minister of education to 'enquire into and report upon the medical, educational and social problems relating to maladjusted children, with reference to their treatment within the education system'. *The Underwood Report* (1955) influenced the style of provision of child guidance services until 1974 when local authorities were issued with what came to be known as *The*

Joint Circular (DES/DHSS/Welsh Office 1974). This was non-mandatory guidance which allowed the development of diverse models of multi-disciplinary work with the adoption of varying therapeutic methods, levels of staffing and financial arrangements.

The powerfulness of consultant child psychiatrists led to their assuming roles as clinic directors, although the educational psychologists consistently challenged this status. Initially, child guidance social workers were trained as psychiatric social workers and were accorded high status on account of their specialist skills in working with parents. By the 1980s the clinics were under threat; new team members such as clinical psychologists and community psychiatric nurses suggested that the work with parents might be done by disciplines other than the clinic social worker whose training was by then more likely to be generic than specialist. Local authority social services departments began to view these clinic social workers as engaged upon optional, marginal tasks, peripheral to mainstream social work with children (child protection) and consequently, re-deployable. Social workers were withdrawn from several well-known clinics, as for example, Avon in 1988.

At the same time social services departments set up record keeping systems in line with the requirements of the Access to Personal Files Act and began to require clinic social workers to conform to these new systems of recording, including computer entry and access by clients. The concept of the 'clinic file' to which all disciplines had up to then contributed notes (often upon differently coloured paper) seemed incompatible with the requirements imposed on the clinic social worker by her managers. The psychiatrists feared their patients would abandon treatment if the social worker were identified as part of social services system, function and stigma. In certain clinics relationships became greatly strained by the issue of record keeping at a time when each discipline was defensive about status and continuity of employment.

This account of social work record keeping shows that themes of accountability and good practice have emerged inter-connected with an increasing emphasis upon partnership, participation and empowerment, and a growing interest in matters of language, meaning and communication which underpin these areas. These themes can be seen in parallel – the style and content of the record developing alongside differing styles of social work practice. The purpose and format of social work recording have reflected the ever changing emphases and pre-occupations of the social work profession. A powerful example is the 'process recording' used by 'caseworkers' in the 1950s and 1960s when a psychodynamically informed diagnosis was reached only in the context of the relationship between client and worker, and which required the supervisor to read a 'blow by blow' account of their interaction.

The widespread adoption of the British Association of Social Workers/ Brunel Institute of Organisation and Social Studies (BASW/BIOSS) model of recording in the late 1980s undoubtedly reflected the social work profession's growing faith in standardised procedures to manage anxiety, maintain and measure standards of service and to involve clients in decision making and service planning. However, social workers in multi-disciplinary settings do not appear to have been given specific procedural guidance about the application of the BASW/BIOSS recording system to team work undertaken with medical and educational colleagues. Social workers in child guidance clinics clearly felt confused and ambivalent about attempts to record their therapeutic work in a standardised format prescribed by their social services department managers. They had particular difficulty in accepting that 'the agency record is not to be used for training or evaluation of workers' performance or for clinical musings' (Ovretveit 1986 p78).

The research upon which this book is based was carried out during this period of great confusion and anxiety about the role of social workers in child guidance clinics. Nevertheless clinic social workers and their clients proved willing to talk at length about the way they perceived the records one made of the other and both communicated a wealth of often emotive material about the meaning which this activity held for them, their families, colleagues and supervisors.

CHAPTER THREE

The Clinic Social Worker's Perspective

Semi-structured interviews with twenty-eight social workers

Although much material was collected from these interviews about the variety of record keeping systems employed by clinic social workers, the real importance of the study lies in its attempt to understand what the recording task represents for the social worker, what the latter feels is its purpose and how far the demands made by client access appear to be consistent with social work practice in child guidance clinics. The interviews were conducted in the social worker's work place, in a semi-structured style (broadly the same topics were covered but not necessarily in the same order), tape-recorded and fully transcribed. The schedule of 'trigger' questions is given in Appendix 1. Social workers held strong assumptions about the scope of the research, often bringing files for the researcher to 'inspect', projecting their anger about clinic politics and managers' expectations onto the researcher or preferring to discuss their case work rather than case notes. Some had never considered the status of drawings, charts and models and were astonished at the implications of treating them as 'records'. On occasion it was necessary to ask a direct question to resume the focus upon record keeping, but on the whole interviewees became deeply involved in the issues of written and spoken communication. They often thanked the researcher, said they had found the time interesting and valuable: some subsequently contacted the researcher to send other thoughts, case material or to share experiences of conflict over social work recording arising in their clinics.

The interviews spanned the period 1986–1991 during which time child guidance clinics were especially prone to changes in management and staffing. The sample was widely selected from clinics in London, the Home Counties, East Anglia and the North and Midlands of England so that different patterns of clinic organisation, clinical practice and lengths of experience could be reflected. The distribution of interviews according to premises and clinical style is given in Appendix 2. The interviews were phased around the implementation of the Access to Personal Files Act so that the first eighteen took place before the end of 1988 and the last ten between 1990 and 1991, when it was hoped there might be evidence of practice changes as clinic social workers began to offer access to records as required by the new legislation. The sample of social workers presented as highly skilled, experienced personnel who were used to working autonomously and having control over their own work space, time and records. Most considered maintenance and storage of records to be their own responsibility and were fearful that 'their' records might become part of a mainstream social service department system. Details of the sample of social workers are provided by Appendix 3.

Descriptions of recording systems

The covers and contents of files

This apparently practical aspect of the task provides a fascinating snapshot of complex relationships between clinic professionals networking with other agencies. The patterns of form and ownership were extremely variable. It appeared that the arrangements for social work recording were different in each clinic precisely because each clinic valued its autonomy, and historical patterns were continued for reasons of inertia, the wishes of consultants or individual preference of social workers. The situation seemed exactly described as 'a wary truce that exists among the several occupational camps as far as mutual demands for proper record keeping are concerned' (Garfinkel 1967 pp194–5).

Where a 'clinical file' was maintained it often contained separate sections for social work, health and education material. Alternatively each discipline recorded on differently coloured papers which were filed chronologically. Where the social services department had insisted that social workers maintain a standard social services department file, reports were photocopied for the clinic file. There was considerable controversy about who should put what where on the clinical files. Handwritten 'private' notes, process records and messages were particularly prone to disagreement. It seemed incongruous that material concerning work with the parents was routinely filed according to the name of the child. A social worker quoted a poignant example of behaviourist work with a mother with learning difficulties being filed on her child's file, as if the mother were herself the client-child. In one area, although the file had two distinct sections (health and social services), it was found that the majority of the material was actually 'shared', as letters and reports about conjoint work were impossible to file in any logical way. In that clinic an initial referral form was completed for each clinic file but the social services required completion of their own referral form, making it 'totally confusing and more work for the secretaries'.

In some clinics social workers were instructed to send information about each new referral to the social services computer. This was usually unacceptable to consultants who feared that becoming clients of the social services department might cause patients to fail to attend appointments with themselves. Social workers were extremely worried about the ethical implications of computerisation. Some disobeyed their social work managers, either directly or by stealth and manipulation, acting like the mutually cheating professionals and patients in the famous study of the tuberculosis hospital ward (Roth 1962). One social worker described how he consistently delayed making up files on cases to avoid the issue of sending pro-formas to the computer. Much of his work was thus recorded in the form of preliminary notes as if the cases 'never came to anything'. There was concern that clients were not informed of their names being given to the social services department, as explained by this social worker:

> The way I have dealt with it at the moment is that I have put my ethics in a cupboard because I should be saying to people that I am a social worker employed by the borough of X but I work in the clinic…I don't tell them their names are going on computer and that's illegal now…I have fantasies that as a team we should be ringing up the legal department to find out if we are personally responsible for breaking the law.

Ownership of the stiff file cover might indicate ownership of its contents but the question 'Who owns your file covers?' often went unanswered and indicated the issue was unresolved in many clinics. A typical response was 'I really don't know…perhaps it's whoever pays the secretaries'. This social worker shared a practical dilemma:

> That's a very interesting question. We have a big tangle from the multi-disciplinary angle – the files used to be the ILEA's, so when the stock runs out we don't know what will happen…but then I don't know if sorting that out will make the file business less controversial.

Commitment to a joint agency file frequently broke down where the social services department insisted upon owning the file cover. Consultants would not then use such a format and had reservations about the levels of confidentiality involved. In more than one clinic social services had used a gap in establishment of psychiatrist or psychologist to rapidly issue new file covers and recording format for clinic social workers. The lack of consultation was deplored even more than the fact that the new file covers did not fit the filing cabinets still provided by the education authority. Levels of confidentiality were seen to vary not only between disciplines but between social workers with different training as exemplified by the worker who observed 'social services social workers stamp the material "open to client" but psychiatric social workers stamp it "confidential – not open to client".'

Such clashes of professional interest resulted in 'knee jerk' reactions rather than attempts to negotiate any kind of new order acceptable to all sides. The difficulties were real, painful and important as was illustrated in an outer London borough where neither consultants nor social services managers were prepared to negotiate over the issue of clinic clients being routinely entered upon the social services departmental computer. Consultants and clinic social workers ultimately worked with different clients, making a travesty of the aim of multi-disciplinary team work. The descriptions of clinic staff struggling, often unsuccessfully, to agree a common format for their records also illustrated the disparate power base from which the parties operated. The higher-status psychiatric social workers tended to work as autonomous therapists and found ways of assimilating the demands of both consultants and their social services managers. However, the generically trained social workers seemed to reflect the powerlessness of their clients (clients were not consulted or informed about the clinic record system). In defying their managers social workers risked disciplinary action, loss of reputation and ultimately loss of jobs. Paradoxically, if they defied the consultant, they faced loss of his willingness to share not only 'his' patients but also specialist expertise. In meetings to address these issues clinic social workers were often represented by managers with little first hand knowledge of the work of child guidance clinics, who, faced with the power of consultants, proved unable to reach meaningful compromises.

Other recorded material

A variety of material recorded the services offered to clients and their responses. Record cards, charts and diaries kept by the secretaries gave information to the team as to who had seen whom, when, where and whether clients had attended. These records, read in conjunction with records of referrals received and cases closed, were not only sources of daily information between team members, but were used by managers to evaluate the necessary level of resource provision. Clients' attendance records indicate motivation and according to one social worker 'state facts, in the light of which, the rest of the case record can be interpreted'.

Individual work with children and adolescents initially resulted in a folder, tray or box being kept separately from the file, often in the social worker's office. Social workers told children that their drawings, life maps and charts were in a special place and would be kept for them between sessions. Much of this material appeared to end up on the clinical file, raising issues of ownership which are explored in the section concerned with direct work with children.

A high degree of anxiety surrounded the use of video as a way of keeping a record of sessions with families or individuals. Social workers advanced many reasons why this was not feasible as part of their practice – too costly, too few tapes, likelihood of being stolen from their cars, storage problems. Some were highly suspicious of the medium and would agree with this social worker: 'We do have video but we don't use it. We don't feel comfortable with video, it's something for the future'. Others considered the purpose of video to be supervision, training and feedback to clients. It is interesting that no social worker mentioned video as evidential recording of work with abused children as required by the Criminal Justice Act (HMSO 1992).

The use of white boards and flip charts to mark out family relationships, links and changes was described most frequently where family therapy was the model of work. Genograms, flow charts and sociograms were used to represent generational information and boundaries, the work in progress and family connections within the community. Whereas work drawn in the session on A4 paper could be photocopied for both client and file, material on wall boards posed problems of duplication. Work on this scale as part of the session usually had a dynamic quality, clients making frequent alterations and corrections so that significant initial material was lost. Having spent hours copying such material by hand social workers had experimented with taking photographs of critical work on wall boards.

One social worker talked at length about her use of the white wall board which she felt was a most powerful tool for use with both groups and individuals. She drew diagrams, made connections with arrows, addressed issues step by step with families and ended with a list of options for future action. She offered powerful case material of her work on the wall board with a seriously ill schizophrenic girl whose access to her social work file had resulted in efforts to remember and make sense of sexual abuse in her foster home. Listing separations, painful life events and their corresponding feelings of anger and helplessness had become a 'three dimensional experience'. The social worker explained:

> The girl had spoken of these things before but to see the words coming up in black letters really tied it into her emotions – it was more powerful than saying it – the power came off the board. We had drawings, diagrams, pictures and arrows all over the board – it was an amazing experience.

For this social worker, the chance discovery of the wall board had changed the nature of much of her record keeping. She declared 'the white board is an extra arm for me. What I do on the board is the most accurate stuff I do'.

Genograms drawn on large pieces of paper were similarly shown to be very powerful in recording change within family systems. However, the medium could also induce strong feelings in the social worker as illustrated by the case of a family of four children whose weekly sessions always started with a generational genogram being pinned to the wall. The social worker explained, with obvious emotion:

> The middle boy developed melanoma and died quite quickly during the course of the sessions. After the funeral, in the next session, with the genogram on the wall as usual, it was a very stiff, jerky interview to begin with and then the mother suddenly pleaded that someone had crossed the name of her dead son off the genogram...and that was what broke the atmosphere and allowed the mourning to start. I never knew who had crossed the boy's name off...but we have always kept that genogram...it's a record for the clinic team of the poignancy of that interview...it's a sort of relic rather than a record...but it really belongs to the family as part of their information.

Social workers in family therapy teams tended to use schematic methods of recording which were incomprehensible to those outside the team. Such material focused upon content and intervention, and special summaries of assessment and future work were written in reply to the referrer and other agencies. Copies of these formulations and action plans were placed on the clinic file and constituted the record of work done. It was difficult to decide if these were social work reports, because the social worker was co-working the case in the role of family therapist and, if functioning as the 'supervisor', may have written the 'intervention' based upon work by a non-social work colleague. Managers of such clinic social workers found this extremely difficult as they were in no position to assess the functioning of their staff member *as a social worker*, the case notes being unintelligible to those not present in the session.

Resource implications of social work recording

It is remarkable that most clinic social workers said they spent the equivalent of one day per week doing paperwork (the range was 1.5–12 hours weekly). Social workers referred to 'doing it in fits and starts', 'having to discipline myself', 'setting aside a day a week', 'driving round the corner to make notes or dictate'. This one fifth of their work was regarded as a support to the 'real' work, an activity for which much self discipline was needed. The following quotation illustrates the sense that 'there was no way round it':

> About one fifth of my time...not as much as I'm supposed to, as I hate doing it so much. If I spent more than that a week I'd feel really great. If I spent a whole lot less than that I'd feel I was skiving. It is a chore – it really is. If I had a reliable memory I wouldn't do it, but as I work in a team people would come after me if I didn't record.

This response was particularly interesting in its paradox that she needed to record only because of her poor memory, yet the social work record was in some way essential to her colleagues.

Reference was often made to the impact of recording on typing facilities. Clinics varied greatly in their secretarial resources; some offered little support to social workers, priority being given to correspondence and reporting by medical and educational colleagues. In better resourced clinics verbatim reported interviews could be typed but there were many anomalies, as for example:

'I prefer it typed as my writing isn't good.'

'I get it typed as I prefer it that way but it wouldn't make much sense to anyone else.'

'In our family therapy clinic the handwritten sessions are only typed up for the students...they need them for their records.'

Scarce secretarial support was often advanced as the reason why the social worker did not use a personal dictating machine; secretaries would only copy-type from long hand. On further discussion it often emerged that the multi-sensory act of writing was difficult to give up in the interests of efficient use of time. 'I've tried to use a dictating machine, but I really can't discipline myself' and 'I'm not very good at it...too long winded' were two typical comments which suggest the need to order and discipline an endless discourse of social work material. However, one social worker did not regard recording as a chore for he had a routine of dictating in the car after each visit and felt 'It's like an analytical tool that I can reflect on...I think I've perfected it myself in such an efficient way that I just wonder how social workers do without it'. His intensive use of the dictating machine was interesting in the way he spoke to it as a person, thereby ventilating feelings between visits. He explained:

It's as if the tape machine becomes like my counsellor. You know, you get it all out and put it in the machine...that's very important for me...it really does allow you to give the feel and to illustrate with some intensity exactly what was going on.

Autonomy and influence in the pattern of recording

Most workers stated they had been free to devise any recording system which was workable in their specialist setting. They had often adopted the format used by their predecessor although one had a helpful line manager who encouraged him to try out different methods. Their comments indicated a sense of abandonment, as for example, 'I'm left to my own devices', but there were indications that they feared their autonomy was likely to be short-lived, as in such comments as 'Personally I don't think it will be too long before I get told...it's impending'. Indeed, in areas where social services were wanting actively to 'manage' the work of clinic social workers, instructions about file formats were beginning to flow and would curtail the autonomy previously enjoyed. Computerisation was strongly resisted, and where social work managers required lists of clients/cases, issues of confidentiality, identity and client access to records had to be confronted.

It was surprising that so many social workers were unclear about the operation of these issues in their area. Many confused statistics and caseload management with computerisation, and were not sure if their cases were on the social services computer or if clients knew that copies of referrals had been sent to social services offices. The following quotation illustrates such confusion. When the researcher asked if families knew information was given about them to area teams, the social worker replied:

> Yes I think they do...usually I tell them...but then that's only if there is an area worker... No no I don't think we do...do we? If you mean do we tell them a copy of the referral has been sent...well, no I don't think we do. Our stationery says we are employed by the child psychiatric service so whether they pick up from that, that we are...well, they probably don't. I've actually never thought about this you know! We do ask permission to request a school report, but this is different, these are our colleagues.

Some of the later interviewees said their social services departments had insisted upon a social work file being kept in addition to the clinic file so that social work records could be available to clients as required by legislation. One social worker described this graphically as 'client access to records trickling into the clinics'. Many examples were given of social workers ignoring or removing those parts of the complex file which they found irrelevant to their task. They resented having to complete forms which were designed for other kinds of work and, consequently, appeared to have developed a range of manipulative devices to avoid their use. There was no support for the process of both social worker and client signing the assessment and interview forms – the dynamic nature of the work meant a constant need to re-evaluate goals, and social workers did not 'appreciate having to re-write contracts throughout the work'. Clinic social workers clearly valued their autonomous styles of record keeping and intended to ignore any instructions from outside the clinic for as long as possible. However their recording was subject to influence from within the clinic and also from their own professionalism.

Many mentioned their poor memories, being concerned that delay in writing up would result in errors in the record. However if time was short, 'doing the work' was accorded greater priority: several admitted to poor spelling and more than one felt their frustration with the task centred around formal dyslexic difficulties. Although clinic social workers felt they had authority over their own notes, they appreciated the opportunity of medical confidentiality and found it convenient to place sensitive material on the medical files. Unlike non-clinic colleagues, they could choose whether to record the item at all, to record it for the medical file, or to record it on their own social work notes. This choice did not extend to cases of child protection, where everything was recorded. One social worker described her decision to record: 'It's the gravity of the case, my own level of experience and the need to keep track of themes and meaning'. There was also pressure from the team to record work done and many members of the sample talked of feeling guilty if up to date records were not available to team colleagues.

But it was also clear that in many clinics there had been long standing attempts to reach agreement about standardised recording in the clinic file. It was common for at least one member of the team to record in an idiosyncratic way which encouraged others also to have personal styles. Little progress seemed to have been made over this and, indeed, as the social services departments were then generally trying to introduce a separate, open records system in child guidance clinics, it seemed likely to fail.

A sense of uncertainty and disappointment seemed to surround recording once social services departments had introduced their requirements. This social worker explained her feelings:

> My gut reaction is to say records don't belong to me now... I suppose they must really belong to the social services...traditionally, if I go back, I used to regard my notes as thinking aloud about what was happening... I haven't thought of my notes as a record that might go to a computer. So I suppose the sense has gone out of it now which is a shame really as they were records to help me to do the work, and somehow now they have become something else...it's confusing. It worries me that it is almost a thing for its own ends...it's become a necessity for itself which is very wrong...it creates a lot of work. It's an attempt to standardise something about the service to the client...but whether it is that, I don't know.

Despite the 18 social workers keeping records in so many different ways there were many common themes: the generous time commitment; the valued autonomy; the lack of procedures or training in record keeping for clinic social workers; the threat of computerisation and standardised format; confusion over ownership of files and expectations of team members. Specialised kinds of record keeping (as for example in family therapy and on wall boards) played an important role which was not usually understood by non-clinic based managers. Records of direct work with children and young people were particularly complex and merit more thorough discussion.

Issues concerning records of direct work with children

The majority of clinic social workers described work undertaken with young people which generated pictures, charts, workbooks and models during sessions. Many had never considered these items to be records and most admitted to confusion about the status and storage of these items. Differences were often perceived between records kept on adolescents and those on younger children. The latter were seen as difficult to construct in a meaningful way and usually comprised written observations of children's play and behaviour. Adolescents were thought to be more interested in the written records made of their conversations with social workers.

There was universal agreement that material produced by children in therapeutic sessions was greatly valued by the child, themselves and the clinic team. However, social workers had great difficulty in deciding its status and purpose which perhaps explained the lack of consistent systems for keeping or disposing of these items. Many workers asked the child 'if you would like me to look after the picture until next time'. This had its problems. Children often wished to take work home, insisted upon it being pinned to the wall (as in a school) or shown to someone else. One social worker described a boy of low self image who needed to have something to show his teacher at the end of each session to make himself feel better – the social worker commented 'like myself, if I'm feeling under-valued, I tend to write things down'. One worker made it clear that work done in the session could not be taken home, but something extra could be drawn to take home. She made the child aware that drawings and diagrams were always going to be used and that the worker might write on them, sometimes with the child's help. Workers faced a continual problem of where to keep this material. Only small pictures could be pinned up in the clinic or filed on the medical file. Pinning pictures to walls meant there was nowhere for the social worker to write her comments or any interpretation. Writing the child's name on the front then identified him as a clinic client which parents might not like. Special cupboards or drawers were used for rolls of larger work: a worker described unsuccessful efforts to obtain a map chest from the planning department. One social worker gave a personal drawing book to each child in the families she worked with and now had 'stacks of these books'. Others used large sheets of paper to explain children's lives with lines, drawings and arrows which were looked at and added to each time. Again, these had to be labelled, rolled up and stored in locked drawers.

The following extract from a transcribed interview with a male social worker graphically illustrates many of these points, and shows him becoming uncomfortable as he considers the implications of his practice:

> If they do drawings I say 'do you mind if I keep them?' Usually they say It is OK, sometimes they want to take them home. I've been seeing a 13-year-old girl for a long time, she's very disturbed and draws a lot...she communicates through her drawings. She's done so many, they are all in that drawer, they are all kept. One day she asked me what I was doing with all her drawings. She seemed pleased when I showed her I'd kept them all. It's a problem what to do with them all when I close the case...I think I may have to talk about destroying them. Some I might want to keep because she is likely to have trouble in adult life...two drawings are particularly significant and could be good for teaching purposes. I might ask to keep those. But with that number of drawings I would say I'd recorded the necessary interpretations of each so they didn't need to be kept so I'd destroy those with the child's knowledge. But then...have we the right to keep the child's drawings? We don't know what the parents think about this either, as the children are seen on their own and they don't actually know what the child does. It's raising something in my mind...I haven't thought of all this...it's an unusual reaction for me.

This worker emphasised the difficulty that the child is the client but 'permission' for him to attend and participate in the sessions is given by parents. Parents may also decide what happens to recorded material if it is 'made' by the child. Some parents may genuinely like to receive their child's work as a 'gift' from him, or as evidence that he 'does something' in the sessions, or, if he is artistically gifted, in case his work may be saleable in the future. (Art therapists are aware of hospitalised patients selling their paintings.) Other parents were said to insist that material stayed in the clinic, regarding it as the worker's responsibility. Another worker felt the issues were 'easier for psychotherapists because there is always a lot of destroying going on in therapy'. He kept children's work in a locker but encouraged them to destroy any they wished, especially at the end of the last session, and explained:

> Just recently one of my children tore up everything he had done over four years except the last picture of himself which I put in the file. He is a very good artist. Should this picture stay there...it could be an important diagnostic item...I've never thought about children's work actually...it's a very interesting topic.

Some social workers fulfilled their own needs by retaining work by children which they regarded as significant or theoretically interesting. The research suggests that on the whole it was social workers who decided the relevance of

pictorial items and destroyed accordingly. One social worker, unsure whether
to regard books of pictures as records, admitted to retaining drawings for her
own needs:

> If I'm seeing small children and I'm having supervision on it, I try to
> hang onto the material for that and it's sometimes become quite a battle
> if the child wants to take it home. I've felt very uncomfortable about that,
> feeling I've got to hang onto it because that's what you do in
> psychotherapy.

Her next suggestion that the clinic constituted a space and 'container' for
children's work which would be contaminated if it went home, might be
considered an attempt to rationalise this conflict.

In sessions with the clinic social worker young people produce a special
kind of record which raises complex questions about the purpose and nature
of this material. Are the drawings, charts and life maps done because it is
beneficial for the child to do that activity at that time? Or are they a record of
progress, an indicator of change as the work proceeds? Or are they essentially
for the therapist to interpret in his search for meaning, to discover what has
happened to the child and to find suggestions for ways forward? Can they be
used as evidence in building a case that abuse has, or has not, been suffered?
Does the material belong primarily to the child and should he be allowed to
destroy this account of work done despite the wish of his worker to preserve
it? The research material indicates that neither social workers nor managers had
considered these issues in any depth.

In using the child's representations on paper, clay or sand, workers were
trying to understand pressures, tensions and growth within his 'inner world',
a concept attributed to Winnicott, Klein and Freud. Social workers stressed
their reluctance to make more than tentative interpretations as to the 'things
meant' by children's drawings and paintings. Whatever the material 'says'
(perhaps more transparently than in spoken words); it also 'does' something
else, that is, it stands for work done with the child and thus represents the
degree to which child patients are admitted to, and maintained in, psychiatric
careers. (Paintings which indicated no disorder of the inner world were returned
to the child or disposed of, whereas those judged to show some significant
pathology were preserved in case of re-referral.) It is possible to view such
clinical material in two ways: as a kind of language, offering workers a
privileged communication with the child's inner world – a view which is
consistent with deconstructionist attempts to take the material apart in search
of its meaning; and as ends in themselves, where the artwork represents only
the activity of child, worker and agency at that particular moment. It should
not be inferred that these two views are necessarily exclusive. For example,
children produce 'acts of creation' (Dubowski 1990) without linguistic skills,

and such marks, if repeated, may hold special meaning for the child. Dubowski explains that such non-representative configuration may be a form of 'action representation', or be produced by rhythmic movements of the hands, or correspond to posture, or include enclosures or circles suggesting the child is exploring concepts of inside and outside; or colour, rhythm and tone be used to express feelings and mood.

The purpose of records kept by child guidance social workers

Near the end of each interview social workers were asked to rank each of 12 purposes as very important, important, not important or inappropriate for social work record keeping in their clinics. Most clearly found this task difficult and consistently required the researcher to provide information and discussion about the uses of records with which they were unfamiliar. One social worker refused to complete the chart and another, saying she 'couldn't think about it', copied the ratings given by her colleague. This task unleashed fascinating items of case material amalgamated with cynical and critical 'musings' which showed the sample's daily experience and practice preoccupations connecting with reasons for which they kept records of their work. The material frequently depicts workers feeling marginalised, disconnected from the practice of *real* social workers, and mourning losses of form and detail allowed before the advent of 'open' records. One interviewee, frustrated with her lost identity, stated 'people tend not to think of us as social workers really. I can tell them my salary is paid by social services and they will still make anti-social worker jokes!'. Feelings of powerlessness and depression recur and evidently relate to confusion about the clinic social worker's role at the time the research was carried out.

It was surprising that so few social workers deemed case records inappropriately used for many of the purposes and were so uncertain about service planning, worker evaluation, financial control and research as valid uses for their records. There were some widespread differences of opinion, for example, in the use of case records for research, 15 workers felt their records were important for research whereas 11 rated research as an inappropriate purpose. Representative comments included: 'that's a real crooked deal to use case records for research', 'research is debatable' and 'researchers could use our files – it might be important'. There was wide agreement that 'fiscal control' was inappropriate but even so, five social workers felt their records could be used for financial control. The sample, in the main, placed a high value upon the use of recording in teaching social work students on placement, many commenting that the combination of video and process record provided the best assessment of students' work.

The scorings were collated for each purpose (see Appendix 4) and those accorded to very important and important were added together and arranged in rank order as shown in Table 3.1

**Table 3.1 Importance of purposes for which clinic
social workers kept records: ranked scores**

Rank	Purpose	Score
1–2	Continuity of casework	26
	Information	26
3	Support worker's own practice	24
4–7	Evaluate agency's work	20
	Legal record	20
	Staff supervision	20
	Teaching students	20
8	Evaluate the worker	18
9	Agency planning	17
10	Worker self justification	16
11	Research	15
12	Financial control	5

It can thus be seen, for example, that of the 26 committed participants, all considered information and continuity of casework to be either important or very important purposes for their case recording. In contrast (as discussed above) there was a particularly striking divergence of view as to the importance of research as a purpose of case recording.

Copious material also emerged during other parts of the semi-structured interviews which did not support data from the purpose charts. It therefore seemed that social workers viewed the purpose of their recording in contradictory and inconsistent ways. They gave the ranked data based on their opinion of what it was 'for', but when talking about the frustrations and meaning of recording within their practice many inconsistencies were evident. Perhaps the best way to illustrate and discuss this phenomenon is to examine more closely some material concerning just three of the purposes in the middle of the ranking – staff supervision, worker evaluation and worker self justification.

Staff supervision

When asked to rate purposes of recording 20 out of 26 clinic social workers scored supervision as an important purpose. During the interviews, however, it was difficult to find any clinic social workers who said their records played a major part in supervision of their work. Most said their supervisors never read case files unless 'something went drastically wrong' or 'I send the file off to be initialled for closure'. Supervision was invariably based upon discussion and the sample of social workers clearly wanted it that way. 'I pick out the cases that are worrying me and then I discuss them with her'. 'We tell them, they don't read the files'. 'Records are not good at reflecting my thinking'. It was suggested that new client access recording systems show only 'that a record has been made' and contains no thinking on which to base supervision. 'The sessions are verbal – I take notes and hide them.' Levels of emotion were high as for example: 'You can see the anger seething in me about it...the chagrin really. It makes me feel like the new girl of the lot'.

Supervision of these experienced specialist social workers clearly posed problems for their employing organisations. Senior personnel in the education departments knew little of social work, and being ill equipped to supervise this work, continued to allow their psychiatric social workers to function as autonomous professionals who provided statistical data at regular intervals to account for their time and resources. But multi-disciplinary social workers employed by social services departments fared little better, as the line managers appointed to supervise them frequently had little understanding of the specialist nature of their work. Such 'supervision' then took the form of discussion about workloads, clinic politics and management of cases with a child protection component. Social workers regarded such sessions as 'contact with my manager' rather than real supervision. It was interesting that most clinic social workers had arranged for work supervision within the clinic system in ways which they found of great personal value. It was common for psychotherapeutically trained social workers to have arranged supervision with other psychotherapists but three other social workers also described their commitment to supervision with the clinic psychotherapist. Group supervision or presentation of cases at a therapy group led by a psychotherapist were other ways of discussing cases so as to advance understanding and personal learning.

Working in the style of family therapy involved a different concept of supervision resulting in social workers feeling further 'supervision' to be unnecessary. Live supervision, video or co-working meant their work was always 'on view', available to constant scrutiny and comment. In one such mode, one worker (or team) is designated the *supervisor* who records the session, noting significant interactions or changes, often diagrammatically. In the conventional sense, the record of the session (called the intervention) is not made by the *leader* (practitioner) but by the *supervisor*. Records of such social workers' practice are thus not used for supervision by line managers when the former function as family therapists. One experienced social worker/family therapist summarised the complexity of these 'supervisors perpetually supervised' (Foucault 1975) in this way: 'It's two things...factual notes about the family, and then the things I'd be using for supervising the therapist. So it's a record of how we were actually functioning as a pair within that part of the therapy'.

Evaluation of the worker

Eighteen out of twenty-six social workers rated their case records important for evaluation of their functioning as professional social workers and local government employees. Yet, with the exception of one who 'felt proud of his records', copious material suggests the sample felt strongly that the standard of their work could not be judged from case recording. The question 'How does your agency evaluate your work?' provoked confused, angry and cynical remarks such as:

> Even after all these years I don't know how he evaluates what I do. It's all so minimal. I've got no idea how they do evaluate me. I am not being sour...but quite honestly I don't know what level of importance is given to child guidance social work.

> I must be being evaluated all the time but it's not explicit. My line manager doesn't read people's records because that's the way she has always worked. So if she doesn't read them she can't evaluate me from them. I don't know how she evaluates me...perhaps from the absence of 'cock-ups' or something. In a small place like this you get a feel about how other people are working. Perhaps it's all extremely subtle...that work keeps coming in and schools keep asking me to take on new children shows I'm doing OK.

Workers referred to evaluation by team colleagues, other professionals, satisfied clients, general lack of complaints, and during co-working where 'there is always someone to report back on you'. In family therapy clinics the considerable observation and feedback by workers' colleagues was largely responsible for building reputation. The tendency to 'assemble the contents of clinic folders...in accord with expectations of sanctionable performances' (Garfinkel 1974) was often given as a reason why records were not used to evaluate workers. Three social workers expressed this forcibly.

> I don't think the record gives an indication of the quality of the work...you can write a beautiful record with all your technical jargon where someone reading it might feel she has really seen all the ins and outs...but the client may have felt no warmth or support...so how the

client feels is missing. So the intangibles are also the unwritable-downs, aren't they?

The process of summarising and the hesitancy to write down interpretation take the feel out. We are all human and because records are selective you tend to record in a way that implies a more coherent interview than probably actually took place. It's just the process of summarising within the mind. It's the condensed paragraph not giving the flavour of the novel.

I think what you evaluate at that point is someone's writing. How someone writes about cases is actually different from what they do...but it's the agency's right to judge standards of work from records.

One experienced senior social worker mentioned appraisal:

More of that sort of management notion. Before, it was more important to have a high standard of work...somehow it felt different...there is now more accountability to time and resources. The senior role has changed, we didn't see ourselves in this authoritative hierarchy...we were much more senior practitioners.

This changing 'culture' was universally resented and resisted by members of the sample. They considered only members of child guidance teams were in a position to evaluate their own practice – a dilemma explained by this male worker:

My records do not reflect the standard of my work and are not used for this. I am not evaluated – one of the real problems is, who can evaluate me? The only one I could trust to evaluate my work is the psychotherapist. Who could see if I am using the counter-transference?

Two social workers in a hospital based clinic expressed their frustration that 'as the powers that be do not read the files, they have no idea if we are being successful or not'. They felt angry that only case conferencing brought their work into an arena where it was open to evaluation by managers and stressed 'we don't want glory but we do want acknowledgement for hard work. Getting across the complexity of what we do is difficult – it's not just pushing papers about'. Many of the sample felt continuous assessment by colleagues had replaced records as tools to evaluate work, which contrasted with their peers in social services teams. This worker stated records played no part in the evaluation of his work and explained that 'in the district team it's the complete opposite...only through the files – no one ever saw you doing anything and the files were used to talk about what you said and did, how you said it, what they replied and what you thought about it'.

Self justification

Self justification was referred to throughout the interviews, sometimes hesitantly, sometimes with emotion and sometimes in the context of keeping records for legal purposes. Social workers referred to 'covering their backs' – a phrase carrying connotations of violence to one who is vulnerable and unsuspecting. This social worker spoke of the agency's ability to 'discipline' social work staff:

> You haven't got a separate purpose on this chart which would be to 'get' people, just to 'get' them, to show that they haven't recorded properly, to discipline them. It might not have been the intention to find fault but it becomes the end result...criticisms are based on the one record. I feel all these purposes are important but that doesn't mean I think they are good...they have a negative significance which can be misused.

If social workers felt relationships with their clients had become more open and trusting, the material suggests this was not so in relation to their managers. They appeared more defensive about managerial than client reaction to the contents of their records, as for example:

> My own priorities have not changed but I have to change my reports because management works differently now – self justification is more important now than when I first started in social work. Then it was the client–social worker relationship which was all important. If it worked for the client, that in itself was enough...now it has to be on paper and justified as well. I'm being forced to think in terms of self justification.

This particular PSW had been unaware that her reports could be used in court as part of legal process and had found that 'in recent cases my reports have been used in detail, nearly verbatim. I was a bit bewildered – the affidavit was pages long'.

As with evaluation, some social workers suggested there was less need in the child guidance setting to use recording to justify their work than in the area teams. For example, 'legal record is very important in the area; my career, my future and my reputation depended upon my files'. Others felt under less pressure to justify themselves in records. 'Oh no, not now...but I did historically.' It was often suggested that with experience there was a shift from defensive practice to trust, and that students were under particular pressure to justify their actions in writing.

One member of a family therapy clinic described the many arguments in his clinic as to whether records were needed at all. The psychiatrist wanted to banish all records and supported Wilfred Bion's view that note taking soon after the session had no more validity than an account written months or years later.[1] However, social workers in that clinic felt the need to produce recorded justification of their work for managers who were described as 'not sensitive or open minded'.

Material from the semi-structured interviews suggested that almost all the sample believed their recording protected them from criticism, justified their decisions and provided proof of their intervention and professionalism. (Yet on the charts, only 16 scored self justification as an important purpose for record keeping.) These three purposes provoked cynical reactions and it was clear that for many the topic was uncomfortable. One social worker produced an article about 'filing families' which discussed the practice of 'stacking' unallocated referrals. He commented 'the irony is, files now assume a great value; the family can have a file but not a service'. Such bureaucracy conjures images of free floating records, unattached to either subject or service and re-shuffled periodically like packs of cards by workers trying to discover their meaning through risk assessment in a vacuum.

It is not easy to explain why so many social workers thought their records important for supervision and evaluation of their own work when quite obviously they experienced supervision based upon discussion, observation by colleagues and input from other disciplines, particularly psychotherapists. Similarly, why did ten clinic social workers deny the importance of records as a means of self justification? One tentative explanation might be that scoring the charts evoked questions of a 'formal' purpose for recording by social workers in general, whereas in discussion of their work, they may have been describing the felt purpose of case recording within the multi-disciplinary politics of their clinics. All interviewees scored continuity of casework and information as the most important purposes for recording. Yet during the interview most asserted, often sheepishly, that they recorded for themselves, for their own use, to support their own practice. It is almost as if social workers

---

1   Wilfred Bion experimented with note taking, becoming interested in the fact that 'in the days when I used to write elaborate notes on my sessions with patients, I found I was no more successful when the interval between writing and reading was relatively short than I do now when the interval is measured in years'.

   Finally he abandoned note taking altogether, one reason being 'my growing awareness that the most evocative notes were those in which I came nearest to a representation of a sensory image; say an event visually recalled. The evocation was not of the past but of interpretations wise after the event. In short the value of the notes lay not in their supposed formulation of a record of the past but in their formulation of a sensory image evocative of the future. The notes did not make it possible to remain conscious of the past but to evoke expectations in the future...' (From *Second Thoughts* 1967 pp123–124)

felt ashamed of such 'selfishness' and scored the chart so as to give the most important purposes as benefiting agency, clients and colleagues.

Issues of communication and language

Throughout the research material an emphasis emerges upon the importance of precisely chosen words. Clinic social workers spoke of a fear of 'getting it wrong', a concern that others attribute different meanings to words said or written, the difficulty in sharing concepts which do not translate easily or satisfactorily into language ordinarily used by clients, and a fear that essential meaning may be lost in attempts to translate or explain. The sample provided material which focuses upon language used in a social context (sociolinguistics as defined by Giglioli 1990 pp7–17) with the social worker's wish to communicate, understand and record ethically as central themes. Modern linguistic philosophers consider it valid to explore complex problems by adopting a focus upon language used to frame the issues – a trend known as the 'linguistic turn', associated particularly with Bergmann (1967).[2] A more comprehensive concern with language in social work seems to reflect this 'turn', and clinic social workers' views about communication which may become part of a written record constitute an important practical contribution to this genre of work.

Vocabulary and culture

The sample appeared to have worked mainly with clients whose first language was English, and were principally concerned about the effect of culture and class upon effective understanding. One social worker described it as a difficult balance between pedantry, clarity, simplicity and condescension. Accent and colloquialism were seen as important, with workers being aware that 'sounding posh' was part of the culture gap associated with the car and bag with which they tended to arrive. Many examples were given of workers who, failing to adjust their language, were seen by clients and colleagues alike as insensitive

---

2   In *The Linguistic Turn* Richard Rorty, in his introduction entitled 'Metaphilosophical Difficulties of Linguistic Philosophy', attributes the term 'linguistic turn' to Gustav Bergmann. Rorty explains that where philosophers have in the past argued with each other about solutions to problems, advancing different propositions, ideas and arguments, linguistic philosophers now argue about the meaning of the words to be used to frame previous arguments, and in so doing, 'short cut' previous methods. Linguistic philosophy takes the view that philosophical problems may be solved or dissolved by reforming language or by understanding more about the language we presently use. Bergmann argues to replace traditional methods of philosophical work by linguistic work and is quoted thus by Rorty: 'All linguistic philosophers talk about the world by means of talking about a suitable language. This is the "linguistic turn" – the fundamental gambit as to method on which ordinary and ideal language philosophers agree. Equally fundamentally they disagree on what is, in this sense, a language, and what makes it suitable.' (Rorty 1967 pp8–9)

and lacking insight. One conference chairperson was described 'asking a client of quite low ability if she would like to explore issues with respect to her siblings'. The client replied 'Oh yes', while gazing at the clinic social worker to check that she had given the right response, which in this case she certainly had not. A Scottish worker was quoted as asking a family if they had 'done a flit', and remained unaware of their anger at his suggestion that they had left without paying rent. Many workers spoke of the need to constantly check out their perceptions, not to rush, to recognise their own prejudices, not to patronise (particularly children), and to show empathy in trying to match the words used by clients. One social worker explained why and how she did this:

> I don't know what my language is like...I'm highly educated – I use complex words and phrases and families would often struggle with those. I'm very interested in things like metaphor and I think it can be nice if you hook into the way a family describes things – to use their style and their language. It's not a conscious decision, it seems appropriate to do it.

Differing levels of language skill among members of the same family was seen as a problem for which there was no ready solution, especially in family therapy.

Only one or two social workers spoke about interpreters for work with clients who did not speak English. There was concern that the agenda of the interpreter might bias translation and thus skew the communication. Interestingly, no one mentioned the use of sign language or makaton for communication with deaf clients.

Representing complicated ideas in simple language is seen as the essential skill, irrespective of medium (speech or writing). It was necessary to recognise the point at which it was impossible to communicate the issue without use of complex or special language (jargon). The sample had much to say about jargon.

Special language (jargon)

Clinic social workers presented jargon as a 'bad thing' to be avoided in order not to disadvantage further the client and, in the main felt that more experienced workers used less jargon but that specialised language used with colleagues in the clinic was an acceptable 'shorthand'. However, although jargon was supposed to simplify or speed up the communication between professionals, it was clear that social workers did not trust each other's usage or understanding of jargon. When reading reports they were critical and suspicious of assessments which contained special language. But without jargon one social worker felt 'my case recording does not sound professional at all – it sounds just like me'. *Just like me* is akin to the concepts of the *I* and *Me* associated with George Herbert Mead (Fisher and Strauss 1979) – aspects of the *self* referred to in Chapter One.

In the absence of specialist professional language the social worker's perception of her interaction with clients was that of the 'ordinary' aspect of her *self.* It seems as if this social worker was ambivalent about 'professionalism' – should she offer the 'real me' to her client, and under what circumstances?

Social workers admitted to expending much energy struggling with words to 'give the right message' to clients. Yet when asked about jargon their responses were invariably similar to the following:

> Jargon? Never use it…it's a long tradition here not to use it…even the psychiatrists…we don't say paranoia when we mean feelings of persecution. That was one of the things I liked about child guidance when I first came into it, that there was no jargon. But I might say something in jargon to a colleague.

> Jargon? I try not to really. When I was at the Tavistock Clinic I used a lot of jargon as I thought it was required of me. It's a stage you go through.

Most social workers could give an example of thinking in specialised language which they then made a conscious decision to say and write in what they perceived to be ordinary language. It is interesting that they spoke as if they categorised words used with clients as 'jargon' or 'non-jargon', as if there were an essential concrete difference. Are there, perhaps, particular words which clinic social workers regard as jargon, or is the category fluid, according to the vocabulary of the client? For example, a nurse who brings her child for advice about bed wetting is likely to have the word 'enuresis' in her ordinary vocabulary. Efforts to substitute a non-jargon word were not always successful – using the material above, was 'feelings of persecution' non-jargon compared to the jargon 'paranoia'?

A social worker offers this thinking about jargon:

> If I want to impress someone I use bigger words, not very well, I'm not into big words, I don't like jargon. Reports have a lot of jargon. Social workers have their own language, don't they…it's there isn't it…the words I'm comfortable with and use a lot might be thought jargon. Because of the experience they have got people talk differently to different people, it's empathy, trying to match the words people use…we have difficulty matching where the other person is. Children are difficult to gauge. It's easy to be patronising to children…most of the time they won't tell you if they didn't understand you. And when two of you are talking to the person or family it's harder; you might be influenced by the language level of the other worker rather than by the client. I hope my colleagues would tell me if I was being patronising to a family.

In trying to avoid whatever it was that they perceived as jargon, clinic social workers had personal strategies when speaking and writing with clients.

Frequent practices were to: use language that would 'fit' an eight year old; stick to the facts; watch the faces of the clients to 'see if there was too much jargon'; create an atmosphere in which clients could ask for clarification; use clients' own words; spend time agreeing on meanings of words.

However, the references to jargon in this research material are essentially pejorative, showing its effect as minimising and detracting from the value of the interaction between social worker and client. But in reality professionals do use jargon, whilst hiding the 'me' behind accent, vocabulary and clothing. It is important to ask not only what jargon is, but also what it is doing within the interactive process. The material quoted above shows jargon not only increasing professional powerfulness but also having the potential to assert equality between social worker and clients who have access to records. Whatever their approach, jargon represented a currency of power relations which was experienced by social workers as both regrettable and inevitable.

The client's own words

It was recognised that in describing the intimacies of the lives and backgrounds of their clients, the clinic social worker's 'posh' vocabulary often failed to give an adequate account. The client's own words were then valued and preserved verbatim in the case record. This experienced psychiatric social worker (PSW) explained:

> People can describe their families, homes and childhoods and I couldn't write it any better because it sums up in two or three words exactly how they thought or felt. So I use those expressions in inverted commas so others know that it isn't my words…sometimes I find people will talk about their home in a certain way, or their parent's home, and the reflection in those words of how they see their childhood, how they were brought up, how they see their parents can be summed up in just those few words. And how a parent often sees their child at a particular time and emphasises over-indulgence or rejection far better than I could in my vocabulary.

Listening carefully, remembering and recording clients' own words were seen as useful tools in building relationships, as this worker says 'people are surprised to be really listened to…if you can quote their own words back to them it shows that you have been paying careful attention'. Family therapists made particularly careful use of clients' words in that they looked back on the reported speech, finding patterns and changes to reflect back to families in the future. This was felt to be a powerful way of influencing change.

Social workers frequently struggled to understand the terminology clients used, or the meaning which they were intending to convey. Clarification often involved a matter of degree, as for example, how much 'taking things' is 'stealing'?; how many 'accidents' is 'wetting'?; when is 'skid marks' 'retention with overflow'? Establishing a common terminology might take some time and noting clients' own words was seen to be important. There were, however, many graphic examples of ambiguity where it was important to record clients' words and hope the intended meaning would emerge in the future. As for example:

> The teenage girl talked about how her father 'held her'. I couldn't tell if she was describing him embracing her or hitting her, so I wrote down her words as I didn't know what she meant. It was something like he fell onto her – it was ambiguous. She was able to repeat it. I knew it was important but I didn't know what it meant.

In writing down clients' own words, social workers clearly made efforts to explain that they were trying to understand the meaning of the communication. One social worker told his clients 'I am trying to understand what you are really feeling. I don't want to be left with a picture of your life which is inaccurate. So I shall write down your own words, and keep them'.

Distortion

In discussing aspects of distortion, social workers often gave refined detail of the process of converting conversation to written records. They had an interest in brevity and conciseness, especially if required to use the British Association of Social Workers/Brunel Institute of Organisation and Social Studies (BASW/BIOSS) format, which they felt 'filtered information at the expense of flavour'. Such economy was itself a form of distortion. In being aware of their own set, they endeavoured to 'record like a verbal camera'. Other workers stressed they were themselves only 'instruments to help people'. Such mechanistic approaches seemed to be attempts to prevent distortion due to personal priorities and emphases, and to deal with feelings that a degree of distortion was inevitable as records were solely 'their perception of what they were hearing'.

The nature of child guidance work was described by one clinic social worker as 'strange' – it reflected peculiar personal situations which required different patterns of thinking to help people become 'unstuck'. Records made of these unusual thought processes would inevitably appear 'odd' to an outsider and it was important not to confuse this 'oddness' with distortion. Another social worker described his concern that 'naming things' for the record pushed the writer into making assumptions. He gave an example of writing 'red in the face' which might imply anger whereas if one wrote 'she blushed' the implication would be embarrassment.

Members of the sample identified six particular strategies which they used to avoid biased recording:

- Write in good faith but be aware of one's own mood, pre-occupations and prejudices.

- Jot down key words during conversation and use them to avoid the record having a different emphasis.

- Do not record uncertainties.

- Be aware that summary may skew the truth by omission.

- Be aware that perceived bias of other professionals distorts recording.

- Routinely remove records found to be inaccurate.

It is interesting that only one or two workers mentioned involvement of clients in checking the record for error and bias. Perhaps because social workers saw records as primarily for their own benefit, they regarded reduction of distortion as their own responsibility. In buttressing their powerful position PSWs, in particular, seemed reluctant to hand over power associated with correcting 'their' record.

Speech versus writing

Social workers appeared preoccupied with speech as the medium in which they worked. Written material was seen as inflexible, oppressive, time consuming and difficult; perceptions which the following quotations illustrate:

> It's a bigger barrier to write it than to say it. It's permanent evidence. You can discuss things in a tone of voice in the one to one where the client has the advantage of being able to talk to clarify things...it's a different feel to have the same things in black and white...very hard to share those written things.

> It's more the talking that clients want...the voice and facial expressions in verbal communication.

> You pitch the records at your own level but you have to adjust what you say to the vocabulary of the client...records don't reflect what sort of client you had.

It is interesting that clinic social workers often spoke of the written form as if it were the product of a chemical process, as for example, 'to *calcify* in black and white makes it appear to have a validity', and 'it's bad enough verbally, but *crystallised* on paper is worse...hardens opinion...'.

Others felt they lacked appropriate skills to communicate well on paper as part of direct work with clients – 'I can't see myself being fluent enough in the interview'. Some described their attempts to clarify elusive ideas by writing for the case record. However, thinking obviously came first, as for example, 'I can only record when the ideas are straight in my mind'.

Graphic descriptions were given by workers using written material as an essential part of therapeutic work. Written lists, often words of one syllable to 'spell out' points were often used with children. Letters written to a family after the session 'constituted a direct message to reflect the way I saw their situation and to check out the difficulties they were experiencing'. One worker felt sure that 'clients actually like you writing it down…it shows you listening and caring…being supremely professional'. However, it was in the area of displaying life histories in diagrammatic form that social workers felt really confident that such writing was better than speech. One worker described 'huge genograms with all family members sitting round the table time after time, all sharing the circles and triangles…it really helped people who are not so articulate'. Another worker, using the white board previously described, felt strongly that the medium empowered her client and declared 'the power that came off that board!'

Rights and responsibilities: access to personal files

The extent of discussion with clients about recording

Phasing the two batches of interviews gave an opportunity to examine practice differences consequent upon the Access to Personal Files Act 1987 (HMSO 1987). It is surprising that no significant differences were detected between the practice of the two groups of social workers. With one exception no social worker in either group routinely described to clients the form of record kept of their interaction. Even those in the second group, when the Act had become law, said they felt under no obligation to raise the matter with clients and that no policy to do so applied to clinic social workers. 'I don't talk about these things, I let them bring it up' was a typical response to the question 'What do you tell your clients about records?'

Many workers, however, felt confused and unhappy that they allowed the initiative to remain with clients. The following selection of quotations expresses this disquiet in their own words:

> I don't discuss it. It's a thorn in my side.

> I couldn't give them a clear picture of what they could and couldn't see as the social work notes are all mixed up with the other disciplines. They would have to see the psychiatrist who is the clinic supervisor.

I feel uncomfortable that I never discuss records, particularly computerisation and the checking if they are known to the area team.

To be honest, I'm fairly sloppy, I only discuss records with adolescents.

Although there was an assumption that clients expected a record because they were used to doctors writing in files in front of them, the material suggests that clinic social workers found it difficult to respond to clients who raised the topic. One social worker made a joke which he felt most people accepted – 'don't worry, unless someone actually dies or there is a dire catastrophe, no one will want to see them'.

Social workers presented some evidence that parents felt the record stigmatised their child, fearing particularly that schools might use the information negatively or that suggestions of inadequate parenting meant being 'pigeonholed for life'. Cases were quoted in which parents had insisted on no record being made as a condition of their child receiving the service. In one case parents explained that a record made of their child's attendance at the (child psychiatry) clinic would constitute a disqualification for emigration to Australia. There was general agreement that adolescents feared the label of 'madness' associated with the psychiatrist and were more accepting of records made by the clinic social worker.

The sample found it difficult to know what their clients thought about the records they kept. As so few had entered into frank discussions on the topic, they could only speculate. There was a general feeling that clients were not interested in recording, considered records irrelevant and would only want to see them to assuage their curiosity. It was thought that explaining the existence of records would: 'make more people want to see them', 'increase clients' apprehension', 'educate people to participate in reading and writing records', 'give them more power by reducing negative messages', 'be a terrific challenge for workers in clinics'. The sample felt clients attributed magical memory skills to social workers and failed to appreciate their need to keep notes in order to retain information. However it was not the writing down, per se, which social workers felt to be feared, but the use to which the material could subsequently be put, as illuminated by the comment, 'they don't fear them being written, they fear them being heard, i.e. left vulnerable to action being taken on what they say'. This is supported by a commonly held view that clients happy with the help they receive are likely to feel relaxed about records kept of their interaction with the clinic social worker.

How would clients be affected by greater participation in record keeping?

The above remarks have a distinctly patronising flavour and serve to reinforce the conventional model of 'clienthood'. It is notable, and interesting, that clients

used many of the same phrases to discuss records, although it is possible that
they were not always referring to the same phenomenon. Given that social
workers thought clients 'should think more about the issue of records' and
could be 'educated' to do so, it was surprising that they felt clients would be
extremely upset if shown their records. It was often said that clients would be
'horrified'. A social worker explained:

> They'd be horrified if they saw the thickness of their child's file – just
> how many thoughts I have which are not necessarily shared in the
> interview. My records pass on my thoughts and feelings. It would be a
> revelation to them. It makes me feel uncomfortable just thinking about
> it.

There was concern that clients would feel patronised and 'laughed at' on seeing
that the social worker had used their own words in the record. Others, however,
thought clients would feel that their conversation had been attended to and
recorded as relevant. One social worker described the showing of records as a
'risky trick' which might inflict pain. Nevertheless, he felt equally concerned
that by omitting to show the record a therapeutic opportunity was lost and
cited the case of a suicidal patient who might be made worse by seeing negative
material in the file. It was also conceivable that the patient could feel helped
by seeing that someone had recognised how hateful and hurtful he felt his life
to be; not to have shown such a written comment discounted all the pain the
client was suffering.

With the exception of statements of special educational need, clinic social
workers had little experience of involving their clients in writing reports,
although their participation in compiling genograms, charts and diaries was
obviously far greater. One social worker set 'homework tasks to record their
coping, a diary of events and their thoughts; it is their property but I take a
copy for the file'. It was felt that clients would not always want to be involved
in writing for the file, or would do so passively. However, many described the
benefit of social workers 'identifying in words what is at the back of clients'
minds', and suggested clients experienced relief from the social worker 'daring
to say it', 'handling it' and 'finding words to write it down'.

Fudging issues of confidentiality

Throughout the research material social workers described ways in which it
was their practice to manage difficult issues of confidentiality by judicious use
of recording systems. As clients could not see the medical file, placing social
work records there avoided problems associated with third party material. In
other cases, sensitive material was not recorded at all which avoided the need
to justify its inclusion in the confidential section of the file. One social worker

explained that if a client asked to see the social work notes she would either 'fish out odd bits to show' or say she did not know the procedure and would have to seek the views of the clinical team. Skilful transmission of coded messages to other professionals also avoided straightforward recording of negative social work assessment, as for example, the phrase 'she urgently requires the benefit of consistent limit setting' which conveyed to the consultant the message that parents were unable to exercise proper control over their spoilt child. Continuing confusion over social workers' identity, exacerbated by their titles and the fact that some PSWs were given the honorary title of senior social worker, allowed clients to assume all the notes were 'medical' in nature and therefore unavailable to them. (Similar medical overtones exist in child guidance teams where social workers are called senior practitioners or social work therapists.) Rather than explain their association with the social services department, some clinic social workers 'allowed clients to think we are doctors instead of social workers'.

Access to Personal Files Act 1987
Social workers were asked if the Access to Personal Files Act (HMSO 1987) had made any difference to their recording practice and what effects they expected it to have in the future. Most complained that, unlike colleagues in district teams, they had received no relevant training, procedural guidelines or leaflets to give to clients. Those participating in training events run by their own department considered that the application to their specialist setting had not been addressed. The phrase 'there is talk of it coming but it hasn't reached us yet' gives the prevailing impression of impending doom. One social worker asked the researcher to turn off the tape-recorder as she said conspiratorially 'Horrors – I really don't know anything about it'. Another confessed 'I haven't bent my mind round all this yet...I suppose, I hope, it's highly unlikely that anyone will ask to read the records'. A social worker said she was 'not yet affected but if social services insisted she would need a ton of guidelines'. Some social workers lacked any sympathy with the ethos of client access to records, angrily calling it 'just a meaningless paper exercise', 'a meaningless task', 'a hassle of piles of files with little in them – 99 per cent will never want to see them'. One worker quipped 'how can we say, hello sit down, have a leaflet!' Ironically, there was sympathy from a family doctor who said to one of the sample 'I didn't know you had the Data Protection Act...how very complicated for you all'.

Making social work files accessible to clinic clients was thought to involve much hard work by the social worker, and delicate negotiation with other members of the clinic team, in order to produce the possibility of advantage to the client. The extra work involved 'thinking extra thoughts...being a lot more

careful…constructing records differently if I thought the family would see
them, and always asking permission before contacting other agencies about
clients'.

Other team members would have to adjust to change imposed by social
workers adopting 'open' files. The social workers admitted to feeling guilty
that it was they who had to disrupt the current clinical file system when they
themselves were not convinced of the benefits. In several cases their files had
been commandeered by managers in social services for the purpose of 'checking
on the progress of client access'. In losing control over their files clinic social
workers felt hypocritical and powerless (one social worker wept when relating
this episode) and were concerned that they could no longer assure families that
files were confidential and would not leave the clinic. The problems of recording
and filing notes of conjoint family therapy sessions have been previously
discussed. Those social workers felt that client access to such records involved
'bizarre' problems, including the one expressed by this worker: 'I'm systemic
so I couldn't possibly split recording among family members'.

It was considered that the social work was, or involved, therapy, and
preservation of the client–worker relationship was paramount. One social
worker felt 'because it is therapy, there is no obligation to share the record'.
Social workers felt responsible for any disruption in relationships with clients
consequent upon enforced change in recording practice. Workers seemed to
expect difficulties, as illustrated by the one worker who mentioned recording
to clients: 'Now I do tell my new clients about records…I have to explain…but
actually they are quite pacified'. It was also feared that bringing recording into
a prime position might interfere with the agenda which the client was
attempting to bring.

In the main, clinic social workers were clear that if clients were to have access
to records, recording practice would have to change. They would write less,
think more, take longer, write only facts, write bland letters and omit their own
thoughts or feelings. This would produce a bland record which had 'no room
for body language' and was constructed 'quite differently'. Quotations from
the work of other colleagues would have to be omitted as they were often
pejorative, for example, 'she sat like a sack of potatoes'. As copies of reports
from each discipline went on the file, other, perhaps verbal, methods of sharing
information in the clinic would have to be worked out. This social worker was
saddened: 'It seems such a crying shame actually. I mean here at the moment
we share information but it would quickly be that everyone was protective and
secretive about their own information, leading to suspicion between professionals'.

There was a strong feeling that already something of value had been lost –
reports reflected only topics covered in the interview and had 'no depth, no
subjective descriptions'. Hunches would have to be carried in the head, 'themes

could actually disappear' and 'encapsulating judgements in two sentences' would be the newly required skill. Concern was expressed that abused children reading their files might find references to abuse suffered by their parents. Indeed, the whole area of recording abuse was felt to be made more difficult within the requirements of the Access to Personal Files Act.

It was interesting that PSWs viewed the demands somewhat differently from social workers having more generic training. The ethos of these very experienced PSWs was that generally everything to be written would have previously been shared with clients who would then experience no surprises. Sharing opinions with clients was seen by this group as a fundamental professional responsibility. Their real concern was the threat posed by 'their' records being considered the property of the social services department.

Contributions to statements of special educational need

Clinic social workers were often required to write an assessment report on the educational needs of a child which, collated with those of many other professionals, became part of the statement specifying the need and necessary resources. Parents were sent a copy of professional contributions and invited to write their own contribution. Many of the children had behavioural and emotional difficulties which were, in part or whole, related to inadequate or inappropriate parenting. It generally fell to the clinic social worker to spell out those factors about parenting and home circumstances which were relevant to assessment of the child's need and to identification and allocation of resources to meet it. Although clinics provided differing degrees of joint assessment, the social worker usually found herself trying to write about the social and parenting factors in ways which, when seen by parents, would not irrevocably damage the working relationship she had with them.

Despite often showing the draft report to parents workers found it extremely difficult to achieve an effective balance between enough honesty to acquire the resource yet not so much as to prejudice parents' relationship with the clinic as a whole. Two quotations illustrate typically strong views:

> It's a farce...I write innocuous rubbish which wouldn't offend a fly and anyone with any sense would disregard it. I have to embroider the truth. I minimise the damning information. I am not in the ball game of destroying people.

> I know they are going to see it so it's really bland. I'll miss bits out rather than risk a confrontation.

Social services managers often felt the clinic social worker had the balance wrong. In one case the worker was criticised for being too brief and bland – when he explained his fear that the parent might attack the child, he was sent some guidelines on contributions to statements and instructed to write in more detail. Another social worker was telephoned by a manager worried that a contribution might damage the widowed mother and cause her to instruct a solicitor. The social worker felt that the child needed to be at boarding school, away from his mother who used him to meet her own needs, and explained:

> Social services were only interested in the legal side, not my work on the case. In the end I changed the report, moved to weaker terminology… watered it down…they felt I had really no need to say those hard things about the poor woman.

The sample agreed that special skills were needed to write these contributions successfully. One worker felt that family therapists were particularly skilled at spelling things out for parents, resource people and decision makers, and regarded the capacity to hold disagreements in parallel to be an essential skill of experienced professionals. She was 'disgusted with professionals who bottle out and fail to fight for resources for children'. She too had been criticised for being too 'strong and contentious' and thought it disrespectful to assume that parents could not tolerate the stress of honest thinking about their child and the reasons for it. Despite variation in clinic practice, the social workers felt they made as professional an assessment as possible and most made real attempts to share their thinking with families before sending off contributions. In only one clinic, however, were families totally involved with all members of the clinic team in both assessment and the written contribution.

The statementing process was then commonly taken over by a panel of non-professional administrators whose poor understanding of the issues high-lighted by contributors was often deplored. The task of the panel was ultimately to allocate scarce resources on the basis of reports received. Whilst having sympathy with this difficult task (one interviewee remarked upon the 'ultimate horror of having to make decisions based upon other people's writings') clinic social workers expressed real fears that their 'professional' writing would be interpreted by panel members so as to justify decisions on scarce resources.

The impact upon parents of receiving the written assessment contained in the statement seems to have been insufficiently examined, although the Education Act (HMSO 1993) now requires local authorities to provide more information and assistance to parents whose child has a special educational need. One social worker had worked as an education welfare officer where part of her role had been to deliver statements personally, and explain and discuss their contents. It seems valuable to include her description of an attempt to mitigate some harmful effects of the process.

> It was my job at the end of the process to take the statement round to the home and explain all the contents. It was just so awful. The different

professionals put in value judgement after value judgement. It was really horrible, having to try and explain someone else's work...it was really...ugh...and sometimes they'd be really upset, saying, this isn't my child. You can't really explain someone else's perception of it...you try to help them make sense of it but it is hard and they get upset. They had a lot of anger about the views expressed...but I could say well let's write something down as your contribution, what would you like to say about this? Otherwise they lacked confidence. I think it just gave them more sense of control that they actually did have a part to play. Otherwise they saw all these pages from other people and they suddenly felt left out.

These complex implications for written assessments by social workers in child guidance clinics, whose child clients include many with special educational needs, are further explored in later chapters, where parents' perceptions reinforce and expand the views expressed in the last quotation.

CHAPTER FOUR

The Client's View

Semi-structured interviews with a sample of past clinic clients

Method of work and sample

This study of client opinion aimed to obtain the views held by parents of 20 past child patients about verbal and written communication with the child guidance clinic social worker, and to do so in the tradition of client opinion studies established in the 1970s. Enabling people to tell, in their own words, of their experience of being a social work client is particularly associated with the well known study dramatically entitled *The Client Speaks* (Mayer and Timms 1970), but research into the perceptions of elderly clients (Goldberg 1970) and families receiving help from Sheffield Family Service Unit (Sainsbury 1975), made clear contributions to our understanding of what it feels like to be a recipient of social work 'help'. Further work at that time (Pinker 1971, McKay *et al.* 1973, Timms 1973) presented client opinion about services experienced by clients of social services departments, but such sampling of customer opinion has been less frequent until recently prompted by the requirement to consult and involve children and parents in planning and delivering new services. Thus adults who were formerly in local authority care have been interviewed (Kahan 1979, Mann 1984, Loveday 1985), young people have spoken of their experience in, and leaving, care (Stein and Carey 1986), children of divorcing parents have vividly expressed the felt effects of separation and loss (Walczak and Burns 1984, Kroll 1994) and parents have shared their experience of participation in both child protection case conferences (Shemmings and Thoburn 1990) and open records (Raymond 1989). This chapter presents clients' experience and perception of the social work recording process and as in many of the above studies, semi-structured interviews were used to gather client opinion.

The sample was obtained by selecting alphabetically, from five child guidance clinics local to the researcher, files which had been closed for one year. It was important to interview parents who had interacted with different clinical teams and, in spreading the sample between all social workers in all clinics in the researcher's health authority, client opinion was more representative than that available from the clients of one social worker in one clinic reflecting the practice of one consultant. Cases having minimal involvement by the clinic social worker or allocated to social workers in other agencies were not included. A profile of the sample of clients is given in Appendix 5.

The sample was approached and invited to participate in one home based interview with the researcher. It was explained that interest lay in what parents felt about records kept on their child by the clinic social worker, and it was stressed that details of the child's problem or family circumstances would not need to be discussed. The researcher did not request the involvement of referred children in the interview but in the event three teenagers were present, interested and participated. Despite the researcher's efforts to invite fathers and male partners to participate in the interviews, there was a feeling that mothers 'dealt with' the research interview just as in the past they had attended the clinic with their child. Two mothers said their husbands feared hidden agendas and had not been in agreement with either of them participating in the research. Both disregarded the objections and met the researcher when their partners were at work.

Thirty families had to be approached in order to obtain the final sample of 20 who participated. The responses of the other ten bear elaboration: two cases were re-opened before being approached, two did not respond, two HM Forces families were posted overseas, one simply disappeared and two families refused to participate because, as one said, 'that painful chapter is now closed. I must refuse to help you as it would open old wounds'. Recognising the reality of such pain, it is surprising that two thirds of those approached so readily agreed to participate.

The semi-structured interviews were undertaken in the homes of the 20 families between July 1989 and March 1991, by appointment, using a tape recorder, and were later fully transcribed. The interview conditions often made recording difficult, in particular the noise of dogs, children and caged or farm yard birds. Some parents were suspicious of the tape recorder, requiring reassurance and clarification about the research topic; several suggested the researcher had been sent to check on their child's progress. Initially parents often felt they would have 'nothing to say', would not be 'able to help', or would 'not remember' but once the interview was underway, clients quickly and freely shared their views with the researcher who introduced topics from the interview schedule (Appendix 6) so as to maintain both flow and focus.

Client attitudes toward thinking about clinic social work records

Interesting and valuable material emerged from each of the 20 interviews but none really resembled another. Neither social class, type of problem, intellectual level nor family constellation proved useful in predicting the attitudes of parents towards the topic. Some were easy to contact, readily agreed to be interviewed and kept the appointment. Others were apparently happy to participate but then unaccountably changed the arrangements several times and in such cases persistence was needed to carry out interviews amid the restrictions of shift work, geography and child care arrangements.

Where both partners were present one usually dominated the interview as was the case with Mr L whose wife needed encouragement to give her views. Neither were thoughtful people. Mr L answered the open-ended questions as if participating in a bout of Trivial Pursuit – there was little sense that the issues evoked any emotion. The couple wished to please, to help the researcher, and located their child's past problems firmly in the medical arena. Their children were extremely precious to them and they would have complied with any requirement to effect recovery. The social worker and her records posed no threat; both were there to help the consultant to help their daughter.

In several cases family members moved in and out of the interview, being joined by friends and neighbours, as in the C family where a large group clustered round the tape-recorder on a small kitchen table. Mr C was unsure whether to participate but he later relaxed and was persuaded to give his ideas. Mrs C told the researcher that she had never heard her husband talk about personal things so openly and had no idea that he held the opinions he expressed so clearly. Other parents joining the interview spoke frankly about communication with the many social workers they had encountered. It was interesting to observe the very high level of agreement shared by these adults about records kept by social workers on their family problems.

Some interviews were carried out with mothers who were clearly depressed, anxious, physically ill or distraught about family problems. Mrs U felt very anxious about being interviewed for the research and needed much discussion about its purpose. The house was in very poor condition, Mrs U was herself unkempt and apparently depressed, and had episodes of trembling at any mention of her past history. Two agitated little dogs gnawed the feet of the interviewer and barked at the tape-recorder. Mrs U required some of the questions to be explained and had to be reassured that there were no right answers. Her particular concern was that the police might see the social work record kept on her son.

Parents whose employment or training involved records, as for example, secretaries, accountants and civil servants often compared their records at work with those kept on their child. This was the case with Mrs J who, during the interview, sat with her own DHSS work spread out around her on sofas – piles of records and a brief case bulging with reports. She frequently alluded to her own record keeping in her job as a home visitor with the DHSS, speaking of 'knowing the system', 'being on the same side as the social workers' and 'doing the same sort of work'. Mrs J was searching in her questioning as to the purpose of the research, wanted clarification as to how she had been selected to participate and seemed upset that she herself had not previously considered issues raised by open records, not only in relation to her son, but also her own work. Mrs J's attitude to the records reflected her attitude to involvement with the child guidance team in general. She took from the sessions those messages which were in accord with her own thinking and seemed to have dealt with the power of the social worker by regarding her as a friend. Dismissing the need for a social worker other than as a friend, Mrs J considered the only important records were medical ones.

Completing the semi-structured interviews required the researcher to gain the trust of parents, rapidly and often in difficult physical circumstances. It was necessary for the researcher to 'join' parents in a participative sense so as to enable painful material to emerge within an atmosphere of sensitivity and acceptance. In talking of records about their children, parents were recollecting events and communication between themselves and clinic professionals – their fears, hopes and disappointments over the child patients. They often wept or laughed as they shared these experiences and needed support to believe that their views were of value to the researcher. They frequently asked her to deliver messages of good or bad progress to clinic staff and sought her advice about the need for re-referral or help with other children. It was evident that thinking about the issues of being known to social workers, 'having a record' and remembering the pain of past problems was highly uncomfortable for parents and this required the researcher to give time for such feelings to be processed before she left.

The material gathered from interviews with the 20 families was extensive and only selective examples can be provided here to illustrate the main themes which emerged. These themes are presented and discussed under six headings to indicate clients' perceptions of: the purpose of social work records, communication by speech and writing, power and stigma, contributions to statements of special educational need, children's art work, and client participation in record keeping.

Clients' perception of the form and purpose of social work records

Unlike clinic social workers, who generally thought about records within a framework of negotiation between medical and social work services, clients were more commonly concerned with the purpose of record keeping. Nevertheless, in talking about the *raison d'être* of recording, most clients expressed confusion about the roles and identities of clinic professionals. This is the more significant because the social workers concerned stated they had specifically explained their own role within the clinic team.

Professional identity

Parents were unclear about the identity of the consultant child psychiatrist; frequently they were unsure what kind of a doctor he or she was. The terms paediatrician, psychiatrist and psychologist were often used interchangeably; one coined the title 'educational psychiatrist'; others referred to 'the guidance doctor', the 'chap at the clinic' or 'the other gentleman'. One mother called the child psychiatrist 'a specialised doctor' or 'counsellor' in case the stigma of mental illness led to her child being bullied in school. Some parents felt they were expected to know 'the set up' and expressed concern that this interfered with the process of getting help for their child, as for example:

> I was beginning to feel I couldn't communicate to people because I asked several times 'Well, what exactly is your job?' and I never did get an answer to that one. I was confused about the psychologist – I didn't feel it went as it should have done.

The astonishing degree of confusion about the role of the clinic social worker was clearly linked to ideas parents had concerning the way in which social worker and consultant worked together. Perceived in a variety of ways, the social worker was seen as a link between GP and specialist, with her records caught up in a confusing web of help offered in managing the child. As one parent expressed it, 'the social worker was part of whatever they were'.

Parents having previous experience of social workers heard the title social worker and made connections with the social services department. Jo's mother had had the names of her other children placed on a child protection register and in the research interview confessed to an extensive involvement with social workers which she had not revealed to the clinic team. An intelligent woman with secretarial skills, she considered the clinic social worker:

> A sort of social worker. She was connected with child guidance but I think she was still a social worker. She was not based in child guidance. Perhaps she dealt mainly with child guidance but she was just a social worker...but then I thought child guidance *was* social services – a different branch, like fostering and adoption.

Such uncertainty extended to the social worker's working relationship with the child psychiatrist. It is notable how frequently parents described the former as a 'sort of' social worker who worked 'for', 'with', 'beside' or 'under' the consultant. This mother's contribution is illustrative:

His secretary actually, like his understudy, came and got the background. Yes well…I think she was the secretary. I don't know whether she worked with him but she was one of the people with him…she was obviously working with him on a secretary basis – or, she could have been his social worker come to find out the background.

The perception of clinic social workers as handmaidens of the consultant has been well documented (Sampson 1980). Nevertheless it was interesting that so many parents viewed her as assisting 'doctor', titling her a secretary, assistant or nurse. Mrs W had known two child guidance social workers and had regarded them as secretary and nurse respectively. She explained:

Well we didn't realise she was a social worker, not until you rang us up and said we'd had social workers. It carried on with the second one, we never associated her with being a social worker either, just someone similar to being a secretary, taking notes like; the first one was more like a secretary than a social worker – now the other lady was more like a nurse, put us more in mind of a nurse…but, no, we didn't know they were social workers.

V's mother considered her daughter's self mutilatory hair pulling to be a medical problem, requiring a doctor, and was reluctant to acknowledge inter-personal factors in its causation:

I was thinking about the doctor all the time. I didn't concentrate on the social worker… I could see she was, like, his helper…to me she could have been his secretary, which I thought would happen, the secretary coming round to take the notes, just to do the background work for him. So, she's not just throwing this in between times then…so she really is what I thought she was but she's called a social worker? She is Dr X's right hand isn't she? And she's doing it for him?

Notwithstanding inferior status ascribed to the clinic social worker, parents commonly spoke appreciatively of her capacity *really* to help them. She was described as nice, understandable, dependable, always there, 'approachable, very good, understanding, reassuring and so nice that we didn't worry about what was written down'. In contrast the child psychiatrists were often perceived as unavailable, unapproachable and difficult to understand; 'they think differently'. Sessions with the consultant were described as painful, upsetting and puzzling whereas parents perceived their contact with the clinic social worker as 'reassuring', 'easing their minds' and 'picking up the pieces'. This good guy/bad guy construct was expressed most graphically by the mother who called both psychiatrist and social worker 'gentlemen':

When the first gentleman turned round and said it was probably my fault
I felt sad…I could have cried but I understood…it was strange, I could
actually see it like a picture. But the other gentleman put us at rest. I felt
quite confident with him. He actually put us more at rest than the psych
gentleman. He reassured us about not taking our son away.

The material showed clearly that parents were confused not only about the
identity of the child guidance social worker but also about her role. There was
a generally held view that her main responsibility was to gather and maintain
information in written form about the child's 'background' for the benefit of
the consultant. Her records were thus seen as important in the diagnostic
process – although one parent commented crisply 'the psychiatrist should get
his own set of notes, it doesn't seem right he should benefit from the social
worker's notes'. Other parents saw her role as reinforcing consultant advice;
'and after, she got in touch with me to see I agreed with it', or to provide an
alternative view of the situation; 'after, they would sit down and cross it all' (i.e.
share their information and opinions), and 'She could be picking up different
aspects of the conversation in the clinic'.

Two parents viewed the social worker as an intermediary, effecting the
referral between GP and consultant; 'She came to see if we needed the guidance
– she had to decide if we needed it. If so she would get us an appointment with
the counsellor'. This suggests a view of the clinic social worker as gatekeeper
and benevolent dispenser of consultant time.

Purpose

The sample was asked why they thought the clinic social worker kept records
of their contact. Replies were usually long and complicated by their confusion
about roles and identities of clinic personnel. Most clients gave at least two
reasons but one said dismissively 'I've often wondered why they do'. Common
perceptions concerned the management of information: the need to provide
continuity, to assist the social worker's memory, to inform other clinic members
and to protect ill-treated children. Some parents saw records primarily as of
benefit to the social worker, 'It expands their thoughts about their job so they
see it from different angles', or for their managers, 'Basically records are for
their superiors or more qualified workers', or for collective decision making,
'They need records to talk about children at meetings', and for allocation,
'Reports go to the social work boss as it takes more than one to make decisions
– they have committee meetings each morning to see notes of the cases that
have come up, to see if they will help you'.

Almost all parents viewed records as necessary in case of 'trouble in the
future'. On discussion this revealed ideas more complex than of mere 'having
to waste time picking up the pieces'. Previous social work records were seen as

evidence that 'there was more of a problem than they'd first thought', and thus important to parents in securing attention and convincing professionals of the reality and seriousness of the problem. Parents stressed the value of social workers' written descriptions of their child's problem so that re-referrals could be interpreted in the light of long-standing difficulties. For example:

> If there is something left they can see it's nothing new. He could kill himself without meaning to; well, at least there is something to show that we have had the problem for a long time – it would be proof no one else was involved if there were social work records of it all in the past.

Others saw the function of records as important evidence that they had in fact done their best by seeking help at an early stage. A mother explained:

> Well, it's for the family's benefit – it works both ways, so if the record is down and if we had a problem (luckily we can get through to him now, got that feeling we are back with him, but if we hadn't have done, at least we had tried) it's on record that probably we had tried with him, that we hadn't just cast an eye at him to leave him until he became a delinquent or something. We came out all right with him but if later on we needed help, they could say 'Well why hadn't he seen anyone before?'. It's a bit of a safeguard I think in that respect if you have got to go on with it.

But a surprisingly large number of parents considered the social worker kept records about their child for reasons concerned with inherited conditions, traits and 'nature' rather than 'nurture'. Comments included:

> Records are in case a brother or sister has the same problem.

> Proving the problem is hereditary.

> It would be a good thing if it showed it was in the family.

> To see what happens if you have more children.

> For if the children's children have the same problems.

> If my child in years to come had something wrong with his child, it could refer back to me – so it should be on record.

There was a sense that parents believed behavioural problems to be inherited and hoped the social work records would vindicate assertions that problems had been 'passed on' and were unconnected with practical parenting.

Two parents felt case notes were kept to assist other families. The comment 'In case another family has the same problem, the social worker can compare' almost suggests a research purpose, which was echoed by Paul's mother when she said 'The notes are needed to put cases together to benefit others'.

Only one parent identified measurement of progress as the purpose of social work recording: 'It is nice to look back – records help you remember where you were'.

'True' communication in speech and writing

Nearly all the parents interviewed praised and valued the social worker's capacity to listen, reassure and encourage them to explain their child's behaviour and their own feelings. Male partners tended to be reluctant to recognise problems with children and, where possible, left mothers to tackle the task of communication with clinic staff. Yet mothers commented that when forced to participate, their male partners were the better communicators as shown by the typical quotation 'he takes things in better than I do'. It seemed that mothers had such low levels of self esteem that they had little confidence in their ability to communicate satisfactorily about important matters. The nervousness and inability of Mrs U to adequately 'explain herself' was cited in the Chapter One but the following quotation alludes not only to difficulty in communicating, but also to the painful nature of the process:

> I can never explain myself completely right, I get tongue tied. I go a long way round to get to things. You've got to be very true to yourself and even say things you don't like saying to get it in a proper picture.

Because it was so hard to 'say some of it', parents felt the attitudes and personalities of clinic social workers were of great importance in assisting them 'actually to communicate with them'. (The extent of what can be written relies upon what has first been conveyed verbally or non-verbally.) The research question 'How easy was the social worker to talk to?' produced relevant material, but, when pressed, parents found it surprisingly difficult to be very specific about qualities which had reduced or fostered their ability to 'say'. Gender was considered irrelevant but all parents valued age and experience in the clinic social workers.

Mr and Mrs C discussed this, stressing how, for them, being easy to talk to connected with trust that their communication would be interpreted in the way they intended. Mrs C valued the social worker sharing details of parenting her own difficult child saying 'She really knew what I was talking about – I think a lot of young social workers let you down on that'. Mr C agreed, valuing life experience, 'not just straight out of college', and said the social worker had made him feel confident telling her 'as her whole delivery was better'. Mrs C had told the clinic social worker 'a lot of things I've never told anybody before' and her husband linked this to a feeling that they were not being judged as being a 'dangerous case'. Mr C felt he could express negative emotions about his child without 'feeling I was putting myself and my family in danger...without it resulting in having people camped on my door step for months'.

Although not all parents appreciated attention being transferred from themselves to their children, for Mrs W effective communication with her children made it easier for the adults to talk:

> They talked to them more than what they talked to myself and my husband, and we was in the background so it made it easier...they made them feel they should be there and were the important ones, that they weren't bystanders. Normally when you go somewhere it's the parents who are the main ones and the children are just there.

Parents appreciated the clinic social worker for being 'very nice', 'more of a friend', 'interested', 'speaking to me as an individual', 'an easy person to talk to', 'doing a lot of listening', 'not making mistakes', 'genuinely wanting to help'. There were frequent comparisons with medical professionals and many statements praising the social workers' communication skills: the material implies clients valued both attitudes and jargon-free talk skills. Mrs C explained:

> Somebody that just makes it easy to talk, that doesn't mind when they've come into a house in a mess, that can ignore all that and sort of say, well...not like doctors talk, they just ask questions. Somebody who cares and just asks the right questions. I think they do, social workers.

One couple described their pro-active approach to 'psycho-babble': 'The social worker was understanding and normal. The psychiatrist, well, he'd been on lots of courses and been up-dated. My husband asked him to broaden it a bit as he was doing jargon'.

Thus the attitudes, personality and communication skills of the clinic social worker were seen as extremely important in assisting clients to find confidence in their own ability both to explain the problem and to access the skills of other team members. The couple above, emphasising the negative effects of jargon, felt 'nervous when they start using words you don't understand, and often if you haven't the guts to ask what they mean, and remain silent, these things go over your head and you are answering wrongly'. Such 'wrong answers' are particularly significant where treatment depends upon diagnosis reached largely through verbal interaction. Most parents expressed fear of harming their child indirectly – by being unskilful communicators they felt responsible for giving information which led professionals either to withhold treatment from their child or to offer inappropriate and hence unsuccessful treatment. Parents felt responsible, 'under pressure to tell all so we would get something for our child', and 'wanting help so we had to tell everything and anything in case it helped'. Parents also worried that their words would be misinterpreted and recorded to convey meanings they had not intended. They frequently blamed their own inarticulacy: 'If you can't explain yourself properly from within, it gets put down a different way'. Clients felt it likely that their words would be 'twisted', 'turned round', or 'turned into something else'. This mother explained her own unease:

> I felt a bit awkward like, whatever I was saying could have been turned round, you don't know how their minds work. You say black and white, well...black and white to me is black and white but I don't know the way they read into it. I just kept thinking 'If I said this, would they think something different?'

On the one hand parents appeared to expect social workers to make sense of the communication in the light of their presumed skill and experience as workers with *the social*. (One definition of *the social* includes the practices of assistance associated with social work and other helping professions (Donzelot 1979).) Yet clients also expected their words to be accepted and recorded without interpretation so as to preserve the meaning they intended. Mrs W was adamant that the significance the social worker attached to her use of the word 'tomboy' to describe her daughter was more than mere linguistic misunderstanding:

> She was trying to say that I described my daughter as a tomboy because I wanted a boy and was trying to make her into a boy. I said I wasn't and she tried to convince me that I was, but I know for a fact that I wanted a boy with both of them and I didn't want a girl with either...so that's not it...they are totally different. She'd got an idea but I knew it wasn't like that.

When invited to express any preference for oral as opposed to written communication, very few parents wished to participate in the act of writing the record but most expressed a deep desire to read the social worker's writings about themselves. Material emerged about their perception of inherent qualities of oral and written material which resonates with the speech versus writing debate of Saussure and Derrida. Is the reporting more 'true' if conveyed by speech and how is it changed if coded into writing? What are the advantages and disadvantages of the written form for parents whose contact with statutory agencies must often now be regulated by written agreement (HMSO 1989: Children Act)? Those interviewed invariably preferred the medium of speech and their comments included:

> I'd rather say – I'm not a writey or a ready person.

> It was the talking that was so important...a Godsend.

> It was easier to say it. I'd need a dictionary if I was to write.

Mrs U, referred to previously, was one of the two parents who had so little confidence in their oral skills that they 'could write better than say it'.

That Rousseau regarded writing as a 'dangerous supplement to speech' is something of a paradox, for Rousseau was an exceptionally prolific and dedicated writer yet condemned writing as the 'destruction of presence and disease of speech' (Norris 1987 p99, quoting Derrida). Likewise, clients often referred to 'dangers' contained in the process of entrusting their own words to written accounts and for some this prevented communication with the social worker, as for example, 'I think it would be very dicey so I'd probably end up trying to keep my mouth shut'. Others considered misinterpretation and mischief making were relatively limited in verbal communication but regarded the written form as unsafe in that their own interpretation might not be preserved by future readers. The parents of J conveyed this clearly:

MOTHER: I'm never satisfied with what I write, I'm terrified of what's going to happen to it if I write it.

FATHER: I feel the same way. I think you can put down some of it, the personal details, if you write it down there in black and white for anyone, to read; but if you've just said it, it doesn't go any further and no one else can relate it to someone else in your own words.

Parents tended to blame their own lack of verbal clarity for factual mistakes made by the social worker in written records. They often likened the process to the whispering game in which the last player gives voice to the multiplied mistakes of the whisperers. Similarly the written record gives the writer/speaker the advantage of 'perpetually having the last word' in their conversations (Norris 1987 p101, quoting Derrida). Mrs Ch explains:

It's like those stories where you pass it on and pass it on and it ends up completely different. It looks blacker on paper than what it is...because they write down what they think she says but what she says is wrong you see...so what they write down is not what she is really saying.

Mrs Ch also describes her feelings about being confronted at some future time with someone who has read previous writing about her situation and thought she would 'feel they are looking at you like summat they heard'. She may well have agreed with Saussure (1974) and Levi Strauss (1961) that speech is the natural, real type of language and writing a poor derivative causing an imbalance of knowledge and power.

Personal information: power, surveillance and stigma

Part of the semi-structured interview aimed to elicit clients' perception of social work case recording as an activity which affected self image, levels of trust, empowerment or reputation. The relevance of the work of Foucault, Goffman and Donzelot to this material has already been discussed in Chapter One: the views and feelings of the sample of parents continue to illuminate ideas about surveillance, stigma and policing of families. However, it is not only philosophers and sociologists whose work bears upon the relationship between clinic social worker and client. Their perspective finds an echo in more popular views of the role of social workers. The crime writer P D James in *A Mind to Murder* has the consultant psychiatrist, Dr Baguely, considering Miss Kettle, social worker to the Steen Clinic, as follows:

> Like many professional social workers she had little instinctive understanding of people, a lack which had gained her an undeserved reputation for insensitivity. It was of course different if they were her clients – and how Baguely hated that word! Once they were securely caged behind the bars of a professional relationship she gave them a dedicated and meticulous attention which left few of their privacies intact. They were understood whether they liked it or not, their weaknesses exposed and condoned, their efforts applauded and encouraged, their sins forgiven. (James 1984 p103)

This passage suggests great inequality: Miss Kettle in control, extracting and then judging the most personal details of the private lives of patients trapped within a professional relationship.

Whilst parents were appreciative of the help given to their children, many considered they had provided information within a framework which was both oppressive and unequal. However 'nice', the clinic staff were regarded as offering help on their own terms, one of which was a right to extract and record sensitive information about parents and relatives of referred children. The vocabulary used by clients to describe this process was interesting (and consistent) in that it underlined a one sided acquisition of information. Examples included:

> Took much personal information away – God knows where to.

> Got our history.

> Take your history.

> Took our background.

> Got bits of information on us.

> She took information, went away and we heard no more.

There was a sense of powerlessness, expressed typically by Mrs L: 'I mean, if you want their help...well, what else can you do? You can't go telling them their job or whatever'.

Parents felt their giving of information had not been reciprocated and considered this in line with their expectations of professionals, as Mrs Ch explained:

> They are very evasive for what they don't want you to know, people like that, they are forthcoming with some things but some things they don't seem to say a lot about. They sort of say it to suit them. They don't come out straight forward...it's all garbled really.

Another parent spoke about the 'reserve of professionals':

> You see, professional people always tend to be, err, well, not secret exactly, but a bit reserved and not really talking about what they think and what they are going to write.

Given that child guidance clinics are in essence psychiatric out patient clinics for children, this material is reminiscent of the 'alienative coalition of next of kin, complainant and mediator' which Goffman suggests underpins decisions about psychiatric treatment. Mediators can be defined in terms of the professional distance referred to so frequently by the sample of clients and are 'professional specialists with experience of handling difficult people, with the ability to distance themselves from troublesome behaviour and proceedings, which comes from professional training' (Burns 1992 p187). Parents complained of particular experiences which it would appear caused them to feel at a disadvantage in communicating with the clinic social worker (mediator) and child psychiatrist.

Professional distancing

Clients felt they did not 'know what others knew' and were thus constantly 'a step behind'. Ignorance of referral routes had frequently made the acquisition of child guidance feel like an obstacle course. This was often exacerbated by the differing geographical areas served by health and social services departments, and the prerogative of general practitioners to refer to favoured consultants whose social work colleagues held no responsibility for the child's home area. Mrs S explained her sense of desperation as she was referred backwards and forwards between three clinics served by different social services offices. She complained of being unable to 'get into the system' and felt outnumbered by the various social workers, school doctors, psychologists and psychiatrists who could decide, or not, that her son 'fell into their area'. She remarked rather sadly 'As you realise, I was on my own'. Parents often felt uninformed about the options available within the treatment process and expressed a need to know 'what usually happened'. Mrs U considered both her doctor and the school had delayed the process of referral and once an appointment was achieved she was 'just as frustrated. I was never told the different steps like, if this didn't work, we can do so and so…no avenues that could have been gone down'.

Although most clients said they were able to communicate well with the clinic social worker, it emerges that this was largely dependent upon discussions taking place in the child's home. Only one parent preferred the clinic setting: most considered it harder to relax, feel at ease and relate to staff in a clinic. Parents disliked uncurtained windows in waiting areas, in that they might be seen by neighbours and friends who might gossip about their child's attendance. Throughout there was criticism of the social worker and consultant talking with them over or round a desk. Some sessions were held in rural satellite clinics which were never designed as premises for child guidance. Although intended to minimise client travelling time, parents recognised only the formality of the desk and seating. The mother of a nine-year-old school phobic boy explained how she felt the surroundings distanced her from the professionals:

> They sat behind one of the biggest desks I've ever seen, could have had a ballroom dance on that thing. That must be terribly imposing to a child – I saw it and…God…it must be terribly…the surroundings could be made more informal. Adults will understand the big desk, but children, it puts a barrier there straight away. We sat in a semi-circle in front of the desk…all my son did was sit on his hands and look at the floor. It's too stiff… I mean at home he did sometimes speak to the social worker but at the clinic, no way, not a word. It was just too imposing.

Both social worker and child psychiatrist were equipped for writing on these desks with files, paper and pens in evidence. Some people considered the social worker's act of writing to be one of distancing and withdrawal of attention, as expressed by this mother:

> She was sat writing all the time and it's hard to talk to someone when they are sat writing. You can't, sort of…you feel that they are not listening…because she was in her writing you don't know if she is listening to half what you are saying. When they look at you, you know if they have got it.

Differences in styles of dress, language and seating between clients and professionals were often mentioned but the material suggests that small inequalities of a practical nature are also perceived as painfully disempowering by adults who attend the clinic. J's mother had felt irritated, embarrassed and relatively ill-equipped because the consultant was able to tap with a pencil:

> If you are sat the other side of the desk and someone is tapping their pencil you feel as if you are a child back in the school room. He just sat there tapping…just a mannerism really…he had a pencil and we hadn't. That in itself was very intimidating.

Parents also commented on communication being 'different' with their social worker when she saw them together with the consultant as part of a family session. It has been shown elsewhere that the practice style of family therapy is not always understood or appreciated by the recipients (Howe 1989). The research material tends to support those findings and shows that one of the factors affecting content of clinic social work records is the extent to which client communication differed in clinic based therapy situations. Mrs Ch felt particularly excluded by professionals speaking to each other in front of her and during the *break*:

> Then he [consultant] talked to her [social worker] like we were not there so that made it harder I suppose 'cos we didn't know what they was on about. We couldn't tell what he was saying to her but she knew what he was saying because she was at the side of him, sort of…we couldn't understand because he was saying it to her, and not out loud, but to her, but it made you feel you were on a test you know…that's before they went out of the room, they went out for five or ten minutes before they came back. It felt like being in a police station and you have done summat wrong. It felt that way, that they had left you to stew, like they do. But you are thinking all sorts of things.

It is clear from such examples that the volume and quality of clients' verbal contribution to such sessions were reduced when they felt disadvantaged by the clinical arrangements. Records then made of such sessions would tend to reflect the lowered level of client involvement and participation, rather than the reasons for this.

Stigma and confidentiality

Clients were largely uninformed about the existence and content of the social work file on their child and family. They had varying ideas about where these records might be stored, for how long they were kept and who might have access to them. As discussed before, some parents felt records should be kept for several generations to trace genetic traits and conditions. Others suggested records be kept for 'a few years' but the majority linked the life of the social work record with the child's school life. Many hoped that the record would be destroyed before the child started, changed or left school. A common fear was that social work records would be sent to the school as a matter of course and the child stigmatised because of clinic attendance. However one parent com-

plained that no information at all had been passed to the school when she had
clearly expected this as part of the social worker's function. Other parents feared
records would be given to the police, especially where their child had a history
of offending, and remarks such as 'that is my biggest fear' were often made.

Whilst frequently saying they expected the records to be 'confidential',
parents conveyed a sense of generalised mistrust. They were particularly
concerned that other parents, office workers and gossips would read the social
work notes. There was a distrust of those who typed the notes – clinic secretaries
being likened to school secretaries who were often said to spread information
in a community. The term *open* records was not understood. Parents took this
to mean that it was open to others to read; 'anyone can get at them', 'anyone
could have a bit of a read'. Mrs W feared confidentiality would be broken to
inform prospective employers:

> It always stems back to the employers. If the employers get rooting about,
> would they give them something? Because now they do vet potential
> employees and is that sort of information available to them? I didn't
> discuss that worry at the time but I thought of that later.

One parent, working for the then DHSS, was amazed that clinic social workers
were not required to sign the Official Secrets Act. Under such an assumption
she had 'automatically thought everything was confidential'.

In contrast to those who felt that in order to help social workers 'needed to
know everything' other parents questioned the need for the worker to 'want
so much background'. One complained that 'She just wrote and wrote'. Some
agreed with Mrs U that workers 'should be allowed to write just on the person
or whoever is just involved, not going back into their history'.

Despite previously giving little thought to social work recording, most
parents expressed a particular fear that its existence or contents might in some
way damage their own reputation as good parents, or disadvantage the referred
child. Some feared, as explained above, that the teenage child would be
adversely regarded by schools, employers, police and peers should the social
work record 'follow'. Several, like Mrs S, whose child had somatic symptoms,
expressed a tentative trust that medical levels of confidentiality would prevail
in their case: 'Nobody would write to them, would they, from university or
anything like that? There is nothing like that, is there? Oh...so...it's still in
the medical world?'. Others admitted to caring 'what other people thought'.
They expected to be criticised for failed marriages and difficult children and
thus giving full information for the social worker to record was often painful.
'It's such an awful thing in a house' said one member of the sample.

For many clients association with the clinic social worker brought anxious
thoughts about her powers in respect of child protection. Parents often referred
to 'Cleveland' and felt records of contact with the clinic might 'tot up' in future

decisions about their adequacy as parents. J's mother contributed this account of feeling labelled by 'having a social worker':

> Three years ago she fell horse riding and broke her arm and we had to go to hospital and I was quite taken aback when they interviewed me and said 'Now, have you got a social worker?', and of course at the time we had the clinic social worker. I was quite alarmed really for them to ask that and I thought, oh blimey, are they going to get in touch? She just fell off her horse and broke her arm but I was alarmed by that bit...the stigma attached to it I suppose, whether they were thinking, does she come from a bad home and that type of thing...it's the stigma of it, having a social worker and for them to wonder why.

In coming to the child guidance clinic parents were motivated to obtain and co-operate with treatment for their child. Most viewed giving information as their part in the process and, it would seem, expected the clinic social worker to record accurately all the material which she had skilfully helped them to 'say'. They were aware that in so doing they might be themselves described in poorer terms than they would have wished, but helping their child took precedence over their own reputation. 'I'd have said it anyway'. Such honesty about failing to solve the child's problem may be most painful if seen later in writing as part of professional assessment. The case of Mrs L illustrates the far reaching effects of seeing herself described as 'inadequate' by the child psychiatrist. Mrs L had given a full history to the clinic social worker and with her daughter had one family session in the clinic with the child psychiatrist and social worker. Her daughter was enuretic and had behavioural problems. Sometime later, Mrs L visited her own doctor and glancing at notes on his desk in his absence, read a letter from the child psychiatrist. This relayed the history she had given to the social worker and reached an assessment of Mrs L as 'clearly an inadequate mother'. Despite the lapse of time, Mrs L explained her feelings with considerable emotion:

> I was seeing on this paper that...inadequate mother...too young...and I was annoyed about that as I thought I was quite a normal mother...made mistakes which everybody does...but you get unnerved by things like that. Inadequate it said! I'd gone first to child guidance about her wetting. Everybody has problems with children, no matter who they are. I thought...well I have admitted that I have got a problem and instead of letting it go on, I wanted to do something for my daughter and for myself as well. It always stuck in my mind that phrase...inadequate. At one stage I wanted to go into that line, there was an assistant occupational therapist job and I'd have liked to have done something like that. But I thought, there again, if they read up on the

> records, if you are inadequate, then how on earth can you help somebody
> else with their problems…so…it stuck in my mind.

This painful example illustrates the assumption by Mrs L that a network of
records about herself, her parenting and her child would connect with those
concerning potential employees. In as far as occupational therapists are part of
the social services department, she may well have been correct. The damage to
her self esteem by seeing herself described in writing as inadequate seems to
be clear evidence of *spoiled identity* (Goffman 1968).

Language and the statement of special educational need

Four of the 20 children comprising the sample had been made the subject of
a multi-disciplinary assessment and issued with a statement of their needs as
required under the (then)1981 Education Act. The child guidance social worker
had provided a contribution to the assessment, as did colleagues from clinics
and departments having 'relevant' knowledge of the child's problems. Parents
of the four children spoke at length about their experience of the process, their
criticisms focusing largely upon issues of communication. All felt they had
experienced high levels of anxiety and anger during the process but were also
generous in their praise for the specialist resources which were eventually
allocated to their children.

Despite this graphic material arising within a primarily educational arena,
it bears examination because it supports findings described elsewhere in this
chapter about professional distance, special language, client participation in
report writing and the need to know what others know. The experience of the
four sets of parents is presented using their own accounts.

A statement was issued to Mr and Mrs A concerning their seven-year-old
son, who had been referred to the child guidance team following his making
of hoax telephone calls. It emerged that he had language difficulties which were
not resolved by extra help in the classroom. The arrival of the packet of papers
(the statement) was a shock for which both parents felt they had received no
preparation. The special language was confusing and the descriptions of their
son conflicted with their own perceptions. Mrs A stated:

> At the time my husband was quite upset. You as parents have got your
> ideas about your child…we knew he had problems, not just one but a
> lot of little problems but when that packet comes to you with those big
> words, I think it made it seem a lot worse than we thought it was at the
> time, even though we knew it was pretty bad.

Mr and Mrs A were unprepared for the multi-disciplinary nature of the
statement. As the educational psychologist had tested their son, they had only
expected a report from him. The presence of substantial reports from many

other professionals was confusing especially as they seemed to be offering conflicting advice about needs and availability of specialist provision. Mrs A explained how they felt:

> We were told he was having a statement but we thought it was just from the psychol...that's all we thought we were getting. Like the speech therapist, that shocked us. But you see, you had, what alarmed us so much was the speech therapist's idea of a language unit but there wasn't one...and then the psychol – he'd got different views. And we were sat there thinking oh my God what an earth's up with the child? There was so much in from different people...we felt pretty low at the time...and then there was the bit from his teacher saying she thought he could attain in the same school. And then some from the paed...children's doctor lady. They were all saying that the boy had specific learning difficulties but they all seemed to be saying different things to do. Like, the psychol had got numbers down, like that IQ thing and the lad was under-intelligent or whatever the word is...lower than average...that upset me, the way it had been put. It wasn't in plain enough language for me to understand. But then again, he seemed to be saying he caught the boy on a bad day and he could perhaps have got more out of him, and with the language difficulties it was hard to say how bad he really was...so where he drew the line with him God only knows.

Mrs A emphasised the need for help to decipher special language and evaluate written professional opinion:

> I suppose all those people have got to be involved but it would be better if it was brought down to one person on a one to one basis. We would have liked someone to talk to us about it. When it's written down it can look more alarming than when you are actually talking. But if that statement had been a bit more plainer English it wouldn't have been such a big shock. All those tests had got special names and we thought well, what the hell are they? And who can I ask? I'm not saying it was all baffling to me but the great extent of it was. Lots of the words I couldn't understand...I mean I was actually sat with the dictionary, some of the words were just baffling to me. I thought it would have been nice if someone had been able to sat down and discuss it...

Mrs B also felt confused and uninformed about the testing carried out by the educational psychologist on her son. She linked her own low self esteem with her son's lack of confidence and felt 'very criticised...looking back now, it's alright them saying you've got to boost the child's confidence but if you are lacking confidence yourself it's not any easy thing'.

It would perhaps be expected that a mother who worked as a school secretary would have access to more information about the assessment and statementing processes. This was not the case with Mrs S who perceived the important part of the process to be a meeting of professionals, after the manner of a tribunal or appeals committee. She was therefore most surprised not to be part of the statementing panel and explained how uninvolved she felt in the process:

> Well the committee when my son was statemented...the case committee...I don't know who is on that committee. I wasn't invited...my boss was convinced I'd be going...he said I'll take you and go with you...he couldn't believe it when we found out it had taken place without my knowledge, and I was the one who had called for help!

Mrs S stressed the lengthy nature of the process and 'felt as if I didn't know what was happening at all, just that we were going from one place to another and there was so long between one thing and another'. She raised no objections to the content of reports when the written statement arrived in the post but thought the clinic social work report left a great deal out and remembered being astonished that no mention had been made of the death of her husband. Mrs S felt professionals were 'aware that we would see the reports and knew they had to be very careful what they wrote'.

The final case shows the process empowering parents to obtain resources from an authority unwilling to accept the concept of 'dyslexia'. Aged seven, J had been referred to the child guidance clinic and treated for tantrums, lack of concentration, tearfulness and sleep problems. The social worker had considerable involvement and made a frank and detailed contribution to the multidisciplinary assessment which was only undertaken after much acrimony between parents and the educational psychologist. Mother complained that the psychologist made her feel stupid by using jargon and professional argument about the exact meaning of the word 'dyslexia'. The couple complained that parents never get all the professionals' writings, only summaries, so the picture is never complete. They felt 'you got nothing off them'. They felt resentful that they had to provide the professionals with personal and sensitive information before they could get the resource. In the event it seemed the professionals had used ideas about traumatic family upsets to explain the boy's behaviour, whereas parents thought he needed help educationally. They felt they were fighting a system which did not work properly and were irritated by a procedure of 'more forms and less action'. When the statement finally arrived, they felt relieved and vindicated that there was actually something measurably wrong with their son which required considerable special educational provision.

J's parents had clear views on the nature of their son's difficulties and had given much thought to their own contribution to the assessment. The task is a daunting one for parents who realise the need to make a case for the resource they consider their child requires and yet are naturally reluctant to describe the child in negative terms. J's parents describe their dilemma:

> We found it difficult. It took ages to write it...when I'd written it I thought, well that looks bloody pathetic...if I could just *tell* somebody properly...but writing it down just doesn't come out right...you can't express the depths of it. You can't put it on paper as you think...well I don't know who is going to see this...which other people see it. I couldn't write down 'I am terrified as to how he's going to cope with life... I don't know how he's going to get on in secondary school...I lie awake at night worrying because he has only got another two years left'. These kids...OK...so it's educational...they can't read and they can't write but there's more to it than that and people don't understand. I worry myself sick when he goes out...he forgets where he is going and he'll have to go on a bus to the big town with his fare and walk through the main street...he's got no road sense and no perception of danger...how do you put that down on a form? How do you tell somebody that, when you don't know who is on the other end of it? These people in authority with the statementing, they have no idea what the kids look like, never spoken to them...how can you tell them on a form? I think you are always worried people will think you are exaggerating so you tend to play it down a bit – instead of telling them the truth. You don't want them to think your child is stupid or something...

This material resonates with that arising in the interviews with clinic social workers on their contributions to statements. Both parents and social workers may be reluctant to write negative descriptions of children and family backgrounds for collation and decision by bureaurocratic functionaries whom they have never met. Yet if they cannot provide sufficient evidence of need, specialist provision will be allocated elsewhere. Part of the price of the service seems to be information, which was summed up neatly by a parent who said 'if you want anything, you have to tell them everything'. In adopting such dependent and child-like presentations, parents were learning how to get the best out of the system and to be 'successful clients' (see Satyamurti 1981 pp149–158).

Communication by children – pictures or records?

Three older children in the sample participated in the interviews and gave their views about the meaning of records for them. Fifteen-year-old H said she had thought about the record afterwards, wondering whether the social worker had written down properly what she had said. She guessed the social worker and consultant would 'write down their thoughts' and she would very much have liked to see what was written about her because 'they thought I had something wrong with my mind and wanted to find out if there was something wrong in the family. I knew there wasn't...that's why I wondered what they wrote... I'd like to see'. H had kept a headache chart (Figure 4.1) with the support of the social worker as part of a programme to alleviate her severe headache. Neither she nor her parents could remember what happened to the chart and had no idea that it had been filed as a record. B, aged 13, said firmly that he'd never thought about any notes being made on him and didn't think he'd want to see them anyway. V, aged 16, felt she would have liked to read the social worker's notes just to see 'if they were different from what they were telling me'.

Other children in the sample had produced drawings, charts or diaries either with the social worker in the clinic or under her supervision as part of an agreed treatment plan. This work generated items which in themselves constituted a record of work done – an indicator of progress at that time and a concrete item of intrinsic significance to the child. It is interesting that parents so frequently underestimated the extent of such items, denied their existence or were unable to remember their child working with art materials in the clinic. When asked what they thought had happened to such drawings and charts parents usually replied that they had 'never given it a thought'. Mrs L and Mrs H were two notable exceptions. Mrs L remembered clearly that she was expected to bring home her son's pictures, regarded this as an inconvenience, and told the researcher, 'They said he was to bring them home. They just automatically came home and we had all these to put somewhere'. Mrs H had an artistically gifted son whose drawings done in clinic sessions both indicated his fearful state of mind (Figure 4.2) and gave the clinic team an opportunity to praise him. His mother was somewhat ambivalent about the drawings being kept by the clinic and explained:

> The chappie said he would loved to have kept them because they were so good. He would have loved to have kept them himself personally. He said to Joe, when you get older you will be famous for your drawings... I would think they are still in his file. Joe wanted to bring them home after he had been praised for them and I don't think he could understand why he had been praised about it if he couldn't bring them home. He asked him to write his name on the bottom – I think he kept them.

It later emerged that Mrs H had seen a TV programme about patients whose art had been found to have considerable commercial value and she wondered whether the clinic retained her son's pictures for their potential as saleable items in the future.

Joe's pictures provided both social worker and consultant with a clear impression of his inner world. His first drawings were of coffins, death, skeletons and so forth (see Figure 4.2) and were perhaps attempts to empower himself against oppressors in the real world. As the sessions went on, he drew a series of dinosaur pictures (two of which are reproduced as Figures 4.3 and 4.4) showing his dreams of being chased by a large beast, dreams which were eventually resolved as he made friends with the beast then drawn as smaller and smiling.

Joe was able to communicate his fears through drawing and his art work was valuable not only as a beneficial therapy for him but as a record of the level of his fears providing reliable information to those trying to help him. Art therapists use the art process as a way of communicating with the *inner world* of the child – a concept developed by child psychoanalysts such as Melanie Klein, Anna Freud and Donald Winnicott. This process can be used in different settings to benefit children with a variety of problems, and using the language of art in art therapy can be understood in terms of non-verbal communication (Case and Dalley 1990).

Undoubtedly the clinic social worker was not claiming to work as an art therapist *per se* – yet in her regular sessions with several children in the sample their communication used the language of images portrayed with paint, pen, paper, sand and plasticine. With the exception of Joe's mother, parents placed very little value upon such activities, often criticising the standard of workmanship of the results: 'She does much better drawings at home'. Mrs W's daughter attended 11 play therapy sessions with the clinic social worker, producing many drawings and paintings, and a diary, with evident benefit and enjoyment. Mrs W commented that she could not understand why this was necessary as her daughter thought it 'a bit of a chore'. It is interesting that Mrs W said the reason for the therapy was that her daughter was not sociable enough and for that she needed a *social* worker. Given such a construct it must have been difficult to appreciate the benefit of play therapy.

The drawings, paintings, models, charts and diaries made by children in the course of their sessions can thus be viewed as records of the therapeutic process. They can also be regarded as evidence of the child's state of mind, which in the case of sexually abused children may manifest their inner chaos in messy chaotic pictures and models (Sagar in Case and Dalley 1990). Drawings may disturb the worker who might be tempted to link apparent sadness, loss and anger with known events in the child's life. A beautifully executed drawing was presented to the clinic social worker by a 15-year-old girl: the social worker spoke of being greatly disturbed by this powerful drawing but unable to arrive at any meaningful interpretation.

The files of the sample of cases showed other interesting examples of recorded work not in the form of a written case record. The dyslexic boy Jon had worked hard on his tantrums, completing a star chart to show tantrum-free days (such a chart is shown in Appendix 7). His efforts to copy formboard shapes constitute a valuable record of developing perceptual skills. Wetting and soiling had lowered the self esteem of nine-year-old R. Behavioural modification work used charts which invited her to draw her success in the form of smiling faces; the qualitative nature of such results can be seen in a similar chart (Appendix 8), where firmness of lines and extent of smiles seem to indicate confidence and achievement. Reference has already been made to the 'unsociable' girl and her 11 sessions of play therapy. At one stage she went on a holiday and the social worker-therapist suggested she keep a diary to show on return. For some reason the social worker retained these 14 pages of very careful writing and illustration, pierced the book with a punch and tethered it into the file. During the research interview, Jo's mother raised the issue of this diary:

> It's just a little booklet but Jo has brought it up several times that she'd have liked to have kept it for herself…just that one thing. Even now she will say, 'That holiday in Wales and I never did bring my diary home, they never did give me it back'. She took it to show them and I thought we would have it back but no…and I thought oh it's gone into the file. She showed it to them and then that was it…it went. I don't think she minded about the drawings and paintings, just the diary.

It is strange that such a caring social worker providing so many sessions of play therapy to this girl should have commandeered the diary. It involved much hard work and was Jo's only 'record' of her holiday (sample page shown in Figure 4.5). It seems likely that for the social worker it represented evidence of her work as a therapist, of the trust and co-operation between them during their sessions and perhaps a significant snapshot of family dynamics during the holiday. It was therefore punched and filed – a record of social work, but also the young client's personal property.

Client involvement in recording and the concept of participation

Service user involvement, partnership and participation are key welfare words of the nineties. The Children Act 1989 (HMSO 1989) espouses a partnership with parents which implies a sharing of resources so as to meet needs without affecting parental responsibility. Elsewhere, a more active participation of the family has been called for (Cleveland Report, HMSO 1987) and, specifically, parental participation in child protection case conferences (Working Together, DHSS 1988). As clients come voluntarily to child guidance clinics for help in parenting children, this agency would seem well placed to examine the extent of their involvement in the service provided. Multi-disciplinary teamwork is potentially more participative than single workers 'having' each case. Such sharing of responsibility in a team can be more easily extended to include the client, opening up potential for second opinions and involvement of clients in managing cases (Glastonbury, Bradley and Orme 1987).

Access and participation are words used by the BASW/BIOSS recording project without a clear definition of their extent and overlap. It is important to consider how far the concepts can be separated in practice, and what they mean to the client. A parallel can be drawn with the issues arising from parental participation in case conferences, and it is helpful to examine this in more detail.

A pilot project on parental attendance at case conferences in the London Borough of Hackney (Shemmings and Thoburn 1990) identified many of the same themes which arise in client recording. The authors refer to work by Schutz (1976) which states two important pre-conditions for the participant to be invited *and* involved *and* contributing:

1. Genuine participants know what others know...they *want* to know and they are in a *position* to know.

2. Genuine participants experience being treated as fellow citizens, otherwise they have feelings of exclusion, isolation and non-partnership.

Thus client participation in the case conference demands knowledge of its existence, an invitation to attend, being present, sharing and being able to make a contribution to the discussion. Similarly, client participation in record keeping requires knowledge of the case file system, an invitation to see the file, reading the records, discussion of their contents and the opportunity to share in the writing of assessments and treatment plans. Just as attendance is not synonymous with participation in case conferences, access does not ensure participation in the process of record keeping – making records available is not the same thing as inviting clients to take some responsibility for their content.

It is possible to envisage a scale of increasing client participation in the social worker's recording which defines some 14 'levels' along the continuum information/access/sharing/compiling (Appendix 9), after the manner of Arnstein's ladder of participation described in Chapter Two. Experience from the action research showed that the level adopted varied widely, both between cases and between records on the same case. Similarly, parents varied in their interpretation of the boundaries to 'seeing' and 'compiling' clinic social work records. In general, they had far more to say about the value of seeing than of compiling.

Exercising a right to see social work records

The research material shows that at the time social work records were compiled on this sample of clients the latter were both unconcerned and uninformed about the file kept on their child and family. One mother said she had never realised they were 'going on record'. No client recalled the social worker discussing the record she was making. Remarks such as 'No, never mentioned', 'No, it never came up' and 'She never explained it' were common. All the parents denied being concerned about the existence of case records at the time when their child was first referred to the clinic. Typically, they said: 'wasn't worried at all', 'never entered my head about the records', 'never gave it a thought'. Equally, most parents said they had not subsequently thought about the record made of their contact with the clinic social worker, that was, until the researcher 'brought it up'. One parent felt she had no energy to think about records and declared 'It's been as much as I can do to think about today and tomorrow'. However, after contact with the clinic ceased, two parents had then worried that the record might have adversely affected their child's life chances.

As the existence of case notes had not been made explicit and such thoughts had not 'entered their heads', it was to be expected that no one had asked to see their files. One parent said she had not asked because she thought the answer would have been 'no'. Raising the issue in the interviews stimulated many parents to consider why they had 'never thought to ask before'. A parent mused, 'I suppose we don't know we can question these things – we sort of leave it in their hands'. Another admitted that she'd always suspected the social worker had a lot more information than it seemed. Only two referred to having a right: 'I think you've a right to know what they are putting down about you', and 'I'd like to have the right, but I'd likely not use it unless the child deteriorates'.

Parents were asked if they would have liked to have read the record if the social worker had offered this. Half the sample replied emphatically that they would have done so. Several were somewhat doubtful, one responding 'In a way, yes, but would it have done any good?' Three parents were sure that they would refuse the offer to see records: 'not my business', 'no need – I trusted her' and 'nothing different in there to what I know'. After the researcher mentioned the Access to Personal Files legislation one mother neatly expressed the difficulty in exercising rights of which one is ignorant:

> It never occurred to me to ask to see. Would they be given the chance or would it be only if they happened to know they had a right? But I'm doubtful if people are told as simply as that…it's probably on a tiny piece of paper put where people don't see it.

The need to see – knowing what others know

Clients gave clear reasons for wanting to read the records. Their statements convey a sense of longing (almost a hunger) to possess, know and get hold of the information and opinion which they felt the social worker had committed to paper. Some parents indicated that curiosity, interest, memory and measuring progress were also factors which motivated their wish to read the notes. Others described a strong need to check up on the social worker's professional integrity, to establish 'if the record differed from what the social worker was telling', 'that the social worker wrote what had actually been said' and 'that the social worker had helped as much as they could'. Parents linked the quality of help given by the psychiatrist with the capacity of the social worker to record all the information offered in discussion.

Generally, parents were unhappy that social workers seemed to withhold information and opinions about the causes of problems and felt sure such conclusions about themselves would be contained in the social work notes. Some expressions of why they wished to share this opinion include: 'to know what people thought of us…how they looked at us', 'another view on us', 'a different light', 'to see their opinion in black and white', 'to see what they really thought the problem was' and 'to let me look at what you think I am'.

This last comment exemplifies many similar indications of a need to gain self knowledge by putting self image alongside professional opinion. Parents seemed consistently frustrated that social workers were not prepared to tell them about themselves orally. In one case the mother felt this was because the social worker was 'too kind perhaps…he wouldn't want to hurt me, like for my sake, not said the bad parts'. In wanting to read their files parents hoped to obtain assessment of problems, personalities and capacities which they felt their social workers had not provided orally. What they really wish to access is the social worker's knowledge and opinion about themselves – to know what the social worker knows and to share in her thinking about the problems presented by their children.

Several parents linked a strong desire to read records with concern about the quality of parenting. Unlike other cases, they *knew* they were good parents and felt confident that the record could not portray them as abusers, ogres, or the direct cause of their child's problem. They were aware that in cases of child abuse less adequate parents might not share their own relaxed attitude to records. Despite their positive self evaluation as non-abusers, it felt to the interviewer that they were nonetheless quite anxious, and reluctant to acknowledge the possibility that the social work file might cast doubts on the standard of their parenting. The following extracts from interviews with clients illustrate the importance they attach to this issue.

Mrs A was the mother of a seven-year-old boy referred to the clinic social worker after he made hoax calls to fire stations, ran away from school and repeatedly hid under stationary vehicles. She hoped the social worker would write down that 'he was from a stable background', and then said:

> How can I put this without it sounds silly. I think the only sort of people who probably want to know everything you are writing down are people

wanting to cover things up, who are not disclosing the full facts about
this that or the other, where a child is being sexually abused or something
and they are trying to deny what has happened to it. Probably people
like that would want to know what you was doing all the time, but not
in a particular case like I was in.

Mother of S:

> If I'd been cruel or that, then I think I'd want to see them. It's not my
> business to read whatever they wrote. I know I'm good with the kids and
> I'd never go round battering them or doing something cruel to them so
> I don't think there'd be anything written that in my eyes would be a
> drastic thing. I've just got confidence in myself that way.

A third parent:

> I thought we'd be down on a record but not for child battering or
> something like that which didn't worry me because I thought whatever
> they have got me down for, I know I'm all right.

One parent felt particularly aggrieved that although her situation did 'not
involve child battering, a record had still been made'.

Involvement in compiling records

Parents were asked if they would have liked an invitation to write the record
with the social worker. Responses showed they interpreted 'writing with the
social worker' to mean any of the levels of participation between 7 and 13 (see
Appendix 9), from discussing with the client what should be written to filing
the client's self-written account alongside the social worker's note.

Most clients thought the act of writing belonged to the social worker. They
felt this to be her job, her responsibility and several parents referred to an
expectation that she would have superior language and literary skills as a
qualification for her role. Comments were made in astonished tones which
suggested that some found the idea presumptuous, and the following quotations
illustrate some of the feeling expressed:

> She should be capable of writing it.

> I'd prefer her to do it. Let me do the talking and her do the writing but
> for me to see the finished job.

> Write it together? Oh no! A file is a thing they write about you – not for
> us to write in.

Several clients greatly appreciated their social worker's skill in finding suitable words to describe, record and reflect back their particular situation, as for example: 'She'd put it a way that I couldn't even write it – definitely summed up what I meant. I explained how I was feeling, she got it and put it into words on paper for me better than what I could'. It is notable that this parent saw the writing of her situation on paper was 'for me'.

It might be difficult for a client to refuse the invitation to contribute to the recording process. One mother's comment well illustrates the potential here for coerced compliance with the social worker's procedures: 'Well...I'd have sat down and I would have done it...probably would have taken me a long time but I would have done it'.

Clients referred to being under pressure during interviews with social workers. They felt any further contribution was beyond their resources at that time. A mother said:

> I don't think I could have wrote it like she did, we were so upset and confused, we'd waited so long for her to come and you get yourself in such a state...so much to tell her and at that time you don't think you could have done writing. You keep thinking and thinking of what you have got to tell them.

The importance of making sure the social worker received the intended communication was repeatedly stressed.

Only two parents would have welcomed an invitation to write a part of the record themselves. Both said they liked writing and felt they communicated more effectively on paper. They had secretarial skills and, stressing that increased involvement in the process would have reduced their sense of helplessness, said they would have liked 'to do something, to contribute towards the solution, to feel less helpless' and 'I'd have felt involved in what was happening'.

Many of the sample mentioned differences of opinion being made more explicit as the level of their access and participation increased. This was seen both negatively and positively. One parent felt such partnership increased accuracy in both communication and recording, and explained:

> Yes, I would have liked to write it together, you're comparing your chats with each other – if she's writing it down you can say no, I don't mean that – that can be sorted out before it's written down, before it can be taken in a different light...a better idea to correct her as she went along.

Other clients were concerned that disagreement between themselves and the social worker over the content of the record would damage their relationship. One mother feared that any disagreement would put a barrier between herself and the social worker; the conflict would upset her and deprive her of a highly valued opportunity to talk freely. 'If I was always thinking oh, she's going to write that down, I'd better not say it...that would worry me. If you are going to start keeping it in, what is the point of her coming?' Concern was also expressed that parents might withdraw their children from much needed help if they became aware that the social worker held, and had recorded, negative opinions of their capacities and circumstances.

Would participation in recording be an empowering experience?

The 'helplessness' referred to previously is clearly only one aspect of the relative differences in resource power between client and agency representative. Where clients perceive the social worker as being able to 'say things better' and 'know things we don't' they are at the same time viewing themselves as the least powerful participant in the process of help being offered by the clinic team. Material from these research interviews suggests that increased involvement in recording the process does engender feelings of powerfulness, but also indicates that issues concerning trust are closely bound up with 'empowering' relationships.

Clients referred to their fear of being judged, of being considered poor parents, of giving information in a muddled, inarticulate way, of being criticised for their child-rearing methods. The need to see records is clearly linked with a need to reassure themselves, to improve their self image and to obtain evidence that the social worker regards them in a positive way, at least in part. Some comments indicated that the invitation to see and contribute to records reinforced a sense of self worth and drew attention to the humanity shared by worker and client. The mother of Jim remarked 'It's a lovely thing to be asked and included, you are a person in all walks of life'. Such remarks support the validity of Schutz's pre-conditions for true participation; knowing what others know and experiencing treatment as a fellow citizen (Schutz 1976). The wish to balance the unequal partnership was expressed several times: this parent refers specifically to the flow of information when 'for good or bad I would have liked to have seen – it does not make it all one way...you are giving information but unless they're giving it back it's a bit lop-sided I think'.

The inaccessibility of the social worker's thinking was seen in various ways. One parent felt failure to share thinking reduced trust in the social worker, saying, 'I mean, we are telling her but we don't know what they think about us, do we?' In contrast another parent felt the professional social worker also had rights and that these constituted the terms on which help was made available. She felt 'they have a right to their own thoughts and to write them in their own way, help was given on their terms, in their hands...you accept their requirements to get the help'.

Three parents were concerned about the effect of the Access to Personal Files Act on the quality of record keeping which the social worker might now be able to undertake. One sympathised with the complexity of the recording task for the social worker, saying 'It's some work involved for you all though'. Another recognised the social worker's duty to decide when to withhold information which might do damage – 'They can't be 100 per cent frank with you for fear of tippling you'. The third parent somewhat despondently stated her view that open access will result in bland records denying a real opportunity to share the social worker's thinking, 'so I don't think you will ever really know now. It will make them a bit more wary about what they write, making sure it is facts'.

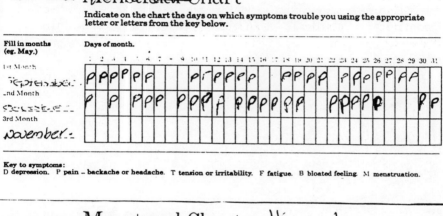

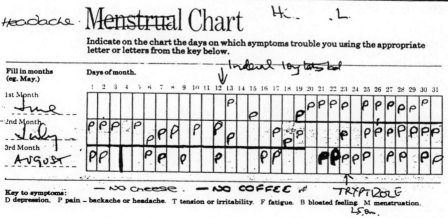

Figure 4.1 Clinical chart by Heather for frequency of headaches

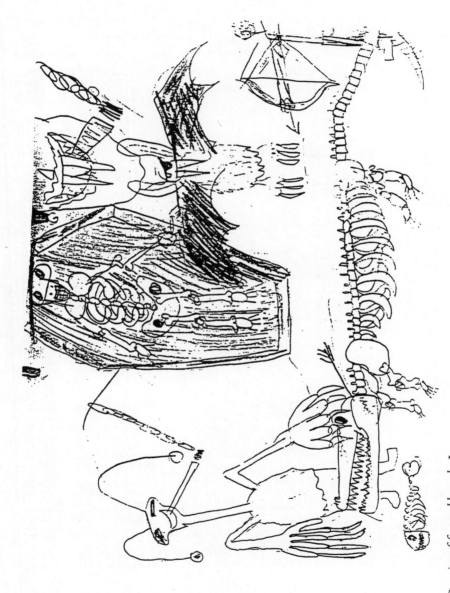

Figure 4.2 Drawing of fear and bones by Joe

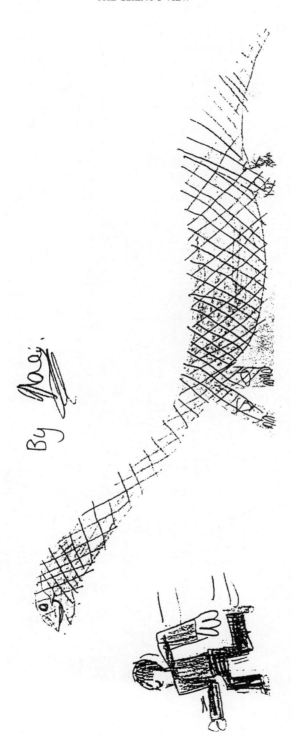

Figure 4.3 Drawing by Joe of his dream – being chased by a huge dinosaur

Figure 4.4 Drawing by Joe of resolved dream – 'Then I made friends with them and they chased everyone else'.

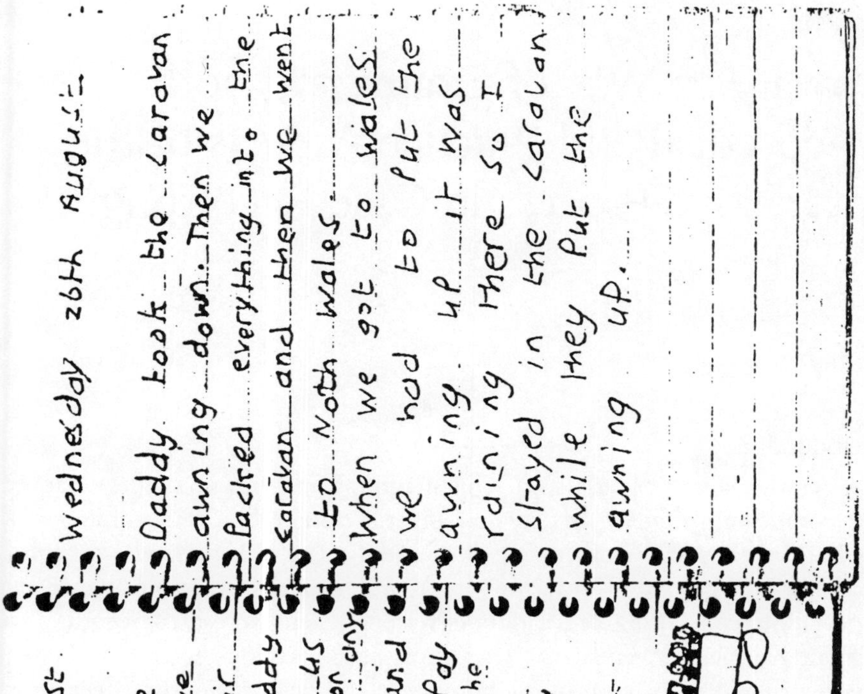

Tuesday 25th. August.

When we wokeup we
had breakfast. Then we
went into the Fun Fair.
Part of the Park. Daddy
bought wrist bands for us
all then we could go on any
ride we wanted to and
we didn't have to pay
anymore. we went on the
snake train. It was my
favourite. It went very
fast.

Wednesday 26th August.

Daddy took the Caravan
awning down. Then we
packed everything into the
caravan and then we went
to Noth wales
when we got to wales.
we had to put the
awning up. it was
raining there so I
stayed in the caravan
while they put the
awning up.

Figure 4.5 Jo records in her diary

CHAPTER FIVE

Towards a Way of Examining both Theoretical and Practice Aspects of the Interactive Process in Case Recording

Introduction

In previous chapters material from semi-structured interviews provides evidence that confusion, irritation, anxiety and anger surround the case recording task for both clinic social workers and their clients. The task itself was executed against a background of insecurity over professional role and management expectation concerning legislation governing client access to records. An account has been given of the way clinic social workers record, and their experience and perception of the purpose of this activity and its effect upon relationships and roles both inside and outside the multi-disciplinary team. The views of a sample of ex-clients about the purpose and process of compilation of written accounts of their interaction with the social work component of the agency proved just as interesting. Clients explained quite precisely what openness and participation in recording meant to them and their families. However, one dimension not directly addressed by these investigations is more detailed thinking about the process of agency–worker–client interaction in participatory social work case recording. The triangular network of relationships between consultant and his medical colleagues, social worker and her local government colleagues, and the child within his family, proved a powerful influence upon the content of records and the extent to which clients were admitted to the process.

It is possible and useful to explore this from two perspectives, which taken together, more soundly address its complexity:

1. Standing 'outside' of the material to examine it from perspectives introduced in Chapter One. In this sense the researcher examines the complexity and multi-dimensional nature of the process concerning

records – its meaning, what it does, the effect of language and power on the identity of both client and professional.

2. Evaluating a specific participative recording practice adopted by the researcher working in her own clinic with 18 newly referred clients. Such evaluation of data, from a therapeutic point of view, draws attention not only to the difficulties of *open* recording in a multi-disciplinary setting but also to the advantages and disadvantages of such a change of record keeping policy for both client, social worker and agency. To explore such interaction the methodology has to be of a qualitative nature, sufficiently sensitive to the nuances of the communication process. An action research approach allowed the researcher systematically to record observations on the process of changing her usual social work recording practice.

It is difficult to effect a complete separation between 1. and 2. However it is the purpose of later chapters to identify and illustrate subtlety within material whose inherent meaning is often contradictory and confusing. A wealth of case material emerged from the 'insider' work of the social worker-researcher and this will also be used to illustrate broader themes from an 'outside' vantage point. This chapter describes the action research approach which was used, the method of work adopted and the sample of cases selected for changed recording practice. Quotations from this action research material can then be used not only to consider the implications for social policy but also to illustrate discussion of more theoretical issues.

An action research approach

Little British research in social work with children and families appears to adopt an action research approach. An examination of ten action research projects describing new styles of intervention with children and youth found all were community based, and American (Rapoport 1987). Rapoport hopes that a partnership between integrated social research and active social intervention by welfare workers and organisations will lead to more reflective practice. This supports a call for relevant research to be performed by social workers in their own agencies as an integral part of their professional work (Whitaker and Archer 1989).

Action research sometimes aims to test a particular form of intervention and to process the results quantitatively. Research leading to the Plowden report (HMSO 1967) concerning educational priority areas adopted an action research method synonymously referred to as evaluation research, social experimentation and project appraisal, under the umbrella term programme evaluation (Bulmer 1982). Much of the data aimed to clarify the effectiveness of changed procedures in educational settings and the implications were of success or failure for use in long term planning. As with the action research methodology used in the central government sponsored Community Development Project, the approach carries the general difficulty of promoting participation in action research which may itself change the specified variables and alter the agreed boundaries to the study (Lees and Smith 1975). Despite not being susceptible to quantitative measures of the 'before/after/control group' type, such open ended initiatives can be described and the material discussed and evaluated to advantage.

Similarly, too great a concern with 'mechanistic procedures that minimise human judgement' would restrict research to areas of study which can be handled by rigorous scientific quantitative methods (Becker 1970). Becker's work on sociological method supports the view that there is no need to apologise for qualitative methodology, a view reflected in Bennathon's inaugural address to Young Minds, which included the statement 'so often it is the method, the certainty of being able to be scientific, which has determined what will be studied. In striving for scientific respectability academic psychology has often seemed arid – method has been put before content and sometimes the next step has been to assume that what cannot be proved does not exist...that to study feelings is not quite proper' (Bennathon 1989 p10). However, it is important that the chosen method be relevant and appropriate to the examination of the specific subject as Becker and others have emphasised.

Action research can be viewed as a cyclical process with five phases: diagnosing, action planning, action taking, evaluating and specifying learning (Susman and Evered 1978). Usually the action researcher and subjects maintain and regulate some or all of these five phases jointly. However, the resources of the small child guidance unit did not permit any of these five phases to be undertaken other than by the social worker-researcher (hereafter referred to as SWR) and the clinic patients. Such telescoping of the action/research/evaluation roles so that practice and research are performed simultaneously carries the obvious danger of excessive subjectivity. Nevertheless, the approach is also seen to possess the following advantages, which can be set alongside the disadvantages of subjectivity:

1. Action research is designed to consider a particular issue in a specific setting and assumes the immediacy of the researcher's involvement in the process. In this case the specific setting of the rural child guidance clinic remained unaltered as no additional personnel were introduced.

2. Action research involves the need for the researcher to bargain his way into the bureaucracy (Lees and Smith 1975). In this case the

researcher was long established as a member of the clinic team and of the wider inter-agency network.

3. The researcher, working as a clinician, is more able to pick out the questions, offer alternative definitions of the situation and to regard side issues positively rather than treat them as obstacles to establishing success or failure in a sharply focused style of intervention.

4. Conflict is frequently found between the neutrality of the researcher and the strong commitment of the action worker to 'success' in the project (Lees and Smith 1975). Amalgamation of role to that of single social worker-researcher avoids such tensions and rivalry.

5. Feelings aroused in the worker by interaction with the client can be regarded as valuable information and should not be dismissed on account of their supposed subjectivity. The extent to which such feelings accurately convey communication about clients' unspoken thoughts and emotions has been described elsewhere (Devereux 1967). The social worker-researcher's close relationship to the client allows such information to be collected and recorded, as it arises, in the context of the casework.

The approach taken to this part of the study is therefore essentially one of action research within the 'programme evaluation' genre (Bulmer 1982). The shifting focus of the investigation and exploratory nature of the initial goals might aptly categorise the procedure as 'experimental social administration'. Limitations imposed by subjectivity and a relatively small sample of cases may be offset by the advantageous position of the social worker-researcher in the clinic, the freedom to pursue side issues thus avoiding criteria of success or failure in evaluating the performance of this particular social work task, and the recognition that feelings aroused in the worker offer valuable insights into the process of client participation in case recording.

The role of the social worker-researcher in data collection

A conceptual separation is required of the impersonal 'outside' agent who is studying the data, from the activity of the object of the study, that is, the action researcher. In effect this needed the researcher to think about herself as if she were someone else. Having coined the title 'social worker-researcher' (SWR) to describe the role of the researcher experimenting with a new method of recording in the context of her usual work, it is possible to think of the evaluator as the 'researcher-observer', studying the research data from a more objective and theoretical perspective. Holding more than one role is always difficult.

Overall three had to be held (social worker-researcher, researcher-observer and evaluator-researcher), simultaneously and for considerable lengths of time.

Such divisions of role may appear tortuous and dispensable but the difficulties for the researcher as she slid between her *work*, observation of *herself working* and evaluation of *her own observations* were considerable and particularly evident in material compiled about her subjective experience of the changed practice. It was to address this problem that a method of work was devised which provided the researcher with detailed written accounts of the action research. Such accounts were compiled by the researcher-observer after each recording session, making, in effect, a record of the recording, but also including the material generated (letters, drawings, memos, charts, artwork) together with detailed descriptions of the SWR's feelings and concerns about particular difficulties. Copies of the 'new style' records, together with such descriptions of the processes which generated them, constituted a huge data resource which was collected together into 18 files, one for each of the sample cases. Each piece of social work recording, together with the SWR's observations upon its construction, constituted a specific 'item' which could subsequently be evaluated from a more objective perspective. It is perhaps possible to consider these 'items' as discrete representations of social work interaction and suggesting they be called *social work acts* resonates most appropriately with the *speech acts* (Searle 1971) mentioned earlier.

The gathering of such analysable data relating to some 232 *social work acts* is detailed later in this chapter and the results will be examined in Chapter Six. An empirical consideration of how far these recorded items were available to clinic clients is presented in Chapter Seven. An account is given at the end of Chapter Six of the negative terms in which the SWR experienced the changed record keeping practice. It is, however, difficult to evaluate the extent to which the SWR's subjective experience of the changed method of practice can be regarded as reliable qualitative data with potential for more general application. Nevertheless if the question 'How does this client make me feel?' is extended to 'How does recording this way make me feel?', ideas of counter-transference justify an assumption that the SWR's feelings about the recording also reflect something of the client's experience. The SWR's notes on her feelings after each recording were voluminous. It must, however, be recognised that subjective factors were inevitably in operation in the identification and selection of significant and illustrative material.

Method of work

The BASW/Ovretveit (1986) project used action research which depended upon the analysis of written evaluation sheets compiled at intervals by social workers and their team leaders. The present study of client recording does not aim to replicate Ovretveit's work but to examine the issues for client, worker and multi-disciplinary agency – continuously, sequentially and in the context of the recording process. Introducing such an action research approach into the work of the child guidance clinic required some care and negotiation. Discussions between child psychiatrist, educational psychologist, SWR and her line manager secured agreement to change the existing style of social work recording on eight cases referred from May 1986 and on ten further consecutive referrals from 1987. Team members had understandable concerns about their own possible loss of access to social work assessment, the protection of third parties and adverse effects upon clinic clients. After some testing for feasibility during the recording of the first case, a procedure was developed and subsequently adopted which addressed the anxieties of team members.

Newly referred parents and children are often especially tense and distressed and it was therefore considered unethical to burden them further with choices about whether they should participate in a new style of recording. The SWR thus presented open client recording as her usual practice so that the client received at least as good a service as those not included in the sample. Other aspects of the SWR's intervention remained unchanged.

Paperwork on the 18 sample cases was physically separated into 'child psychiatry' and 'social work'. Recording by the SWR which was open and/or participative was kept in a detachable social work folder clipped inside the back cover of the clinic (child psychiatry) file. Items of recording which could not be shared with the client were filed in the psychiatric section. Details of each such usage were documented by the SWR as were any covert notes or decisions not to record sensitive information.

During the first case it was realised that a more structured case recording format would help the SWR and client gather and write down the salient points of their sessions in a more succinct and purposeful way. The BASW/BIOSS format was therefore adapted to meet the specific requirements of the child guidance clinic. The SWR completed contact sheets for each case and then used first assessment, review and closure summary forms as appropriate. The front sheet of the clinic's social history form was retained and paper headed 'social worker's progress report' was used instead of the BASW/BIOSS 'incident' form. There was no intention to test the performance of the BASW/BIOSS recording system in the child guidance setting or indeed to consider the merits of different styles of paperwork and filing arrangements. The SWR merely selected and integrated pro-forma from the BASW/BIOSS system which she felt most helped the open recording process in each case.

At some point during the first interview the SWR explained to parents that time would be put aside to make a record of the session and to discuss what was to be recorded in the social work part of the file. The SWR made explicit that she was a social worker, that it was her social work records which were open to clients to read, that they could not see other parts of the clinic file and that they could be denied access to material involving other people or items which the SWR judged to be damaging to themselves and their children. The SWR attempted to sit near to the client, side by side, so that both were in a position to see the material being written down as points were discussed and agreed. This ideal arrangement frequently foundered and the importance of such situational factors cannot be over-stressed.

After the case notes had been compiled and clients departed, the SWR made careful notes about her experience of recording that particular session and how far she had involved clients in the process of compiling case notes for their own files. It was recognised that the degree of parental participation was extremely variable and that it existed on a 'sliding scale' of user involvement which ranged from informing the client of his right to see all or part of his record (level 1), to accepting the client's own recorded item, be it drawing, diary or report, as the sole record for the file (level 14). Such a scale of user involvement was previously discussed in relation to the interviews carried out with clients and is detailed in Appendix 9.

The SWR aimed to note her own feelings about the changed practice, the difficulties and conflicts encountered and what those meant to her in the context of her usual professional work in the clinic. In gathering a mass of observations about problems of timing, place, language, third parties and work with the education authority the SWR was concerned not merely to describe these as obstacles to open recording, but to discover the meaning they held for clients, colleagues and other agencies. The degree of 'openness' was considered in each case using the contact sheets and reasons for denial of access examined. She looked in particular for evidence that case recording undertaken with clients had enhanced or diminished the quality of her practice and such, albeit subjectively judged, occasions were documented in the context of the case material from which they derived.

In effect this method was adopted in order to investigate a new technique using the researcher as both action researcher and clinic social worker. It was important that the action researcher had the clinical skills of the experienced child guidance social worker and was also trusted as an established member of the multi-disciplinary team. However it has also to be recognised that without other research resources, there was no other feasible way of proceeding. The difficulty of 'studying oneself' is further explored in Chapter Six.

Description of the agency in which the recording method was changed

Closer examination of the process of participative case recording was undertaken in a very small child guidance clinic situated in the high street of a busy town in a rural shire county. The district health authority considered it appropriate to deliver child psychiatry through the establishment of child guidance clinics based in the community and there were, in consequence, no hospital-based departments of child psychiatry. The premises were provided by the education authority under agreements dating back to the 1974 DHSS circular (Joint circular 3/74 from DES/DHSS/Welsh Office on Child Guidance). The facilities and secretarial assistance left much to be desired and were constantly being threatened with either review or reduction, or both. All three professional staff believed strongly in the value of a multi-disciplinary team and indeed the majority of the clinic cases were held in common by the social worker and consultant in child psychiatry There was considerable argument as to whether the educational psychologist was in fact a third member of the multi-professional team or whether the concept of a child guidance network more properly described his contribution to the work of the clinic.

The consultant in child psychiatry journeyed 50 miles to this clinic once a fortnight to see some six children and their parents in the one session, with no allowance made for time to travel, confer or eat lunch. The consultant rarely brought the senior house officer or registrar to this distant clinic although occasionally a nurse from the adolescent unit would accompany him. His work was therefore essentially performed with the social worker as a co-therapist in a situation of considerable professional isolation. The acute lack of time for thorough discussion even between consultant and social worker increased the dependence of both upon histories and notes each compiled as part of the clinic file of records This child psychiatrist saw himself as providing an opinion on puzzling cases largely referred to him by medical colleagues and immediate team members (educational psychologist and social worker). Treatment was then undertaken by himself and/or the social worker using psychotherapeutic, behavioural or family based approaches in places and ways which were geographically and practically possible.

The educational psychologist had a base in the clinic, although his main office and indeed his records were some 30 miles away at another child guidance centre favoured with more secretarial time. The work of the clinic had a highly 'educational' flavour; a high proportion of children seen had special educational needs which the local schools found difficult to meet. The psychologist tried to be present at some point during clinic sessions to discuss educational issues raised in the cases seen, especially those in which he himself was personally involved. He rarely read clinic files but a considerable number of letters flowed between himself and the child psychiatrist and were filed in their separate files 30 miles apart despite the child being seen by a tri-partite child guidance team. This psychologist spent considerable time discussing cases with the social worker and received lists of children to be seen and notes of plans made after each appointment. Despite his commitment to working as a team, his own department favoured the idea of withdrawing educational psychologists from their bases in clinics, and operating such multi-disciplinary work on the lines of networks.

The social work establishment of this clinic was a 0.75 specialist social work post permanently seconded to the child guidance service. This was the post filled by the SWR. Three full-time social workers and a senior social worker were similarly seconded to three other clinics in half of this large rural county. Supervision was provided regularly by the senior social worker and, together with monthly team meetings of these clinic social workers, this went some way towards reinforcing professional identity and reducing isolation.

The clinic secretary had been in her half-time post for many years and took pride in a fairly complex system of differently coloured typing and note papers to denote discipline and task of the writer. The education department employed this secretary and provided all office equipment and file covers. The health authority provided the headed stationery and the consultant considered the files to be 'medical' files, despite most of their contents being written by the SWR. Four months after the research began this secretary retired and three months elapsed before a replacement was appointed. The post of secretary in a child guidance clinic demands an ability to cope with administrative requirements imposed by three separate departments all focusing on the same child, albeit on a rainbow of differently coloured and headed papers. The induction of this new secretary was made more difficult by the supplementary set of instructions relating to the records of the 18 cases in the action research sample.

Selection and description of the eighteen sample cases

Three criteria were applied to selection of the cases in which the method of case recording was to be changed:

1. Re-referrals were not allocated to the sample. Using newly referred cases avoided problems of retrospective access jeopardising participation in the current referral.

2. The SWR had to be the sole social worker – cases with current input from other social workers were not included.

3. Cases selected should appear to require more social work involvement than one initial interview.

The first eight cases, referred consecutively from May 1986 and meeting the above criteria, were recorded in the new style for a period of four months. Three of these cases became 'long term' while the other five had only ten interviews between them and active work was concluded within the four month period of study. The cases selected for the sample are described in some detail not only to give an overview of each child's problem and professional input, but to help readers put extensive quotations from the *social work acts* into the context of work on each case.

Ronald P was an eight-year-old boy who, with his parents, was referred by the educational psychologist for advice concerning his killing of chickens, soiling, stealing, aggression and acute learning problems. The case remained open for some years as this emotionally rejected boy needed help from all three disciplines.

Joanie L Six-year-old Joanie was referred to the clinic by the GP because of parental concern that she lacked self confidence, was weepy and fearful at school and had difficulty in sleeping. Joint work with the family by the SWR and consultant in the clinic augmented work by the SWR with parents at home and in liaison with school staff.

The Godfrey family The health visitor referred the parents of three demanding pre-school children for help in managing their behaviour. The referral was to the SWR by name and one long chaotic family session took place in her office. Home visits later revealed that the family had precipitously left the area. These young parents were in urgent need of housing and money – being in a state of crisis their interest in recording was minimal and only basic information was gathered.

Alex W was referred by the hospital after this 16-year-old grammar school lad took a serious overdose prior to examinations. The consultant child psychiatrist saw him on the ward and then asked the SWR to assess the case prior to follow up in the clinic. The mother, a business woman, displayed only shallow emotional investment in her son, seemed to intellectualise his problems and, perhaps because of this, participated enthusiastically in recording a full history.

Leon B Leon was ten when parents asked the GP to refer him to the clinic team for assessment and advice about dangerously aggressive behaviour rendering him liable to expulsion from school. The parents had adopted their two older children so were well used to social workers and their files. The father in particular was keen to participate actively in the record keeping but he worked away from home six days a week. The mother had a chronic illness – being unwell and very anxious reduced her capacity to undertake any further burdensome activity. Considerable input was required by all three members of the clinic team and although the outcome was ultimately good, resolution took far longer than four months.

Dean W Thirteen-year-old Dean also became a long term case. His GP referred him to the clinic as truanting, fearful of being bullied and thought a 'poof'. The parents complained vigorously that their son refused to attend school, stole, was violent to his mother and ran away. They gave different accounts to the SWR on different occasions and presented the child psychiatrist with yet other versions. The parents were known to the clinic – they were foster parents and had appalled the same team with their sudden rejection of a very deprived foster boy whose removal they demanded with no preparation. It was clearly painful for them to present with their natural son only weeks later, this time as 'clients', not 'fellow professionals'. The father avoided the SWR as far as possible; the mother manipulated every situation so as to 'professionalise' herself, as for example, insisting that the SWR meet with her at her own work place, over her desk. The SWR had several roles in this case, not all therapeutic. There was real concern that the boy was inappropriately treated and required removal from his rejecting parents. In addition, the SWR felt a responsibility to advise that no further foster children be placed which provoked much conflict and raised issues of confidentiality and ownership of information given to the SWR.

Jay T The GP referred Jay for management of behaviour problems. Although his mother clearly wanted advice about her 'wild' four-year-old son, she would not proceed with the referral until satisfied that records made would not follow Jay to his primary school. Because she was concerned about records, it was particularly easy to involve this mother in the new recording process. It eventually transpired that the boy's behaviour was a paradoxical reaction to drugs given by the GP and parenting was not an issue.

John M The educational psychologist referred John who, at 15, had serious problems: stealing mortgage money, stealing and selling bikes, addiction to gambling machines, hoarding food and his mother's jewellery, fraud, truancy and damaging the school bus. The mother was overwhelmed and, having no satisfactory partner with whom to share her distress, needed the SWR to process her torrent of angry, guilty feelings, in particular those relating to the family 'myth' about John's paternity. She had neither interest nor energy to devote to keeping a record of the very sensitive information she gave.

In the spring of 1987 ten further cases were selected in the same way and recorded in the new style until closure. In this way it was possible to examine issues raised by record keeping practice during the complete 'life' of the case rather than a fixed period of four months. The cases remained open from a minimum of three months to a maximum of three years and five months; the mean was fifteen months.

> *Daniel B* was a 13-year-old lad, referred by the GP for 'behaviour problems at home and school'. In fact he was seriously out of control of his lone parent who could not enforce his school attendance or prevent his gambling in the arcades. The mother over-protected and colluded with Daniel who was eventually placed by the team as an in patient at the adolescent unit where a full assessment led to his placement at a private boarding school for boys with emotional and behavioural problems. The social work (and hence the records) spanned a long period and required liaison with colleagues of both health and education departments as well as the boarding school.

> *Lily J* was an eight-year-old girl, referred by the health visitor to the SWR at the request of the mother. Pains, crying, reluctance to attend school, food fads and obstinacy had developed around the time of a grandfather's death. However, Lily was never seen as the father did not consent to the referral, feeling that 'it would go on her record'. The SWR saw the mother for individual counselling about parenting this bossy little girl and the case was closed after nine months.

> *Carol G* was nine years old, the only daughter of a woman who had fled from an urban area to drift between temporary accommodations. The GP referred Carol because of her stealing, not sleeping, being anorexic and having poor school grades. The focus of the mother's concern was very different. There were child protection issues in this case and the SWR had to negotiate conflicting demands of openness, confidentiality and sharing of information with colleagues worried about child abuse. The focus of the SWR's work was with the mother who left the area as suddenly as she had arrived.

> *Steven H* was a 13-year-old school phobic boy, the eldest of five children, who was referred to the SWR by the education welfare officer. The focus of ensuing work was the acute separation anxiety and enmeshed relationship of the boy and his mother. The SWR undertook some individual work with Steven but her input was largely with the parents, various agents of the education system and staff of the in patient adolescent unit. The case remained open for well over two years with some support and monitoring by the SWR in order to maintain the placement in a very expensive independent mainstream boarding school some 200 miles away.

Justin W was referred by the school doctor after his mother admitted to longstanding soiling and bed wetting problems with her ten-year-old son. The parents were divorced but lived in the same house, creating difficulty in establishing who was actually taking responsibility for supervising Justin. Lack of compliance with treatment programme and clinic attendance, mistakes over factual information and an abrupt closure created many obstacles to consistent open recording.

Roy G was one of nine-year-old twins in a strict Jehovah's Witness family where the mother had deserted and then been disfellowshipped (cast out) for being unable to follow the strict Witness code. The children were sad about her disappearance and saw her only under the supervision of Witness relatives. Roy was a tense little boy whose eye blinking, head nodding, depression, enuresis and speech problems had worsened as the father found the task of bringing up the family alone more taxing than he had first envisaged. His belief system separated the children from life in the ordinary community – similarly he attached no importance to the systems surrounding the SWR and consultant. He brought all the children to the clinic for joint sessions with the SWR and consultant. Eventually Roy became more confident, less sad and did better at school.

Jim E was a four-year-old 'little basher', referred by the GP as his mother was quite unable to manage his over-active, mischievous behaviour. The SWR visited the home and observed Jim to be very bright, bored and perfecting the art of winding up his mother, day and night. His repertoire included catapulting her out of her wicker rocking chair by leaping off tables onto the rockers. Work was done over a short period to obtain funding for a playgroup for Jim, to counsel the mother about child management and to press for early school entry. The parents were separated, and the father lived nearby and came every day to help to control his son's behaviour. The SWR had problems of role in this case as she blurred the boundary with the social services department office in tasks connected with financing the playgroup.

Molly C was a six-year-old girl referred to the SWR by the health visitor after her mother asked the latter for help with her daughter's behaviour problems. The family lived in a very middle class area, were Italian and had built up a well-known business. They felt isolated socially and emotionally. The mother was depressed after the stillbirth of her second child. It emerged that the referral was made without the knowledge or consent of the father – hence work consisted of counselling the mother; Molly was not seen.

Lawrence W was a toddler when the GP referred him to the team saying that his mother could not handle him, he was violent at playschool and threw things about. Assessment revealed a very tense and over-involved relationship by a mother who never felt good enough to meet the needs of an over-precious child. Issues of trust and confidentiality arose when this mother applied for the job of clinic secretary using her maiden name.

Graham S was referred to the SWR by the head of the local grammar school requesting that she draw the consultant's attention to the problems exhibited by this severely epileptic 13-year-old boy. The case proved difficult, both to help and to record in an open style. The father suffered with manic depressive psychosis and returned to mental hospital during the period of child guidance clinic involvement. The mother was exceptionally anxious, denied the obvious problems to the point of irrationality and became locked into conflict with anyone attempting to help her seriously disturbed son. Interesting issues arose as the school tried to manipulate the clinic team into validating their wish to exclude Graham.

How far did these eighteen cases reflect the client group usually referred?

The sample was examined from six perspectives and compared with the profiles of either 100 randomly selected past referrals to this clinic or the 300 cases referred to the area child guidance service in the same year.

Social class

Due to high numbers of one parent families (39%) attempts to match for social class have to be tentative if based solely on current occupation. Thus both educational and occupational histories of sample cases and 100 randomly selected referrals were used to allocate each to a middle class group (1, 2 and 3a), or to a working class group (3b, 4 and 5).

Class	Sample	Random 100
Middle class	27%	26%
Working class	73%	74%

Sex

Sex	Sample	300 Cases
Girls	22%	43%
Boys	78%	57%

The low proportion (22%) of girls in the sample was its one unrepresentative feature, as a figure of around 40 per cent would have been expected. Two factors might account for this. First, excluding cases with involvement by another social worker probably skewed the sample by avoiding referrals for treatment of sexually abused children, who tended to be girls. Second, the sample was gathered before the height of the holiday season when a high proportion of referrals concerned out-of-control teenage girls.

Age

Age Group	Sample	300 Cases
0–4 years	22%	12%
5–10 years	44%	39%
11–16 years	34%	49%

Pattern of work

Pattern of Work	Sample	300 Cases
SWR/Consultant/ Educational psychologist	39%	24%
SWR/Consultant	44%	63%
SWR	17%	13%

Clients saw one, two or three professionals in a pattern of intervention regarded as usual for that clinic. There was a high concentration of educational problems with which it was expected the team would become involved.

Source of referral

Orientation	Sample	300 Cases
Family doctor	50%	70%
Health V/school doctor/self	22%	15%
Education	22%	10%
Hospitals	6%	5%

Focus of the problem

Orientation	Sample	300 Cases
Home	50%	54%
Medical	33%	25%
School	17%	21%

Considering the small size of the sample it is remarkable how closely it matches the profiles of previous referrals, particularly so in respect of social class.

CHAPTER SIX

Discussion of the Action Research (Theoretical Perspectives)

Who is the client?

Before presenting issues from the action style research, it is necessary to explore the difficult question of who is the client in this specialised form of social work. Lack of clarity about the case subject pervaded and bedevilled logical attempts to apply legal guidelines with respect to client access to records, confidentiality and third parties. The psychiatrist considered the child to be his patient, labelled the file accordingly and was (at the time of the research) under no pressure to reveal his written records to clients. His patients were normally under sixteen on referral: they could not legally consent to their own treatment and the agreement to consider their needs was between psychiatrist and those with parental responsibility.

The social work records reflected the fact that the SWR spent much of her time helping parents to meet the needs of the index patient (child) and thus the true subjects of her part of the file were parents. Parents, not children, usually sought help with their own inability to meet the needs of a particular child in the course of ordinary day to day parenting. Although the file was opened in the name of the child, it contained far more information about other family members, particularly parents. Strictly, all family members could be considered third parties, having little right of access to the information in a file whose subject was a child. In the case of a child over 14, DHSS guidance required the child subject to give permission for parents to see what was recorded about him. Conversely the permission of all third parties was needed before he could see items in the record relating to his parents, siblings, relations or any other identifiable person who was not the file subject (HMSO 1984).

One major paradox therefore was how to establish the subject of the file in a clinic which offered psychotherapy and individual counselling rather than systemic family therapy, and where health and social work agencies accorded differing rights to those aged 14 to 16. The focus of social work intervention was essentially the interactive space between referred child and others, usually adults and parenting figures who had sought referral. (However, a focus upon the family system, as in family therapy, allowed the possibility of all family members having subject access to a family file labelled accordingly.) It was difficult to give a name to the focus of work on essentially symbiotic relationships within an egocentric network binding index patient and nurturant figures. In many ways the named subject of the file, as printed on the label, was not in practical terms the subject of the work recorded as having been performed. The majority of social work recording concerned work with parents' practical and emotional difficulties in managing to care for the index patient.

The dilemma is summarised by asking the following questions:

1. Who were members of the child guidance agency for the purpose of access to information?

2. Who was the client, that is, the access subject?

3. Who or what was the focus of the SWR's work?

The SWR found herself largely unable to answer these questions – a fact which perhaps accounts for the conservatism of her decisions as to material she felt able to make available to clients. Her inability to formulate procedural rules around the question of 'Who is the client?' maintained the number and complexity of moral minefields to be negotiated afresh as she wrestled with issues of access and confidentiality in each item of recording.

Confidentiality and protection of third parties were complex inter-related duties

The British Association of Social Workers has given much attention to the issue of confidentiality, and distilled the recommendations of its report (1972) into Practice Principle X1 of the Code of Ethics (Appendix 10). Section 7 of the Local Authority Social Services Act 1970 dealt with identifiable personal information held by local authorities and the circumstances in which it might be disclosed. In 1988 the Department of Health issued guidance (LAC[88]17, DOH 1988) to local authorities under Section 7 which was intended to formalise long standing conventions governing the handling of this type of information and its exchange between professionals. The guidance recognised the fundamental importance of donated information to both service users and providers by stating 'Informed judgements rely on the supply of information in confidence by clients, and on exchanges of information between social services departments and other organisations or individuals' (paragraph 15).

It was, however, the Local Authority Circular (83) 14 (DHSS 1983) which provided general principles on arrangements for the subject to know what was held on file about him in local authority records, in clear anticipation of the Data Protection Act 1984 (HSMO 1984) and the Access to Personal Files Act 1987 (HMSO 1987). Section 6 of the latter detailed five conditions which would justify the local authority refusing to disclose recorded information. It is this provision which requires the local authority to protect third parties who have given information on the understanding that their identity and/or communication would not be disclosed.

Thus the legislation and its accompanying guidance have treated confidentiality and protection of third parties as separate topics. Experience in the action research did not find it possible or helpful to separate considerations of subject access from more general ethical concerns about the confidentiality of donated information. Two aspects of agency function exerted a particularly strong influence and merit some elaboration.

First, the multi-disciplinary nature of the agency made it difficult to have agreed administrative arrangements to guard against misuse of information in a team with flexible and shifting boundaries. This setting, in which social work was not expressly the principal function of the agency, involved a group of professionals diffusely networked to yet other professionals whose involvement with the case regularly produced voluminous 'third party' contributions to the clinic file. For example, the inclusion of the educational psychologist in work by the core team of child psychiatrist and SWR stimulated a flow of written communication from his colleagues in the education department. Similarly, the consultant was part of a chain of communications involving paediatricians, school medical officers, psychiatrists and other consultants who freely shared information about children and families. Second, as discussed above, in the confusion between children and parents, patients and clients, families and individuals, it was impossible to arrive at an agreed system which accurately identified the true subjects of the files of records. There was therefore confusion and conflict over who were subjects and who were third parties.

Protecting the confidential nature of clients' contacts with the child guidance clinic imposed a constant pressure upon the SWR. She had initially told clients that she would not approach other agencies without their permission, making specific reference to schools. It is notable that she did not always abide by this promise. In practice there was pressure to obtain school reports in time to assist the consultant with his initial assessment and it was easy for the SWR to forget to ask permission for this when preoccupied with other aspects of the case, as occurred with Alex W. The SWR's upsetting confrontation with the elder brother of the overdosing Alex W was probably what led her to forget to ask the mother's permission to contact and discuss with the school. This led to an unrecorded 'clandestine' telephone call with the head teacher who blissfully dismissed the SWR's scruples, saying there was no issue about confidentiality as the mother had insisted she expected the school to sort matters out.

It might be argued that the SWR should have been more persistent in gaining the mother's permission to obtain a school report. However, she had to balance conflicting priorities; disregard her commitment to confidentiality and rely upon the head teacher's assertion that the mother would not mind, or, by adhering to her promise, cause the boy to be seen at the clinic in the absence of information, which might adversely affect his treatment.

Some clients feared that the information they gave might stimulate an interest by statutory agencies in the welfare of their child. Parents having other, or past, contact with social workers were perfectly correct in suspecting that statutory agencies viewed their parenting in a negative way (Jim E, Carol G, Leon B, Dean W, John M). Other parents were anxious to avoid being so judged. The fathers of Molly and Lily both refused to allow their daughters to attend the child guidance clinic because they feared stigmatisation by records and escalating interference by welfare agencies as 'one thing led to another'.

It may be that other clients in the sample were actually less happy with arrangements for confidentiality than they initially appeared. Mrs W's mistrust of the SWR's capacity to safeguard her personal information was revealed four months after referral. This mother suddenly expressed her anger that she had not been selected for the job of clinic secretary. She was highly suspicious that somehow the SWR had 'leaked' information to the interviewing panel that she was not able to cope with her child and was therefore 'on the wrong side of the desk'. Small rural communities increase the prevalence of such problematic situations and it is interesting that several parents interviewed during the research (Chapter Four) mentioned fear of their records being seen by gossiping office staff who were neighbours or relatives. Such was in fact the case with Daniel B whose aunt became the clinic secretary: parents' fears may be well founded.

Information as an index and source of power

Ownership of personal information about the lives of clients is central to discussion about issues of power in record keeping. In knowing about clients the SWR increased her powerfulness in respect of them. In contrast, clients knew little, if anything, of her personal life and the research material often demonstrated that even knowledge of her professional role was scanty. From the perspective of civil liberty, personal information belongs to the subject who should have access to written accounts about themselves (Cohen 1974). However, the records in this research remained in the possession of clinic staff and clients sometimes lacked knowledge of their content or existence. Yet the clinic social worker was free to share them with colleagues, decide to withhold their contents from clients or to provide edited summaries to clients, colleagues, managers or other agencies. 'Notifying by standard letter' and the spread of information between agencies are two examples of ways in which manipulation of information about the client tipped the balance of power in favour of the professionals: both need further discussion.

Clinic social workers and clients spoke of being 'known' to the clinic, and to the social services department. 'Standard' letters by clinic personnel to 'notify' other colleagues of new and closed referrals, and to request information, formed part of a network of surveillance. Rarely was this trawl for personal information made explicit to clients who were largely unaware that an appointment for their child to see a consultant in child psychiatry also resulted in the family becoming clients of the social services department. The response from the social services department was also of a standard format in language suggesting potential for wide surveillance by an organisation which could decide to inform or show papers according to mysterious criteria. The letter asking if the W family were 'known' resulted in this typical reply: 'I write to advise you that the above named family is not currently supervised by this office but I can let you have further information upon request. Your social worker might like sight of the papers'. In another case the reply stated the child guidance social worker was 'welcome to peruse' a file of information from another local authority.

A long-standing agreement with the health authority not to place non-statutory clinic cases on the social services department computer caused problems with filing and retrieval of these 'standard' letters. Given fully computerised records there was no reliable way of retaining or recalling communications from the SWR about clients not on computer. Such letters were commonly destroyed on receipt. In offices with manual records a miscellaneous file of the SWR's letters were referred to on an ad hoc basis which depended upon the senior social worker remembering the contents of this unindexed folder. One unfortunate result of this arrangement was that clinic clients subsequently seeking help from the social services department often became aware that information about them had already been given by the clinic social worker without their knowledge or consent. The harassed duty officer's chance remark 'And how is your daughter getting on at child guidance?' was met in one case with the retort 'And how the hell did you know she goes to child guidance?'

A high proportion of the sample had previous involvement with social services departments. It was striking that parents did not usually disclose this to the SWR themselves, fearing perhaps that such past contact might stigmatise them as poor managers or inadequate carers before they had had a chance to present their current situation to clinic staff. Referral letters from doctors rarely included information about involvement of social services despite this being at times of a statutory nature.

Letters were not routinely sent to schools asking for information until parents had given permission. However, when the referrer was not a doctor, the GP was sent a 'standard' letter seeking 'approval' of the consultant seeing the child, and 'any information you feel could assist in my assessment or a clinical note'. Parents were not made aware of this correspondence which was initiated and signed by the SWR on behalf of a consultant based 40 miles away.

The spread of information within and between departments was rarely known to clients. Information on closed cases was readily given if there were issues of child protection, as for example, in the Carol G case. When another local authority investigated allegations of sexual abuse, the SWR felt the needs of the child over-rode her commitment to confidentiality. The strength of information networks within the social services department had not been appreciated by the parents of Dean W. Their services as local authority foster parents were terminated after the clinic social worker gave negative information about them to the family placement section. In this case the clinic social worker offered the information to support her professional view that Mr and Mrs W should not act as foster parents. Sometimes the social services department required the clinic social worker to submit her case records to senior officers. Her notes often referred to aspects of the consultant's work or opinion which he did not wish shared outside the clinic team. This issue erupted also in the W case when the SWR was instructed to hand over her file to residential workers who had agreed to care for Dean at short notice. The SWR refused to comply, considering that half her file contained medical and educational material which was not hers to give. Her own notes had been written on the assumption that clinic team members would read them in the way she intended them to be understood – the 'shared, practical and entitled understanding' referred to by Garfinkel (1967 p201).

Records and correspondence between social services and the clinic thus comprised the system of 'intense registration and documentary accumulation' described by Foucault (1975 p189). Families and individuals 'referred' became 'cases' to be 'seen' during 'examination', their 'social history taken' and the resulting information retained. Foucault's concepts of the 'discourse of power', 'disciplinary techniques to manage bodies', 'hierarchised surveillance' and 'the examination' are useful and vivid ways to consider what such diligent information gathering was actually doing to the balance of power between worker and client. It is in studying such 'micro' transactions within the recording process that the Foucauldian approach (described more fully in Chapter One) elevates the case recording task from that of a 'boring chore' to one in which 'power is exercised rather than possessed; it is not attached to agents and interests but is incorporated in numerous practices. Power can thus work from the "bottom up" and Foucault uses the notion of the capillary to describe the operations of power at micro level' (Barrett 1991 p135).

It is interesting to consider why the SWR did not inform clients that her first action on receiving the referral had been to institute a trawl for information about them, especially her standard letter to the local social services department. This had been a much debated issue, not only in the SWR's clinic but for many clinic social workers interviewed in Chapter Three, and was one which crystallised the dilemma about responsibility for cases. Essentially the consultant considered referrals were to himself, but for logistical reasons the SWR acted as an intake facility, offering an initial assessment visit before clinical examination. The consultant feared the reaction of his patients if they knew social services had been made aware that they were seeking help in parenting one of their children. His patients often wished to keep secret their connections with other welfare agencies and to present their child as the focus of problems. The consultant, whilst wanting information about any other involved agencies, hoped that the SWR would not imperil clinic attendance figures by revealing her information network with the agency, which was feared for its statutory powers and reputation for 'interfering'.

Whatever the degree of client participation in the process of closing the case, standard letters routinely 'notified' the social services department that the case was closed. These letters were logical sequelae to those sent initially announcing the involvement of the clinic social worker. The final sentence of the standard closure letter offered 'If at some future date (child) should be referred to your department I shall be pleased to give further details of our past involvement upon request'. The same moral dilemmas arise for the SWR as in the original notification, for parents were never made aware of this communication, with its suggestion of significant information becoming available if the family failed to cope with their child.

Recording and negotiation between professionals

1. Within the clinic team

The research data illustrates vividly how the social worker's recording could be viewed as a process of manoeuvring and bargaining. Team members noted the writings of others, discussed the wording of letters and sought tacit approval that their contributions to the file reflected matters agreed verbally. There were long established, informal understandings about who recorded what about whom and who wrote to whom about which topics. Therefore although the purpose, content and format of the SWR's writings reflected her role at the time, their full significance and effect is only understood in the context of communication between clinic staff as they 'juggled' their joint resources and responsibilities in each case. Thus social work records were not merely 'made' – they were the subject of negotiation and containers for powerful messages to team members; they managed political strife.

The SWR and child psychiatrist negotiated the content of their respective records particularly in respect of 'bad' things. The consultant usually recorded clinic based sessions in which the SWR acted as co-therapist. As his notes were not seen by clients, he could, and did, record for both of them those things which clients would find punitive. Thus the SWR was spared the necessity of dealing with such opinion in the context of an open social work record. Clinic notes about the parents of Justin W are illustrative. Frustrated by the parent's inability to supervise effectively their boy's toilet training, the consultant wrote on behalf of the team that 'mother is out at work therefore she does not give any supervision', 'mother was hesitant and giving excuses' and 'it is their job to give supervision and they should stick to it for six weeks'.

Such manoeuvring and bargaining is reminiscent of the way in which those who live and work in psychiatric hospitals continually revise, defend and subvert the 'order' within their institution (Strauss et al. 1963). Consensus is lacking both within and between groups of workers and Strauss shows that the apparently weaker groups (patients, ward orderlies) actually have considerable power to change the 'order' laid down by consultants and senior nurses. The idea of such a 'negotiated order' is helpful in understanding the way in which unspoken attitudes and interests governed the day to day practice of the child guidance clinic. The social worker's recording can be seen as an important arena in which such negotiations were played out, one example being its use as a vehicle for coded communication.

Transferring meaning between team members was an integral part of their careful negotiating, one around the other, over particularly sensitive issues. One such area was the consultant's wish to offer personally 'his' in patient resource, in his own time and own words. Unfortunately professionals outside the clinic frequently pre-empted this by describing the unit to parents and teenagers in an attempt to engender positive feelings about what the clinic had to offer. When recording a social history with the parents of Graham S, the SWR felt that an in patient assessment was urgently needed but could not say so to the parents in case the consultant disagreed. She therefore wrote that she felt it necessary 'to exclude the possibility of a psychotic breakdown and to help with the separation/independence problems'. This made the consultant aware of her own view. In fact the parents knew of the in patient unit and involved the SWR in discussions about it. In then writing 'the parents are aware of the existence of the adolescent unit' the SWR was sending a strong message to the consultant, 'don't blame me...I didn't tell them...but I have had to discuss it as one of the options'.

Phrasing things so that the consultant would understand the meaning she intended to convey enabled the SWR to understate situations so that clients reading the record would not feel criticised and withdraw from the service. In the social history on Carol G, the SWR wrote 'Mrs G is concerned to be a good

mother to Carol' which conveyed to the consultant that mother was defensive
and over-protective. In the same case the SWR wrote 'I have advised mother
to be honest with Carol', which meant in effect that the mother was telling her
daughter lies. A further device to alert the consultant to items of significance
without alarming clients was the use of inverted commas. In the case of Jim E
remarks were quoted without professional comment or interpretation. At that
stage the SWR felt unable to share her thinking but used inverted commas to
send 'messages' to the consultant, as in these two examples: 'Jim was bottle fed
– "mother's milk was no good".' 'Father lives nearby, visits daily – "Jim does
not realise he has gone".'

The apparently strange attitudes of the SWR and consultant towards
construction and ownership of clinic records appears to relate to the strength
of feeling about whose work, and therefore recording, was of the greatest value.
The differential power relationships in child guidance clinics have been well
documented (Sampson 1980) but the work of Everett Hughes and associates
has, since the 1930s, shown the importance of occupational status in maintaining individuals' sense of value and self esteem. Their series of studies of people
working together in professional occupations illustrates ways in which occupational behaviour aims to enhance self esteem. Throughout the research the
SWR's record keeping seems to take into account the high status-power of the
consultant, sometimes explicitly and sometimes manipulatively.

It was evident that team members and colleagues routinely depended upon
the opinions and judgements of certain other professionals. As Everett Hughes
observes, one profession tends to depend more upon the views of some
colleagues than of others (Hughes 1962 pp.119–127). Professionals of the
child guidance network constantly referred issues to each other using the SWR
and her written record as a kind of buffer zone between their problematic
situation and the desired advice. In several cases education professionals
engineered referral to the team hoping that the consultant's recommendation
would vindicate action already taken or provide ammunition in their differences
of opinion with parents. Sometimes the SWR herself harnessed the inherent
power of consultant opinion to the plough of fighting for resources for clients
whose circumstances she herself knew well. In the case of Jim E the SWR knew
the most effective way to acquire early school entry for the lively Jim was to
invoke the power of the senior clinical medical officer for child health services.
The SWR therefore supplied the consultant with the written recommendation
'If Jim is always at home things may deteriorate and then it will be difficult to
establish him in a normal school situation'. It is interesting that this item of
social work reporting was reproduced in the letter sent by the medical officer
to the county education officer as if it were the sole thinking of the consultant.
One important consequence of this was that its copy, and the SWR's recommendation which generated it, were filed only on the clinic file and became

inaccessible to clients. Such shifting of social work material into reports and letters of more influential consultant professionals seems to parallel the reluctance of clients to incriminate themselves by too frank accounts of their personal lives.

2. Between the clinic and other agencies

The SWR's records were caught up in interaction between clinic members and many 'outside' others. Two examples will highlight the role played by social work recording: admission to the adolescent unit and the problems posed by referral letters.

ADMISSION TO THE ADOLESCENT UNIT

The SWR's written communication with nursing and social work staff of the in-patient unit reflected the complex negotiation needed to balance client need with managerial dictate and multi-professional power relations. The unit social worker co-ordinated social work to children during their placement, notwithstanding any involvement by child guidance social workers. Unlike the latter, who were line managed by children's services, this social worker belonged to a mental health team whose manager considered admissions to the unit should follow procedures commonly accepted as appropriate for adult patients. In contrast the consultant considered it his prerogative to admit by agreement with parents after an introductory visit. During the action research the mental health manager and child psychiatrist remained locked in an unresolved power struggle over this issue which greatly influenced communication between child guidance and unit staff in the sample cases admitted to the unit.

The way written material played a part in managing the inevitable tension is well shown in the case of Daniel B, the out of control school refuser. The mental health manager required full reports on any proposed admissions to be sent to him by the child guidance social worker so that he could allocate the stage managing of the introductory visit to 'his' unit-based social worker. When writing to the mental health manager about Daniel it was necessary to assert confidently that the SWR had herself assessed the situation and regarded admission as necessary and in the boy's best interests – that is, an assessment had been made independently of the child psychiatrist's opinion, as in the adult model of involuntary admissions to mental hospitals. The SWR referred to 'much maternal over-protection', 'the need to make a full assessment of the obese boy' and 'six to eight weeks of complete school refusal'. The SWR knew from experience that references to the boy being out of parental control could lead to the mental health manager insisting that Daniel's needs be met by district child care resources. Her letter concentrated upon emotional disturbance rather than delinquency.

This letter was never shown to Mrs B nor its contents discussed with her. The SWR felt references to maternal over-protection and obesity would be unacceptable to Mrs B who was not ready to deal with plans involving further separation. The present task was to help the mother accept the need for Daniel to go to the unit and the SWR judged that the contents of her letter would be detrimental to that end and indirectly damaging to Daniel's interests. Knowledge of the 'in house' strife as to which arm of the social services department should provide social work would not have helped this mother to develop confidence in either worker. Thus by careful choice of words the SWR was simultaneously managing the politics of her own department and those of the health professionals, striving to obtain a resource and present it in the way most acceptable to Daniel and his mother, and assessing what effect sight of the letter might have upon the mother's relationship with the agency and her capacity to parent the boy.

LETTERS REFERRING CHILDREN TO THE CLINIC

The SWR acted as the intake facility for the clinic, 'receiving' referral letters and undertaking an initial social work assessment. The way in which the referral was made and the information conveyed in these letters had a profound influence on the way material was shared and recorded in the first session. If the SWR copied the gist of referral letters onto a first assessment form, it was frequently difficult to share that page with clients ignorant of the contents of the referral letter.

Letters from referring doctors were extremely variable in both form and content. One, of two illegible lines, was handwritten on the second copy from a flimsy referral pad. One arrived on a drug company 'give away' pad, depicting gnomes jumping over toadstools. More than one referring doctor apologised for 'troubling' the consultant with a minor matter of apparent concern only to others. Such was the case in the brief letter from the GP referring the obese out of control truant, Daniel B, in which he mentioned 'unsatisfactory behaviour at home and school' and then asserted 'As I have listened to the history of these incidents they do not seem particularly worrying and I hope I have not sent them to you unnecessarily'. The message that 'I am asking you to see this boy but it is not a serious request and I am only making it to allay the anxieties of others' reflected the mother's own wish to play down serious problems and to protect her son from all authority and accountability. The mother and SWR thought about the problem in different ways; they defined it differently and both were convinced that their own definition was correct. The SWR believed that sharing the GP's letter would support mother in her denial of the problem and make her unlikely to accept assessment or advice which felt uncomfortable or threatened to reduce her over-protection of Daniel.

In addition to eccentric presentation and apologia, referral letters were sometimes completely at variance with the client's perception of the problem. The discrepancy in problems ascribed to Carol G was startling and difficult to share without reducing parental confidence in the capacity of the sole, rural GP whose intervention for physical health might be needed urgently in the future. Problems as referred were stealing, not sleeping, anorexia and poor school grades. In contrast mother stated that Carol ate and slept well, had only once stolen pennies and had a good school report. *She* wanted advice about her daughter's defiant, attention seeking behaviour after disappointing contact visits with her father. The mother was quite articulate and the SWR was puzzled by the extent of the failure of communication with the GP. Because the social history and initial assessment forms both required a statement of the problems as referred, the SWR decided not to show mother the sheet on which the GP's letter was summarised.

The GP's letter about Lawrence W provided a typical example of alarmist, contradictory and incomplete referral information. It was difficult for the SWR to commit the tenor of this letter to social work records knowing the mother might then see how the GP had interpreted her request for help and advice. The GP quoted the mother as saying she could not handle her two-year-old son, that he was violent at playschool and threw things about. The letter continued: 'For a quarter of an hour I observed and played with this child and found him to be a quiet and pleasant child and could not believe he could be aggressive'. The GP then postulated various causes including food allergy, mother's slight deafness or something else 'to do with the mother'. The letter concludes:

> In our opinion therefore the problems seem to be mainly with the mother and not the child but I should be grateful for your assistance with this matter as I feel this child is under threat and the mother has said she cannot cope much longer. The child is totally suppressed both in his speech and in his actions.

Extraordinary aspects of this referral include no reference to the child's father or to the fact that Lawrence was under the care of the ear, nose and throat (ENT) consultant and had recently had both ears drained and fitted with grommets – clearly relevant to the language delay. The SWR asked the mother what she wanted advice about and the following was recorded with her full participation: 'Lawrence very aggressive, awkward. Is he hyperactive? Very demanding of attention; mother wonders if she needs to manage him in a different way'.

As in the case of Daniel B, the SWR felt unable to share the contents of this GP's letter with its implied criticism of the mother's coping abilities and suggesting her deafness as the cause of the toddler's language delay. Whether the mother made different complaints to the GP or whether the GP put a different construction upon what the mother said, each emphasised very different aspects of the child's behaviour. One explanation of this phenomenon is that of 'competing definitions' of the same situation (Hughes 1958). Such competing definitions arise repeatedly in the research material, not only in letters of referral but in the way both clients and workers, as well as separate disciplines, have presented different facets of the same situation, verbally and in writing.

Doctors were not the only professionals whose referral letters expressed views unshared with parents or which adopted a focus denied by parents. The research material provided evidence of head teachers writing frankly and subjectively about children on the assumption that their letters of referral would not be shared with parents. The case of Graham S illustrates the difficulty experienced by the SWR in deciding how to deal with this communicated material and its constraining effect upon sharing file contents with anxious and ill parents, let alone a disturbed epileptic boy.

It was common for problems to alter in the time between referral and the SWR's initial visit, sometimes in severity, sometimes in symptomatology. Parents then considered the referrer's out of date description to be 'wrong' and objected to its perpetuation on the first assessment form. Such insistence upon the client's own definition of the problem illustrates a pattern of attempts to preserve, and maximise, their own sense of worth at a time when their levels of self esteem were lowered by seeking help with parenting.

The SWR found little difficulty sharing referral letters which were so brief, bland and understated that they posed no threat to GP relationships. However, such letters provided an inadequate basis for initial action by the SWR in new cases. For example, the GP referring Jim E presented the problem as one of a 'disturbed' little boy, hyperactive perhaps, with advice needed upon his 'psychiatric state'. The letter gave an impression of the mother as an experienced parent of two other teenage children and gave no hint of anything other than a very stable family whose four-year-old had begun to exhibit unusual behaviour. The contents of the referral letter were easily shared but failed to alert the SWR to the fact that the family had multiple social, economic and personal problems, and previous involvement with another child guidance clinic. Thus although bland 'medical model' referrals labelling the child as the 'sick' index patient were easier to include in an open record, they did little to help the SWR approach the case in a realistic and well-informed manner.

It was clear, in the variety of ways described above, that the form and content of referral letters between medical colleagues greatly influenced the SWR's recording practice in initial sessions. She was unable to share their contents unless the client's perception of the problem matched that given by the referring doctor. Referral letters not postulating causes were easier to share with parents.

Examples included the health visitor's short referral of Molly C to the SWR which was readily summarised on the social history sheet as 'jealousy of new baby – behaviour and attitude problems'. In the case of the Jehovah's Witness family the SWR found that, despite the referral being from the GP and addressed to the consultant, she had no difficulty sharing its purely factual contents, with which the father agreed.

Referral information about the school phobic Steven H was used very positively and the practice adopted suggests a more effective model to address difficulties inherent in handling initial referral information within open recording. The education welfare officer had referred Steven to the SWR over the telephone and requested the SWR undertake a joint home visit to assess the 'crisis'. The SWR offered, instead, an appointment for the family and education welfare officer to meet with her at the clinic. At this initial meeting each member's statement of the problem was recorded in their own words, there were no 'secret' referral letters and the referrer was herself facilitating the family's telling of the problem whilst giving reality based school attendance statistics as her own contribution to the meeting. Perceptions of the problem were very different and all were attempts to define the problem in terms of causes. Father felt society should allow him to use greater physical force on his son; mother defined the problem as insensitive surgical treatment on Steven's ears; Steven blamed bullies at school; the education welfare officer stressed unusual home tuition arrangements made by another education authority. The explanations are interesting in that members connected the location of the problem with the 'system' for which they were not responsible. Thus all three family members located the problem out of the home (society, health service or bullies) while the education welfare officer and SWR indicted respectively, other education authorities and the family themselves. However discrepant, these competing definitions of the same situation could be recorded in their own words, demonstrating that each had been 'heard' by the SWR.

Notwithstanding these few exceptions, the action research revealed substantial difficulties attached to the SWR sharing contents of referral letters with parents of children attending the child guidance clinic. Case material showed that the medical style of referral, client denial of problems as stated, and the explicit opinion of the referring doctor as to causes or parenting capacities were all factors which obliged the SWR to withhold social work records containing such referral information. It is helpful to view the differences of opinion in terms of competing definitions of the same situation but problems surrounding these letters of referral are also related to power relations and aspects of control exerted by the consultant over other disciplines. The letters were invariably addressed to the consultant: it was his opinion which was valued as his diagnosis could then be used to obtain resources and services from other departments and disciplines. Thus the relative levels of authority were being played out in the referral letters, with the SWR caught up in transactions of status and control as she attempted to incorporate their contents into her own shared recording.

3. Negotiation between clinic and education agencies

Material discussed above has introduced something of the complexity of paper negotiations between the clinic social worker and other agencies. A plethora of 'social work acts' described in the SWR's notes showed the clinic/education system boundary to be the focus of the most difficult interaction between workers on behalf of their clients. Two particular aspects merit detailed discussion as acute examples of the ways in which 'professional' behaviour shaped information which the SWR felt able to record and subsequently share with clients.

PROCESSING INFORMATION BETWEEN CLIENT AND SCHOOL SYSTEM

Schools varied in their understanding of the SWR's commitment to confidentiality. Two head teachers of day schools attended by children in the research sample regularly made angry demands that they had a 'right to feedback', preferably written, following clinical assessment of children in their schools, regardless of parental consent.

The SWR was unsure of the level of confidentiality she could expect from the two privately-run boarding schools with whom she negotiated arrangements for the placements of Daniel and Steven. She wondered if she should give boarding schools in the independent sector more or less information than those run by her local education authority. How 'safe' would it be to give sensitive information about the boy and his family? The SWR therefore attempted to balance a cautious approach to unfamiliar private schools with a 'professional' conviction that staff caring for maladjusted youngsters should be as adequately informed about their emotional and family lives as about attainment and educational difficulties. Head teachers of both these schools insisted upon the SWR giving such information over the telephone and, in the case of Steven, demanded an assurance that parents would support his placement.

Considerable information, therefore, passed in conversation between the SWR and heads of boarding schools during the placement process. The message from head teachers, 'Don't bother with a written report on the family circumstances – we will just discuss', prevented the family from knowing exactly what information had been passed to school staff. In contrast, the contents of a more formalised written social work report would have been discussed and shown as part of joint recording practice.

Practical matters in the early days of boarding placements tended to generate social work records which were easy to share with parents – arrangements for uniform, equipment, travel, visits, fees, and formal school reports and circulars.

Subsequent reports compiled with the participation of parents often reflected in a straightforward way stages in the process of separation and adjustment. This example, made on a visit to the home of Steven H after his first exeat weekend, was compiled with the full agreement of the participants: 'Mother tearful, dislikes Steven's long phone calls...he puts pressure on her as he moans, complaining of everything he dislikes. He agrees! Mother to listen sympathetically but not take it to heart. Really, he is doing well'.

Issues about open recording overlap with those concerning client involvement in case conferences and reviews. The SWR attended reviews held twice yearly on children in special boarding schools but interestingly only the two private schools invited parents and sent them copies of review forms. Nevertheless the ideology did not always promote true client participation and empowerment, according to the criteria espoused by Shemmings and Thoburn (1990), as is shown by this extract from the research notes concerning the review held at the private boarding school on Daniel B:

> The reviews were of an open style with the school insisting that parents were present all the time. Such an admirable policy of involvement and participation by parents was on this occasion spoilt by the fact that the staff seemed not to have done their homework beforehand. Given no reports or preliminary discussion, details of the home circumstances were not known to the participants, especially an educational psychologist sent to represent the sponsoring education authority. In order to get a 'grip' on the case, the staff and psychologist asked sensitive questions of the mother which she clearly found embarrassing and annoying...her defensiveness and distress were evident...she flushed and trembled, frequently turning to the SWR for help.

The SWR was concerned that the subsequent blandness of the review did not address any difficult matters about Daniel's manipulative behaviour and felt it was odd that although this private school put great value upon the participation of Daniel's mother, it was not seen as appropriate to involve Daniel.

Material from the sample cases described numerous situations in which the SWR adopted the role of intermediary between client and other professionals in order to 'take care of' sensitive communication. Collaborative work with professionals in the education department provided particularly rich material which depicted the clinic social worker explaining, expanding, rephrasing, timing, storing and generally managing the information and opinion which converged upon her pivotal position between client, clinic and school. The research material therefore reflects a process of evaluation, filtration, interpretation and participation across the boundary between clinic client and education authority.

Teachers conveyed a considerable number of negative, sometimes pejorative, verbal and written reports to the SWR which she felt unable to share with clients. Criticism of belief systems (Roy G), references to 'spoilt brats' (Daniel B), 'smelly' (Roy G), 'strong body aroma' (Carol G), 'impossible, nutter, zombie, mad' (Graham S) typify the lack of restraint of many exasperated head teachers in describing their more difficult pupils. As fully demonstrated by the research notes on Graham S very few of the school's reported views were shared with his ill parents, partly because they denied the gravity of the problem, but mostly because school staff attempted to manipulate the SWR into communicating 'bad news' on their behalf and consistently obscured the extent to which they had actually spoken frankly to parents. This exchange between headmaster and SWR arose when the latter telephoned to ask if the parents of Graham S had seen his referral letter:

HEAD TEACHER: No, but they know it all.

SWR: Even the bit on masturbating in the cloakroom?

HEAD TEACHER: Well…sort of…

SWR: Did you tell them the details?

HEAD TEACHER: I don't know. The PE teacher dealt with it…I can't be sure what *he* told them.

As this case progressed the same head teacher continued to demonstrate his inability to say the bad things himself. He repeatedly 'softened the blow' in conversation with parents, believed he had conveyed his views but in reality left others, principally the SWR, to present upsetting information to Mr and Mrs S. This was well illustrated by his ostentatiously leaving a 'school report' in sight, but out of reach, of parents at the end of a joint meeting in the SWR's office. The SWR challenged this by asking if he had forgotten his papers but the head replied 'No, it's for you' and abruptly departed leaving the SWR to deal with parents' demands to read the distressing report on their son.

Thus information which cannot be passed further accumulates with the SWR, either in a file or in her head. Questions must be asked as to the effect of this residue of acquired secrets upon her communication and relationships with clients and other professionals. What happens when she meets with both together and adopts the role of intermediary, deciding upon and maintaining the status of each item of communicated information and opinion? It appeared that the clinic social worker was acting not only as an advocate, a facilitator of communication between client and school, a custodian of confidential reporting, but had also assumed the onerous responsibility of assessing the impact of each part of the recorded item upon the often vulnerable client. If shared, would it be likely to damage him, or by reducing his trust in other professionals, undermine their endeavours on his behalf?

It seems that participatory open recording precipitates the issue that sensitive information is uncomfortable to hold, the SWR having to establish who has given permission for who to see what, whilst constantly predicting and coping with the results of sharing upsetting facts or opinion. It therefore underlines the extent to which the SWR was used by clients and professionals (especially schools) to facilitate communication about painful and frightening issues, a record of which they wished to 'lodge' with the SWR in lieu of direct expression to one another.

RECORDING CONTRIBUTIONS TO ASSESSMENTS AND STATEMENTS
OF SPECIAL EDUCATIONAL NEED

The report of the Warnock committee (1978) reviewed educational provision for children and young people who were 'handicapped by disability of mind or body' and provided the basis for the Education Act 1981. This legislation, the implementation of which is well reviewed elsewhere (e.g. Cox 1985), imposed a duty upon local authorities to identify children with special educational needs, make an assessment of the latter, and 'if of the opinion that it should determine the special educational provision' issue a *statement* to that effect. Although research for this book took place whilst the 1981 Education Act was in force, it should be noted that the new 1993 Education Act has 'reformed the statutory obligations but adopts the same approach' (Friel 1995). Both pieces of legislation depend upon written advice from multi-professional assessment before determining the child's special educational need and the provision required to meet it. Advice from social services departments must concentrate upon those factors which contribute to his special educational needs, is submitted in a prescribed form and is generally written by a social worker who knows the child in the context of his family and home environment. Thus contributions from child guidance clinic social workers are included with those from district and hospital social workers knowing the child.

The educational authority undertook assessment under section 5 of the 1981 Education Act (section 167 of the 1993 Act) in six of the eighteen sample cases and proceeded to issue statements of special educational need in respect of Ronald P, Daniel B and Steven H. Special boarding provision was determined for these three boys with specialist help with learning and behavioural difficulties, emotional and behavioural difficulties, and specific learning difficulties, respectively. In all six cases the SWR involved parents in preparing her written contribution to the assessment and, despite varying levels of participation, felt able to state her advice frankly and usefully because it had been openly negotiated with parents beforehand.

It was interesting that the social services manager who vetted advice sent from his department expressed great concern that the language used by the

SWR in describing factors likely to adversely affect the education of Daniel was 'too strong' and wondered 'what we should do if the mother exercised her right to see the assessment'. As the social work contributions were always reproduced in full in the appendix to the statement and automatically sent to parents, this was illogical and suggested that the senior manager had only a superficial understanding of the procedures. This experience supports research findings about the extent to which social services and education departments held similar interpretations of the 1981 Education Act (Goacher 1986). The manager was astonished to learn that the SWR wrote this, and other, contribution(s) with full parental participation and readily admitted that the results were more useful than bland efforts of social workers daring to write only those comments which they judged unlikely to provoke parents into making complaints and appeals.

Most contributors to the assessment quite properly confined their written advice to descriptions of the child's mental, physical and cognitive functioning. However, the social worker was expected to grasp the nettle of linking home background and parenting with the child's ability to benefit from ordinary educational provision. The SWR's written contributions were always included in full in statements, and her 'advice' was therefore available to parents. In contrast, submissions by the child psychiatrist were collated by the district health authority with advice from other medical colleagues. Thus only their 'recommendations' were included in the resulting aggregated submission of advice from health professionals; in this way the child psychiatrist was able to submit written opinion which influenced the medical contribution but was not a constituent of the statement sent to parents. Such unseen influence was clear in the psychiatric advice on Graham S which was requested in a letter from the senior clinical medical officer asking, 'Is there any contribution you wish to make to the medical report which will be seen by the parents when completed?' The consultant replied:

> Whenever I saw Graham the parents denied any problems, therefore it is very difficult to do any effective work. My feeling is that Graham cannot be helped at home and in a normal school. The best way to help this boy will be a residential school which caters for epileptic children who have good endowment, but I am not sure whether parents will agree with this. I would not like this report to be seen by the parents.

The SWR had no such protection. Her contribution stood alone, reproduced in full under her own name as part of the appendix, and was open to challenge by parents who disagreed with it. This rendered the task of the SWR complex and contradictory. On the one hand she needed to convince the education authority that expensive resources were needed, that aspects of the child's background prevented his educational needs being met by ordinary provision and that the facilities needed were not those of the social services care system. On the other hand, the written contribution had to avoid many things: raising levels of parental defences, guilt or anxiety so that provision was refused; jeopardising future work by damage to the SWR's relationship with the family; reducing the child's chances of acceptance by the specialist provision by over-emphasising levels of emotional disturbance or social problems. The SWR was constantly wrestling with words to make a good case for resources in a way which parents could tolerate, without loss of trust in her ability to help them in the future.

The SWR's accommodation to the defences of the mother of Daniel is a graphic illustration. The SWR really wanted to write that Mrs B had protected Daniel from all forms of authority but Mrs B objected saying that her protection had been necessary because of bullying at school. During lengthy discussion she said that she still felt too close to Daniel and this made it difficult for her to discipline him appropriately. Finally it was agreed that the SWR should write in the statement 'Mother had found it necessary to over-protect and indulge Daniel because of his unhappiness in school'.

Writing the social work contribution to the statementing process on Steven H also demonstrated the complexity of the task. Initial confusion reigned when a clerical officer acting as collator for social services tried to find the part of the system whose social worker knew the family and could 'contribute'. The request oscillated between desks of social workers in the adolescent unit, district team, hospital and the SWR's line manager (who left before allocating the task). Thus, as often happened, there was then a need to complete the contribution quickly as the several professional groups accused each other of causing delay in completing assessment, statement and allocation of provision. It was tempting, under such pressure, to rush the social work contribution but the research commitment to participation required the SWR to discuss the content with Steven's family at the earliest opportunity. Steven was unexpectedly at home and once again the SWR had to manage the dilemma of how to write about the boy's need for boarding education without further raising his anxiety and parents' defences to levels which might lead them to refuse the provision. It was impossible to proceed with a frank discussion of the proposed content in front of the anxious and tearful boy. The SWR discussed in general terms, delivered the long awaited contribution to the social services department and returned to show a copy to the parents four days after Steven had commenced at the boarding school. The following extract from the research notes gives their interesting responses:

MOTHER: *read the copy through, folded it twice and said:* I see why you thought it might upset Steven.

SWR: Does it upset you?

MOTHER: Not really, I suppose it is all true. Can we have a copy?

SWR: Yes, one will come with the full statement but I prefer parents
          to know what I have written and to tell me if they thought it
          was not true.

MOTHER: *re-reading the copy, triumphantly*: The date of birth is
          wrong, people always get it wrong…usually 20 instead of 2
          for the day…but you have got 3 instead of 8 for the month.

The SWR was surprised that mother had picked out this detail – perhaps Mrs
H felt that people making such an error might make others of professional
judgement…was the SWR's advice reliable? Could she be trusted? How fallible
was she?

The father then read the report and said jokingly: 'It's very mild really
considering what happened. Do you remember me tying him up with the
clothes line and him escaping down the beach…it took three bloody days to
get him to that unit…still we did manage somehow, didn't we?'

Parents made no comment on the final sentence which stated 'The SWR
continues to offer ongoing social work support and parents are accepting of
this'. However, as she left the house both parents sought reassurance that the
SWR would still remain their social worker; they feared being left to manage
Steven on their own now he was at boarding school. It seemed that their
intellectual involvement in the written contribution had not enabled them to
raise the issue which was apparently their greatest concern.

The SWR was frequently surprised by the items in contributions with which
parents disagreed. As detailed above, Mrs H found acceptable some quite painful
material about emotional and personal matters but attached importance to the
inaccurate birth date. In contrast, Mr H used the material to reminisce over past
difficulties, defining for himself a baseline for measuring progress. Perhaps
because recording practice on these six sample cases involved parents in
negotiating the content of contributions by the SWR they were more accepting
of the final document, found fewer factual errors and were already aware of
what were, in the SWR's opinion, 'factors in the child's environment which
lessen or contribute to his needs'. These six families did not therefore appeal
against the content of statements but the SWR was aware of other cases where
parents formally appealed against the social work 'advice' and in so doing
expressed powerful feelings of being stigmatised by information and opinion
with which they disagreed.

As was illustrated previously the SWR used her written contributions to
convey her own ideas to the local education authority, particularly concerns
over lack of appropriate provision. Undoubtedly in most cases involvement of
parents in writing the social work advice prevented error, enhanced the

relationship between parents and SWR and allowed the SWR to offer frank, negotiated opinion about the child's needs and provision required. Nevertheless such participation did sometimes appear to weaken the impact of contributions in arguing the case for expensive resources. The case of Graham S provides a good example. Given that his parents denied the existence of a problem and refused all offers of treatment, the SWR had no alternative but to send the weakest of communications to the panel; 'it is difficult to make any specific recommendations'.

Conversation, language and text

Selecting the 'right' words to describe the client's situation proved a demanding component of joint case recording. The language used by the SWR had to be meaningful for parents in the way it expressed difficulties with their children, and once agreement had been reached that the suggested vocabulary accurately reflected their situation, it was easy to proceed with writing the record. The case of Jim E illustrates the SWR establishing that words chosen to record her observations of the mother's inadequate limit setting held equivalent meaning for the parents. This extract was part of a record fully discussed and agreed with parents at the end of the session:

> I watched Jim winding up mother, clearly taking satisfaction from the contest in which he always emerged the victor. I felt their battles were not games. Jim persists in challenging, outwitting and wearing down mother, all with the speed of lightning.

The words 'winding up', 'contest', 'battle' and 'wearing down' were chosen to convey to the mother that the SWR did understand the true impact of Jim's demanding behaviour.

The content of conversations between the SWR and her clients dictated what could subsequently be recorded. The research material thus reflected such conversations and one way of considering what these descriptions 'amount to' is the ethnomethodological approach of Harvey Sacks and Emmanual Schegloff. Sacks drew attention to the importance of studying mundane conversations as a way of examining the 'organisations of talk'. He focused upon ways of achieving possible descriptions and analysed two short sentences from a child's story: 'The baby cried. The mommy picked it up' (Sacks in Turner 1974). The apparently common sense observations upon this quotation remind us that the natural initial hearing of these sentences amounts to a cultural accomplishment (the mommy is the mother of the baby rather than an Egyptian mummy), that we infer the connection between mommy and baby, that quite complex hearings are made without any contextual information, and that the eight words constitute an understandable description of an everyday event.

Sacks used the idea of 'category', conceiving of members selecting one category from collections of categories in order to arrive at common sense, taken for granted descriptions. For example, when we hear 'baby' in the above sentence we are hearing the category 'stage of life' as well as the category 'member of family'. The description 'cried' is also seen to be consistent with the category 'baby' and the two taken together encourage the hearer in their sense-making activity. A graphic example of failure to attain 'correct' understanding appeared in the research material when the SWR, taking a social history, heard with amazement the father of Roy G describing his vast number of brothers and sisters. Her common sense hearing did not take account of Mr G being a Jehovah's Witness whose members are known as Brothers and Sisters.

Schegloff looked in detail at the concept of place (Schegloff 1972). He showed how members in a conversation display ability and sensitivity to descriptions of 'where', 'who' and 'what topic' so that sections of their talk fit together to become hearable. Schegloff also considered the sequential organisation of conversation and illustrated the taking of turns to speak by analyses of telephone conversations between two parties, the caller giving the summons and the receiver the answer. The summons/answer sequence is extremely powerful in generating conversational interaction: those summoned feel compelled to answer (Schegloff 1968).

The research material shows the significance of apparently mundane matters concerning choice and use of words in conversations which then become the 'nuts and bolts' of written reports. If this material is viewed with the work of Garfinkel, Sacks and Schegloff in mind, it can be seen that the 'skill' of the social worker is not the only factor responsible for the effectiveness of conversations with clients.

Finding and offering particular words which precisely fitted the client's own conceptualisation of the problem seemed to be an acceptable form of verbal reframing. In defining the problems of Lily J the SWR discussed her wish to write that the mother was bullied by her powerful daughter. The use of the word 'bully' was highly appreciated by this mother who emphasised that bullied was exactly how she felt in relation to her daughter. The SWR felt quite overwhelmed by the extent of the mother's excited gratitude that her predicament was understood so accurately and defined by the short word 'bullied'. It is interesting that 'bully' was a word which frequently required careful negotiation both in discussion and in record writing. This seemed to arise from the poor self-esteem of many parents and children who tended to blame others for problems. Considerable verbal ingenuity was needed to manage their defensiveness whilst struggling to record a realistic version of events. The mother of Daniel B was typical. She denied the headmaster's observation that Daniel bullied other boys and insisted that her son had been bullied by others. The SWR felt unable to support either school or mother on the subject of bully or bullied and resolved the issue after much useful discussion about low self esteem by writing 'Daniel felt bullied', with which mother was able to agree.

Establishing a common vocabulary which could allow reliable communication about embarassing topics was especially difficult where parents felt disgraced by their child's problem (stealing) or where physical problems required frank talk about body parts (soiling, wetting and sex abuse). The Justin W case provided illustration of the SWR's efforts to find words with which they could all be comfortable. Not surprisingly, the mother found daily soiling by her large ten-year-old son very distressing, combined as it was with bed wetting and the deliberate leaving of faecal lumps on her best carpets. She had difficulty getting the words out to explain what he was actually doing and it eventually emerged that she had no idea what the school doctor meant by enuresis and encopresis. The SWR asked if she understood the word 'soiling', but Mrs W denied that Justin 'did soiling' saying he 'just mucks himself'. Words for the enuresis were less difficult as mother accepted the SWR's 'bedwetting' as the equivalent of her 'pees the bed'. The whole family referred to the soiling as 'mucking', which term the SWR found herself very reluctant to use. In the end the SWR said soiling and bedwetting and the family said mucking and peeing.

This difficulty can be viewed from an interactionist perspective: both mother and SWR clung to competing definitions of the same situation. The SWR defined the problem as the mother's emotional rejection of an otherwise 'well' child: the mother's vocabulary showed clearly her definition of her 'bad' son as full of 'muck' and 'pee' which he was deliberately voiding or retaining in order to make her unhappy. The SWR wondered why she herself found it so difficult to adopt the vocabulary used by the family. For her, 'mucking' had connotations of manure and animals and it seemed unacceptable to liken the boy's distress to the bowel habits of farm animals. Perhaps she was trying to reduce the level of condemnation for the boy's 'filthy' habits, being very aware of his desperate need for support and encouragement. Or perhaps she was too appalled by the cold and angry way that mother and Justin's elder brother spat out their accusations about his mucking, the smell, the filthy hidden underpants, the clods of dried faeces. Perhaps adopting their vocabulary might in some way reinforce their attitude to the problem. If the mother's description seemed to present the SWR with the category 'farm yard animal', it is interesting to speculate about the effect of the professionals' 'encopresis, enuresis, soiling and bedwetting' upon the mother. What category might she have in her mind which was in fact *worse* than these to describe her son's behaviour – 'sick, mad or damaged' perhaps?

The material indicates that articulacy, choice of words to convey exact or equivalent meaning, verbal reframing, paraphrasing pejorative reports, the special language of both client and SWR, commas and caveats to attribute particular significance, use of clients' own words and the struggle to find and adopt a common vocabulary are all part of a complex web of conversational interaction between clinic social worker and client as they took pains to attribute meaning to what is said and what is then written. It may be that there are qualitative differences between spoken and written communication which have not emerged in this part of the research. This was touched on by Joanie's mother who, having participated most diligently in recording jointly with the SWR said rather wistfully 'Oh, it looks all funny written down'. Such a significant remark resonates with the views of clients presented in Chapter Four. Clients worried that their spoken words would be 'twisted and turned into something else' and that people would 'read something else into a written record'. Whilst relying upon the SWR to capture the sense of what they said, clients still distrusted the medium of writing, preferring 'talk' and holding a widespread view that 'things look blacker on paper'. Further consideration of records, both as 'acts' and as texts, is therefore justified.

What was social work recording actually doing?

It seems that record keeping mirrors the clinic social worker's professional activity and in that way functions as an index of child guidance social working. The conflicting demands of recording reflected the considerable confusion of workers, clients and colleagues about the role and identity of the clinic social worker: how far was she the consultant's secretary, a nurse or some kind of therapist and how exactly did her work connect with that of the district social services departments? The act of inviting parents to participate in decisions as to what should be recorded makes explicit not only that a record is being kept but that the person with whom they are involved is a social worker. Recording often crystallised what the social worker was *really* doing. Jim E's parents expected to meet with a team of therapists and were confused and annoyed to discover the SWR to be part of an information hot-line to the social services department, undertaking financial assessment for playschool fees and offering written accounts for countersigning. 'Just like the KGB' was the mother's angry retort.

It was difficult for the clinic social worker to maintain her ambiguous and flexible role: in working with the sample cases the SWR often interacted with clients while uncertain of her mandate to do so. She met clients in informal settings who insisted upon discussing their children. Clients having themselves more than one role, for example an ex-foster parent who attempted to discuss 'our colleagues at HQ', caused the SWR to adopt a very strong 'clinic team therapist' role. The mother of Daniel B emerged as the sister of the clinic secretary and the SWR found herself having professional roles in respect of both at the same time. Mrs W applied for the job of clinic secretary under her maiden name and the SWR had to switch roles from therapist to processor of a complaint that Mrs W had not been short listed. Making records of such work was difficult. The SWR often felt she had no firm basis from which to write; when between roles she had no right to write.

Although the social worker's role certainly affected the nature of the recording activity, the communication between client and social worker, whether spoken or written, proved the more important factor. Arguments for the privileged status of speech were outlined briefly in Chapter One: written language was felt by Saussure, Rousseau and Levi-Strauss to be solely a derivative of speech. Speech act theory, in its various forms, offers a useful alternative insofar as the 'acts' of speech/writing can be viewed as a 'unit' without concern for the method by which the linguistic communication was produced. Speech act theory conceives of illocutionary acts performed with particular intentions and governed by rules (Searle 1971 p39). Thus speaker/writers and their hearer/readers are engaged in an activity as they, for example, question, assert, predict, wish. Records of communication between the SWR and the sample of clients describe what occurred but they also do many other things, for example, keeping to the rules of the SWR's role, dealing with conflict, processing feelings, establishing and maintaining status, forcing decisions, to name but a few. An examination of one page, selected at random from the research data (social work acts) showed the wide scope of speech acts being performed between SWR and her client as they talked, read and wrote together: disclosing, referring, giving, retorting, involving, fearing, making aware, initiating, signing, receiving, processing, replying, recording, presenting, defining, asking, alerting, informing, saying and thinking.

It is not appropriate to attempt an in-depth application of speech act theory to social work record keeping but merely to demonstrate the usefulness of the approach in understanding communication between the SWR and her client as they actively spoke, wrote and read material concerning their interaction. It has perhaps been easier to ask 'What does it mean?' than 'What it is doing?' and examining social work acts from the latter perspective reveals yet another layer of complexity within the communication. It will be helpful to discuss in more detail the extract of material already quoted concerning a contribution to the statement of special educational needs for Steven H. The SWR was showing it to his parents.

> Mother read the copy through, folded it twice and said 'I see why you thought it might upset Steven'.

Mother's first sentence is in the form of a statement, she is pushing the idea of upset onto Steven, giving the SWR the responsibility of causing upset and denying any involvement of herself in the process.

The SWR then asked 'Does it upset you?'

> This question is specific, forceful and probing. It has to be answered, and by the recipient. It is purposeful – it returns the ball into mother's court, preventing her avoiding the pain of the situation yet also providing a therapeutic opportunity to share feelings.

Mother responds 'Not really, I suppose it is all true. Can we have a copy?'

> Mother ignores the opportunity to share feelings and without being overtly rude casts doubt on the veracity of the SWR's contribution to the statement. The eight words were felt by the SWR as physical acts of discrediting, undermining and distancing. The request for a copy is a direct question, testing the SWR...are these records available to parents or not? Is the one being shown just a token to be whisked away, or worse, altered back at the office?

The SWR promises 'Yes, one will come with the full statement'.

> This promise fulfills the conditions set out by Searle. Principally, the promise is a promise, not a threat; the client would like the SWR to send the copy; the SWR intends to send it; the sending is not to be expected as usual practice; having uttered the promise the SWR is under an obligation to send the copy; the semantics of their language and dialect are such that an understanding of a sincere promise can be conveyed.

The SWR explains 'I prefer parents to know what I have written and to tell me if they thought it was not true'.

> The SWR is defending her professionalism, yet at the same time wanting parents to recognise her offer of real participation.

Mother complains, re-reading the copy, triumphantly, 'The date of birth is wrong – people always get it wrong, usually 20 instead of 2 for the day...but you've got 3 instead of 8 for the month'.

> Clearly no one can be trusted with even the most basic information items. This utterance conveys to the SWR that she has made an error of enormous significance – she has not even made the 'usual' error but has displayed a high level of carelessness and fallibility. In complaining 'triumphantly' mother conveys that she has won a battle. Yet was there a battle and who were the combatants? Perhaps mother's agenda was to catch the SWR out.

Father jokes 'It's very mild really considering what happened...do you remember me tying him up with a clothes line and him escaping down the beach!'

Father's humour negates mother's complaining, puts things in perspective, asserts that the error was only mild. His contribution shifts the conversation from negative to positive, suggesting that they too have made mistakes. Images of bondage and escaping teenagers wipe out the SWR's error over a birth date and draw attention to the father's own difficulties.

Father reminisces 'It took three bloody days to get him to that unit... still...we did manage somehow didn't we?'

It is not difficult to see what this reminiscence is 'doing'. It remembers, relocates, re-evaluates and conveys the pride of having coped in the past. 'Three bloody days' resonates with ideas of 'battle', suggesting that they managed alone without the clinic social worker. In the end they do win their private battles.

The above example concerns verbal illocutionary acts. However the SWR's contributions to statements of special educational need also demonstrate that written communication is also doing far more than is immediately apparent. The written recommendation 'a boarding hostel would have best met his needs' acts in one sense as professional opinion, second as an admonishment to the local authority for recently closing the one such resource, and third asserts 'as you have closed this resource I can make no other recommendation to help you meet his needs'.

Case records as texts

This chapter has stressed the need to consider the research material from a variety of standpoints and has indicated the value of conversation analysis and speech act theory as approaches to client–worker communication within the recording process. Such plurality of approach should include a post-modernist concern with the text of case records themselves, that is, as pieces of writing which can be read and re-read over time, by different people giving different attention, values, significance and understanding to the symbols used by the writer to represent their thoughts at the time of writing. Among both academics and professionals there has recently appeared an emphasis upon the importance of the text itself rather the situation in which it was produced. Michelle Barrett (1991) explores the ways in which neither Marxist ideology concerned with class, work and economics, nor Foucauldian concepts of discourse and power, adequately address current intellectual preoccupations of present society. She describes the recent movement towards greater emphasis upon textuality (the linguistic turn) and gives examples of historical, medical and legal documents being scrutinised as texts in themselves. It is therefore appropriate to think about case records as items of text, rather than to concentrate entirely upon their role within the child guidance network.

Changes to social communication brought about by electronic symbolic language in post-industrial societies have been addressed (Poster 1990). Whereas Marxist thinking could be seen as emphasising the 'mode of production', Poster argues that current culture gives importance to information. Coining the term 'mode of information', Poster describes the encoding of language to generate the massive data bases without which society cannot now cope. Such electronic language is at one step removed from the human communication which generates it. This poses major new questions, for example, about its use for surveillance, problems such as computer viruses, TV advertisements, the fate of non electronic writing as we now know it, and the powerfulness of those specialists in computer science who will decide future possibilities. The flexibility of language allowed by the computer makes the written word less concrete. Poster argues that such changes provide new communication experiences, an interaction between humankind and a new kind of reality.

Whatever future developments, it is clear that welfare and educational professions describe their human subjects through symbolic language and that case records contain such texts. The development of video and audio-taped interviews and the use of personal computers for social workers might be thought to radically alter the basis of the 'record'. Nevertheless the work of these professionals seems to depend upon language and communication held within the text of their records.

The SWR's negative subjective experience of the changed recording method: surrender of power?

The impact of changing the method of recording upon the SWR is described at this point as the material makes vivid many of the issues dealt with so far. The SWR noted her subjective experience in almost entirely negative terms: unfamiliarity, stress, guilt, pressure, role conflict, responsibility, and an endless need for diplomatic playing with words. She had to hold in her head complex thinking about confidentiality, power, negotiation, language and textuality whilst simultaneously carrying on social work and social work recording. Her own discomfort appeared to parallel that of a client seeking help, in that the situation exposed the 'self'; participation involved them both, the SWR could not so easily protect herself against too painful exposure to the client, and writing her own account of their interaction alone in her office became a forbidden luxury.

Unfamiliarity with the new task was evident from the outset and the SWR's uncertainty proved that old habits die hard. Over many years her case recording practice had become confident, automatic, integrated and thought-less routines. The new task required major unlearning of these old habits and constant vigilance and attention to the minutiae of the method within an unfamiliar framework of openness and participation. The SWR felt deprived of her previous carefree record keeping arrangements and, instead, burdened with a more onerous and complex task whose outcome she could not predict. She felt self-conscious explaining the method, often foolish and apologetic in carrying it out; stripped of professionalism, operating more like a student on placement than a competent experienced child and family specialist. The research material makes explicit many things which the SWR previously took for granted when recording. With increased understanding about recording as an activity, the SWR found her perception of the task shifted to include constant checking back on the effectiveness of her communication with clients.

Increased feelings of stress were induced as the SWR worked with the 18 cases: the method introduced an additional strand to the work requiring constant attention, enhanced communication skills and a flexible 'tailor made' response to the recording needs of each person in each case. Carrying out the unfamiliar task felt particularly difficult under the curious eye of another professional, as for example, the education welfare officer in their joint interview of Steven H and his parents.

In many instances her uncertainty centred around an absence of a defined working procedure for the task; a felt lack of 'how to do it' expertise, as exemplified by this quotation from her research notes in the same case:

> The summary of work done provided an opportunity to look together at how far the treatment was addressing problems initially identified by the parents. The SWR felt unsure whether it was necessary or desirable to write the obvious...she did not want to squander mother's limited attention on recording ponderous practicalities...

A feeling of being under pressure pervaded the SWR's experience. There was often pressure to work fast, as for example, before the father of Molly C returned to disrupt the shared history taking, or before time available for the interview ran out. Situational conditions made participative recording difficult, as for example, noise of children, televisions, dogs, visitors and inadequate seating. The SWR found herself growing tired as she tried to listen, choose words and write at the end of interviews. She felt she missed aspects of the conversation, while lowering her gaze to write. The 'extra' task then felt stressful, burdensome and counter-productive.

A constant pressure concerned the necessity to summarise in one sentence that which the client had taken ten minutes to explain. The SWR often felt she was marshalling large volumes of spoken communication in her head and considering their import whilst simultaneously making succinct verbal and written summaries. It is not surprising that on occasion, under such tiring conditions, her attention wandered, confidentiality was breached and the therapeutic focus was lost. For example, the SWR 'forgot' her commitment to open participatory recording with Mrs W, in the same case was 'put off her stroke' by discovering her client was an applicant for the post of clinic secretary, and in the case of Alex W was side-tracked by an upsetting confrontation into ignoring the rights of the 16-year-old file subject. The effort required to maintain the extended concentration felt uncomfortable during many of the interviews.

The SWR recorded many instances of role conflict where her duty to alleviate distress and protect children seemed in opposition to an ideology of participation. Attempting to involve parents in open record keeping meant, in practice, deciding how high a priority to give this task: deal with distress or collect information? In this no-win situation she frequently felt guilty that participation in record keeping could be achieved only at the cost of ignoring therapeutic needs. On occasion her ideal of openness and participation collapsed as she returned to her office and indulged in a spate of negative recording about a client. Thoroughly infuriated with the Daniel B case after an unsatisfactory ward meeting, the SWR concluded her record with a swinging attack on Mrs B's capacities, a record which she never mentioned to this mother. The most likely explanation for this lapse seems to be that the SWR absorbed and shared the anger of ward staff watching the boy deteriorate, and then displaced her feelings into recording criticisms of his mother. The SWR had run out of patience, she was exasperated with the lack of inter-departmental liaison and could not summon the energy to sustain the previous level of openness. She was later quite surprised at the extent to which she had used the record as a repository for her feelings of anger and frustration in this, and other, cases.

Such a desire to off-load poisonous feelings onto paper was not always unconscious, in which case it could be more readily contained. In the case of the overdosing grammar school boy the SWR was very aware of her negative feelings towards the mother but felt quite unable to share her assessment. She would have liked to have recorded her subjective impression of the mother as 'an unrealistic child-like lady, roaming the world in search of the good life, who, despite her wealth and middle class attitudes has only a very shallow emotional investment in her son'. Instead, she recorded her description of the informant as 'mother is an intelligent articulate woman, worried about her son and is pleased to have some follow up. She is a teacher of equitation and therefore experienced with teenagers'.

The SWR considered whether writing during interviews would damage work with parents and children and was cautious about 'experimenting' within a therapeutic process concerned with delicate parent–child–therapist relationships. She felt under some pressure to 'make them participate' and somewhat guilty if she omitted participative recording from too many sessions on account of damage to clients or other therapeutic priorities. There was a sense of failure if interviews were recorded later in the privacy of her own office as this denied the client openness and participation. The SWR worried particularly about the effect of recording about children in their presence. It was natural that parents, angry and fearful over the behaviour of their difficult children, should wish all their 'badness' recorded in graphic terms but the SWR felt protective of the index patient and worried that her introduction of participative recording provided an extra opportunity for parents verbally to 'bash' the child. She sometimes felt that her own agenda had shifted to place record keeping into too prominent a position so that she was less sensitive to, or in danger of ignoring, clients' priorities. Despite obtaining tacit agreement of clients to 'use' some of their interview time for record keeping, the SWR felt she had imposed a 'chore' upon them and that in reality they were in no position to refuse to co-operate with the agency's new system for recording.

The SWR felt responsible for feelings induced in clients as a result of involving them in record keeping. When feelings of optimism and pleasure in children's good progress were shared, the SW felt confident of the method and convinced of its therapeutic value. It is natural that clients would wish recorded those things with which they are in agreement, that is, where they share the SWR's opinion. Such harmonious interaction was relatively rare and the SWR felt a high level of skill and diplomacy was required to decide the content and phrasing of material which would be bearable to the client on that occasion. Thus the SWR continually monitored the material to assess its likely impact upon families, and considered whether sharing her opinion and thoughts would cause unacceptable distress or damage her working relationship to the point where the child-patient was withdrawn from the service. Constantly weighing the benefits of openness and participation against the possibility of further damage to clients was a parallel process to that of considering what words to say and whether seeing them in written form would be helpful, distressing or destructive. Holding the two strands in her mind, whilst playing with the meaning of words, felt onerous and tiring.

Reaching agreement on words to use aroused feelings in the SWR with which she found it surprisingly difficult to deal: her reluctance to use the W family's word 'mucking' for soiling has already been mentioned. Similarly the language used by the father of the Jehovah's Witness family made the SWR feel uneasy and self conscious about saying or writing the words he used. In this case the client subjected the SWR to Witness jargon from which she found it difficult to obtain a clear picture of the family. The SWR felt uncomfortable about showing him her written report in which she had put inverted commas round his special language. Father did not accept the SWR's interpretation of his son's problems, stating this was 'of no consequence as the SWR's system was irrelevant to The Truth'.

The research material showed clearly that both clients and SWR often felt uncomfortable with each other's language and that it was an onerous responsibility for the SWR to predict the impact of showing them her written reports containing assessment and opinion. It was also notable that while subjectively the SWR felt most of her records were fully available to clients, this was not supported by the evidence. Only 48 per cent of items of social work recording were fully accessible to their subjects.

This suggests that there were considerable barriers to participation which the SWR had erected to protect herself, her agency and her colleagues. The method used to share recording with clients appears to have protected the social worker against too great an exposure to the feelings and emotions of clients; the new procedure allowed the SWR to decide when 'sharing' would 'damage' relationships, work with the child or parent's emotional state. In this sense it could be felt that the SWR acted in a paternalistic manner, deciding what could be shared, and 'holding all the cards' (that is, records). However it could also be thought that the SWR's discomfort in having to consider these issues forced her into a more participative dialogue with clients which, although stressful, indirectly empowered them as fuller partners in the process of assisting their children. The act of making clear the existence of the record, giving energy to agreement upon meaning, and recording in clients' homes, are examples of ways in which the SWR surrendered professional power and became more exposed to the reality of the client's situation. This issue is further explored at the end of the next chapter, a chapter devoted to a more evaluative examination of the changed recording practice.

CHAPTER SEVEN

Description and Evaluation of the Experience of Open and Participative Recording Practice

Introduction

Findings in this chapter are discussed from a therapeutic perspective to facilitate some evaluation of the changed record keeping practice. The way in which the practice caused the SWR to feel stressed and vulnerable was addressed at the end of Chapter Six and emphasised aspects of client recording which the SWR had previously taken for granted. The account now asks whether open participatory recording made a difference to the service offered and considers parental response to participation, factors limiting or facilitating their involvement, and issues of power and ownership of information. Some benefits and difficulties are identified and implications for the clinic team and other agencies are explored.

Material in Chapter Four showed that clients felt excluded from the record keeping process: they would have liked information about records kept on their child and family, an opportunity to discuss the content, and to access the social worker's thinking which they assumed would be reflected in her reports. They had less interest in, or understanding of, the complex issues of policy, third party confidentiality, and identity or status of the social work record, which so concerned clinic social workers. Clients said they wanted to feel more involved in the process of care for their children. They were also needing overt signs of respect for themselves as parents, capable adults and citizens. Seeking help for their child usually meant help for themselves as parents, a painful process which in itself tended to further reduce low levels of self esteem. In nuclear families, especially a lone parent and one child, capacity to parent becomes all too easily the prime measure of self worth. As the material illustrated, attending the clinic involved examination by unknown professionals whose unseen writings remained an undefined but permanent threat.

Chapter Two outlined the development of client access to records and the ways in which social services departments and other agencies responded to the legislation requiring files to be 'open' to their subjects. In many ways the term 'open' records is unfortunate as it implies a loss of confidentiality – much reassurance has been needed that 'openness' relates only to subjects. However 'openness', with its attendant bureaucracy, does not meet all the needs and wishes of clients. Their wish was to be part of the process, to discuss the language used to compile records, to have access to social workers' views about themselves; in short, to preserve some sense of equality in their interaction with clinic personnel. For these reasons social work recording practice was changed to offer participation as well as openness.

Parents' responses when invited to participate in compiling case records

However thoughtfully, sensitively and carefully the SWR introduced the idea of time being given to joint compilation of a record, client reaction was not usually one of interested enthusiasm, although there were exceptions. In general, clients did not accord priority to case recording and required considerable encouragement to focus time and attention on this issue. Parents seemed surprised that the SWR required their involvement in an activity they had hitherto expected to be her responsibility.

Nevertheless, as they had a general expectation of there being a price to pay for help received (fares, loss of earnings, emotional stress, spoiled identity for example) they apparently took for granted that 'falling in' with a system of clinic routines was a non-negotiable requirement. The father of Steven H illustrates such trusting acquiescence when he said 'The record is quite OK...very true...but then you are the professional...we don't really know, do we? It's you that has to give the advice...we know you know best what has to be written'. In contrast, Lily J's father evidently considered the price too high when he refused to allow the clinic team to see his daughter, stating that he did not want such involvement 'on her record'.

Despite inevitable overlap it was possible to identify four types of response by clients when they were invited to participate in writing case notes.

1. Passive acceptance and lack of interest

Clients in this group typically responded with remarks like 'that's nice', 'please do' and 'that's fine'. There was subsequently considerable variation in how far they shared the SWR's perception of the nature of the task and to what extent they could be held to it. The father of Ronald P, difficult to hold in family interviews at the best of times, always evaded involvement in recording. Jim E's mother, construing the heading 'social worker's aims' most concretely, escaped the shared writing by asserting 'Well, you won't need me to do that bit, I'll go to the loo in the meantime'. Mrs B conditionally aligned herself with the SWR's recording system in the same way that she agreed to co-operate with any agency's processes, that is, unless and until they challenged her own construct of Daniel's behaviour. The belief system of the Jehovah's Witness family resulted in Mr G regarding the files of local government bureaucracy as of no account whatsoever. He dismissed the invitation to participate saying he did not care about 'other systems' unless they interfered with the values of Witnessing. The SWR could write whatever she liked, their life was not affected by such things.

2. Too overwhelmed to participate

In many of the sample cases parents were initially 'full up' with emotions aroused by their child's problem, the process of seeking help or their personal circumstances. To engage in any extra activity would have required resources they simply did not possess. In Bion's terms, they had no space in their minds (1965 p106). The young Godfrey family were in urgent need of housing, money and support with basic child care. They were unable to think clearly about anything at that time and a minimal interest in case notes can only be seen as highly appropriate considering their chaotic state of crisis. Agitated weeping (Mrs G), defences, fear and mental pain (Mrs B) and emotion (Mr and Mrs H) prevented these clients from taking in the implications and expectations connected with the SWR's invitation to become involved with compiling case notes. The mother of delinquent John seemed totally unconcerned about the content and confidentiality of the sensitive information she poured out. She felt overwhelmed, anxious as to her son's future and guilty about the intense anger she felt towards him. She had neither interest nor energy to give to record keeping.

3. Interest, enthusiasm and active participation

This sometimes developed suddenly after several contacts, apparently as a consequence of progress in the case and trust in the SWR. In a rare opportunity to sit with the mother of Carol G, side by side in her office, the SWR felt they were working together on the recording, drawing together the strands of their interaction in previous sessions so as to agree on how they should summarise. Mrs H participated so enthusiastically in detailing all the items of good progress that time ran out and the SWR had to make another visit to complete the work.

It is to be expected that clients would enjoy recording good progress: the writing serves as reinforcement for their hard work and celebration of desired outcomes. However, over-enthusiasm for the task at the outset seemed, to be one way in which parents managed extreme anxiety, assumed a position of 'fellow professional' or distanced themselves from painful emotional involvement. Some extracts from the research material will illustrate this important point.

The articulate mother of the 16-year-old lad whose suicide attempt led to referral found the recording very congenial. The SWR became aware that in concentrating upon recording family history the mother rarely mentioned her son and displayed no emotion or concern for him. Leon's parents were used to social workers and said their chief memories of adopting their first two children were of the paperwork. They always sat round the table with the SWR, the focus of the interview becoming the 'paperwork' as Mr B suggested bigger and better phrases to describe the situation in general and Leon's behaviour in particular. Both parents were exceptionally anxious people and their nervous concentration upon the recording seemed to be the way in which they attempted to 'manage' stressful involvement with the child guidance clinic. The ex-foster mother, whose own deprived son was out of her control, used every opportunity to present herself as a fellow professional and to discuss her boy as if he were a foster child. When asked if she would like to participate in the recording she replied 'Yes, of course' and set about it in a way made even more business-like by manipulating the SWR into agreeing to meet in *her* office. Her enthusiasm for recording was an opportunity to avoid the pain of becoming a client, unable to parent her son. A final example concerns the parents of the epileptic boy who supported the idea that the SWR record carefully the views of 'both sides' in their meeting with the school staff. The mother said 'Please do that – I feel angry if I go to see a professional person and they have forgotten all I said last time – I do resent giving information twice'. Nevertheless as the resulting record did not accord with their views, the validity of its contents was denied. In this case, openness of the record and parents' expressed wish to participate in its compilation could not reduce the intractability of the problem.

4. Initial concern about records

In one case, mentioned above, 'having a file' was felt to be so stigmatising that it prevented the child being seen directly. Two other clients in the sample raised the same concern with the SWR at an early stage which provided an easy way for her to broach the subject of their participation in recording the social work. The mother of the soiling Justin W seemed tense, agitated and angry and the SWR's first question exposed concern that records might stigmatise. The following process record of the conversation is reproduced here as illustration of clients' fear that clinic records stigmatise children as mad or bad.

SWR: Are you in agreement with Justin being seen at the clinic?

MOTHER: Yes, but I am worried about records…will it go on his record? I don't want him labelled.

SWR: Which records do you mean?

MOTHER: Will the school know what you write, do copies go…will it be on his record for *ever*?

SWR: What is worrying you really about it?

MOTHER: It's the psychiatrist bit. I don't want anyone to think he is mad…if it goes on his record that he has seen a psychiatrist…also I don't want the secondary school to know about his problem, he goes there in six months time. He will be called smelly.

Concern that the education system should not know about the referral was a common theme, also exemplified by Mrs T seeking reassurance that records of clinic contact would not 'follow' her son to his primary school.

Timing the recording task in the life of the case

During the first interview the SWR had to decide when to introduce the topic of recording and to do so according to the degree of client distress, nature of the problem and situational factors. There seemed to be no 'best time': whenever introduced in the first session, talking about recording practice added to the volume of information which the over-burdened client had to absorb from an unfamiliar worker. Ideally, clients' rights would have been best protected if information about records could have been given before they said anything at all (in the style of a police caution) but this was rarely feasible. Most clients seemed determined to plunge into an account of the problem and expressed resentment, non-verbally at least, if the SWR attempted to interject information about social work records. Several parents confessed that they had over-chastised their children or feared that they might injure them. Therapeutically, it clearly benefited parents to be able to articulate such fears of endangering their children. However, information given initially about what they said becoming a permanent record would have empowered clients to make an informed choice about what was 'safe' to say. Raising the topic of records after clients had incriminated themselves through pouring out sensitive material effectively removed their right to make a fully informed decision.

Hazards were also experienced in leaving the issue until the end of the first interview. Clients and SWR were more tired, interruptions increased and one or both parents often left unexpectedly to fetch children, deal with crises or catch buses, so that the topic of records had to be postponed until the next interview. The conflict for the SWR in attempting to combat such procrastination is discussed later, but was essentially the first dilemma over timing which she had to resolve in each of the 18 cases.

Deciding when it is professionally appropriate to share opinion or assessment involves balancing the often conflicting demands of honesty and openness with a responsibility not to damage the client or impair his relationship with the agency or worker. The importance of such timing to the sharing of assessment was recognised in the BASW/BIOSS (1986 p24) study but was viewed in terms of the 'social worker's wish to control when and how they shared information with the client'. The SWR detailed many examples of struggling to decide whether the client would be more damaged by 'honesty' in the form of unpalatable diagnoses or by paternalistic 'secrecy' withholding opinion until a relationship of trust had been established. In some cases, as for example Graham S, no amount of shared recording could influence parents' massive denial of their child's need for treatment either at the beginning, middle or end of their contact with the clinic – parents continued to refute the professional view that Graham was ill.

The stage reached in the development of a trusting relationship between client and SWR often determined how far the latter felt able to share her own thinking and written opinion. After seven months the SWR identified a 'turning point' in her relationship with Mrs B when she felt she could speak and write frankly about Daniel's difficulties. The research notes describe the development of a 'shared perspective':

> From this point on it seemed largely unnecessary to protect mother from the hurtful effects of the SWR's notes. Quite why this interview proved such a turning point is debatable...perhaps after seven months the mother felt she could trust the SWR to deal gently with the painful feelings from which she had been so strenuously trying to defend herself. Perhaps the unit placement of her son, bringing control and order after chaos, gave her confidence that the agency could, and would, offer good things to help her and her son. Perhaps she was beginning to stop blaming others and could appreciate the SWR's focus upon Daniel's needs. Certainly the SWR felt that a shared perspective was being developed.

Many factors appear to have influenced such turning points. In the Carol G case a combination of lack of distractions, helpful seating arrangements and a more trusting relationship enabled the SWR to involve Mrs G in recording the session. Improvement in the child's progress or a feeling of hopefulness may have made it appropriate for the SWR to share the writing of bad news previously withheld. The information about school phobia was appropriately given to Lily J's over anxious mother only at the point when the SWR judged that it would not be experienced as an added burden or source of fear.

The potential for written records to exacerbate low self image and reinforce anxiety was evident in the material and exemplified by the case of the 'suppressed' toddler Lawrence W whose referral by the GP was previously described. The SWR had shared own observations of some inconsistent handling and mother had been able to accept these in the context of a non-threatening home-based interview. The SWR felt that mother's own account of her difficulties with Lawrence was too important to omit from the record if the assessment was to be of value. She thus recorded the mother's words:

> I feel driven to make sure he gets every care and attention. Lawrence hits and bites me...I feel angry and disappointed that he doesn't respond to my efforts...he resists cuddles. I always need to see if he is alright. I couldn't wait to leave hospital and begin but then after two weeks my nipples cracked and he had to have a bottle.

The SWR judged that this mother's sense of inadequacy and 'not being good enough for the precious child' would only be reinforced by seeing the above comments recorded in black and white. She felt that her role was to help the mother perceive normal attention seeking behaviour as less persecutory and to convey a sense of hopefulness that mother *was* good enough and that she and Lawrence would find ways of getting along together. Such work with parents of low self image was common in the sample cases and sharing recorded material had to take into account their high levels of defensiveness and sensitivity to criticism which constantly resonated with deep fears of their children hating, punishing and intending to make them unhappy. Showing records of how well their child behaved in day care or school settings might be experienced as further proof that only 'others' could secure appropriate behaviour.

Gauging the effect of sharing painful information was a constant theme. The SWR often felt more time was needed to assess the parents' capacities, attitudes and motivation to help their child. A typical example arose for the SWR in writing down part of a school report on Roy G: 'He does sometimes smell...on occasion, the school is aware he is enuretic'. The father was wanting to hear that the boy did not smell, that is, he had washed properly. If told that his son smelt, might he not over-react and inappropriately punish this withdrawn nervous boy, or would it motivate him to allow the school nurse to help? A decision to share that recorded item required better assessment of father's 'readiness' to hear painful information without loss of his co-operation preventing the child receiving help.

Keeping a record and sharing it with the client has to dovetail into a network of other tasks expected of the clinic social worker. Appropriate 'pacing' of the sharing of information and assessment had to balance 'client readiness' against the SWR's need to use written assessments in negotiating work within the clinic and resources from outside agencies. Interestingly, the clinic social worker's job description carried a requirement to 'provide the consultant with a written assessment of the history and social circumstances of the child' and the SWR therefore felt obliged to convey to the consultant issues and ideas which she judged to be salient, whether or not they could be shared with the parents early on in the case.

The SWR used her judgement and experience to 'get the best out of the system' for her clients – a process which entailed writing resource requests before relationships with clients could tolerate differences of opinion. For example, in order to secure the scarce resource of play school fees to help Jim E, the SWR completed application forms with material which she felt it premature to explore with parents. Deciding when her relationship with clients was sufficiently trusting to absorb unpalatable opinion seemed less to do with concrete timing than with shared meaningful experiences which were 'review-able', 'account-able' in Garfinkel's terms. Jointly recording a review or summary contributed to the process of aggregating shared memories of 'how things were'. Mr and Mrs H participated in recording a review at three months which gave an opportunity to look together at how far in-patient treatment for Steven was addressing problems initially identified by the parents. So much had happened since referral and some 13 significant events were identified, thought about, discussed and listed by the SWR, parents and eldest daughter. The printed heading 'changes in people' prompted a useful discussion and mother's words 'The whole family is more relaxed, we can plan and get on with things…we can think straight again' were recorded verbatim.

The ability to make, share and record a joke appeared to be a reliable indicator of the point at which the SWR and clients felt able to acknowledge their common humanity – a shared recognition that the difficult time also had its funny side, to laugh together, to take the risk that the humour may be unappreciated or the joke misfire but nevertheless to attribute good intentions to each other. In the same case, the sentence 'Mother's fractured arm is mending but she cannot wrestle with Steven' was a jointly recorded joke, hugely appreciated by both mother and father. It referred to unhappier times when mother had broken her arm by hitting Steven while trying to assist father's vain attempt to prevent Steven absconding. This same father explicitly linked issues of timing and trust with his expectation of 'fair' recording. When the SWR asked him if he trusted her to write it fairly, Mr H said 'I do now, 'cos we know you…at first, no, I didn't want anything to do with your lot, you know that…now, you are like, more, one of the family, even the pony likes you!'

The stage reached in the life of the case was therefore shown to be a most important influence upon the clinic social worker's ability to involve clients in recording the work. Explaining the recording system, sharing contents of referral letters and giving opinion and assessment all required careful timing during the initial and middle stages of the work. Recording practice in the final phase of work on the sample cases was strongly influenced by particular issues surrounding closure summaries. Records of closure work were either planned and jointly recorded, recorded after a final ad hoc meeting with the client, or constituted a bureaucratic 'closing of the file' in a case which had drifted, moved away, failed to keep appointments or was 'cured'. Where a child's genuine recovery was the reason for closure, joint recording appeared to enhance the celebratory quality of the final session. With Mrs B the SWR used BASW/BIOSS closure forms to structure discussion, refer to the problems originally outlined by the mother and to celebrate Daniel's completion of secondary education. An extract from this closure summary read:

> *Aims achieved*: Now copes with bullying. Feels is not always blamed now. Temper tantrums have gone. Lazy? – a little. School attendance – has complied with the requirements.
>
> *Aims not achieved*: Smokes, still…so does mother! Overweight but is more conscious of his appearance.
>
> *Reason for closure*: Nothing further to do!

The SWR wanted to close the case on an optimistic, informal, 'jokey' note and she ignored items on the form which carried the risk of resurrecting mother's previously high level of defensiveness. She felt unable to invite Mrs B to sign the closure form – such a quasi-legal activity felt out of keeping with the relationship of mutual trust which had taken three years to build.

Where it was possible to record jointly, completing 'reason for closure' often prompted frank discussion about progress and the need for continuing intervention by clinic staff. It was not always appropriate to 'celebrate' closure. Some parents, as the mother of the encopretic Justin W, asserted that their child was cured when the SWR did not share their optimism. Others, for example, the parents of epileptic Graham S, felt that they were not being helped by the clinic and themselves requested that no further appointments be sent. In the cases of Lily and Molly, closure centred around lack of consent: in the latter case joint recording addressed the matter of closure with the mother. Further intervention was not being offered, the reasons were shared and recorded as follows:

> *Aims not achieved*: Father doesn't feel there is a problem…only that mother is too weak. He will not allow support to be given by the clinic. Mother feels it best to follow his wishes.
>
> *Reasons for closure*: Consent of father not obtained – mother feels involvement of clinic would not work if he resents it. SWR agrees.

Quite frequently the SWR wrote incident reports on final sessions which occurred in unplanned circumstances without the file and closure forms available for joint review and recording. Examples of such ad hoc discussions about closure took place in a bookshop (Steven), a supermarket (Lawrence), at a school open evening (Graham), in the house of another client (Justin), over the telephone (Dean) and in the road (John). Although the SWR and client agreed that closure would occur, these clients never had the opportunity to see the final entry on their file or to discuss the SWR's perception of why the case was to be closed. In general, records made of closure negotiated in chance meetings felt less satisfactory than the jointly recorded closure summary where progress could be measured by comparison with earlier recordings.

The third category of final record felt even less satisfactory, compiled as it was in reaction to an abrupt termination of the case by either client or consultant psychiatrist. Such unplanned closures were often the result of families precipitously leaving the area and effectively disappearing, as occurred with Mrs G and her daughter Carol, who departed as suddenly as they had arrived. In some cases contact with clients simply drifted, with clinic appointments unattended, letters unanswered and home visits by the SWR failing to establish the current position. In the case of Jim E, both work and recording drifted so that it was not clear from the file exactly how or when the case had been concluded. Other cases lacked a social work closure summary because the consultant summarily decided to close the case at the end of a clinic session. Roy G and 16-year-old Alex W were cases closed by the consultant in a peremptory fashion which effectively denied the SWR any opportunity to involve parents and children in recording a closing summary of contact with the social worker.

Conversation, language and text

As conversation between client and SWR greatly influenced the content of subsequent records, the application of conversation analysis and speech act theory was discussed in Chapter Six, where some case material was also introduced. However, it is necessary to illustrate specifically how use of the 'right words' was so fundamental to client participation.

The capacity of clients to converse easily and effectively varied widely, sometimes for physical reasons. Mrs W was partially deaf, the mother of Ronald P had paralysis of her face and vocal cords, and the homeless Mr and Mrs Godfrey were too distraught to discuss coherently. In contrast the intelligent, articulate mother of Jay T easily described and recorded the history of Jay's difficulties, using language which the SWR found easy to share. The defensive Mrs B was also intelligent and articulate. Her vocabulary in jointly compiled reports was sophisticated, rather than technical, referring for example to the 'feasibility' of Daniel joining the RAF; he was to be 'confronted' rather than 'faced' with his obesity being a bar to passing the medical.

The SWR deliberately chose words to lower anxiety levels or reduce hostility. For example, 'avoiding school' was used instead of 'school phobia' with both Steven H and Lily J. Unkind or pejorative remarks in reports given by schools and other agencies were frequently paraphrased by the SWR so that they could be part of an open record which informed the team, benefited the child and was shareable with parents. A school report obtained over the telephone asserting 'He is a foul-mouthed evil little pig, but we are winning with his reading' was committed to paper as 'Swears too much but his reading is coming on well'. The SWR had to consider what effect particular words or phrases might have upon defensive, ill or vulnerable parents – in some cases her assessment precluded the whole or part of reports being shared with parents. Such was the case with a school report on Carol G which, although mostly very positive, drew attention in the last line to 'her strong body aroma'. The SWR judged this to be unkind (if true) as the mother and daughter lived in one roomed temporary accommodation with poor washing and laundry facilities. She did not to share the last comment about 'body aroma'.

Having decided that items were not shareable with parents there was a strong tendency for the SWR to lapse into special language in recording reports which could be read and discussed by team colleagues. The following extract, from the social history compiled on Steven H, is a typical example of such a 'lapse': 'Opinion. Parents have colluded with Steven's promises to attend. Mother and Steven seem enmeshed emotionally…I suggest in patient admission to the adolescent unit is needed to assess and manage the separation and non-atten-dance'. The words 'enmeshed', 'colluded', 'manage the separation', were examples of special language normally used by team members. The SWR would have had to find ordinary equivalents if the report had been shared with parents.

Special language was not entirely the preserve of the professional SWR! The strict Jehovah's Witness father of Roy G subjected the SWR to Witness jargon from which she found it difficult to extract a clear picture, and which made her feel self-conscious and uneasy. Words like 'The Truth', 'Witnessing', 'Fellow-ship', 'Brothers and Sisters' had particular meanings for this father who made no attempt to describe his situation in 'ordinary' language. Mr G eventually made it clear that he did not recognise his own relatives who were not Witnesses, his real family being the Brotherhood. The SWR used inverted commas for many of these words which, with hindsight, conveyed something of her own scepticism about father's belief system.

Inverted commas gave particular significance to clients' own words. The SWR certainly felt uncomfortable about showing Roy's father the written report in which she had put commas round his special language. However, commas were not the only devices used to distinguish material which the SWR could not validate. The questionable use of caveats was highlighted by Mrs H when she denied the truth of the SWR's opinion 'mother attributed her own feelings to Steven' and vigorously objected to the SWR's recorded item 'mother alleged throughout the day that she and Steven were feeling sick'. Mother felt the 'alleged' implied that she was not being truthful and asserted that her view should be recorded without caveats which 'put meanings different to what she had intended'. The SWR then realised how frequently she prefaced recordings of clients' own words with, for example, 'parents told me that', 'mother is adamant that', 'father believes that'. All cast doubt upon the validity of what follows.

Accurate verbatim recording of clients' own words seemed particularly important when said in the context of confused family relationships, especially by children to parents. In the case of the soiling Justin W, the boy's own words to his mother were seen by the SWR as very important evidence of anxiety that his 'badness' did not cause mother to totally reject him. When the smell led her to discover hidden evidence of his soiling, Justin asked her 'Do you still love me?', and later, 'How can you love me when I do it like this?' and 'Would you love me more if I didn't do it?' Despite the emotional impact upon herself, Mrs W did agree to these significant remarks being recorded in the file.

The effect of physical circumstances upon client recording

The physical context of conversations often determined the extent to which it was practically possible for the SWR to involve clients in the recording task. Situational factors such as time, space, location, privacy, interruption and inconsistency shaped the SWR's experience of the changed recording practice, and tended to undermine her best efforts to establish shared, open recording as a routine component of each meeting with family members.

The SWR often failed to establish a consistent pattern of case recording and it was then necessary to adapt the method to the practicalities of each client contact. Such inconsistency was caused by a variety of case-specific factors, but the following extract from the research notes on Daniel B describes a particular difficulty:

> The interests of the boy and his mother were frequently in conflict. There were two clients being seen, usually separately but occasionally together, in a bewildering variety of situations sometimes involving other professionals or even other clients. No single system of open record keeping could be sustained against such a background of erratically spaced client contacts involving different people in different venues.

Unscheduled meetings with clients, including final ones, inevitably meant that files of past records were unavailable to show or discuss and that the SWR was not equipped with forms for 'on the spot' completion. In such situations she was reduced to searching her handbag for scraps of paper to note down important facts, changes, or areas of progress which would later justify decisions to continue or terminate her involvement. In the case of Justin W, Mrs W was unexpectedly present during an interview at the home of another client and after acknowledging their mutual embarrassment, the SW asked about Justin's progress and the reasons for unattended clinic appointments. With Mrs W's agreement the SWR wrote notes in the back of her diary about 'where things had got to'. A typed copy was later made from the diary page, constituting an account of the situation according only to the mother. Important areas of difficulty and doubt were not recorded, but then, they were not fully shared in conversation.

Such material illustrates the difficulty of compiling records within the session when clients from more than one case are being seen at the same time, either by accident or design. Much of the later work with Daniel B and his mother occurred during long car drives to and from a private boarding school, always accompanied by another disturbed boy and his stepmother. The SWR had equally well-established relationships with both families and viewed work done on the car journeys as essentially that of a small group in which mothers and boys shared their experience and problems of boarding school life. The presence of the 'other' family consistently prevented the SWR from using journey time to record important issues about Daniel and his family, and for geographical reasons she could not return the other family home first.

The research notes reveal enormous practical difficulties faced by the SWR in attempting to secure sufficient privacy and space in homes, schools, cars and cafes to enable shared recording to be undertaken and completed. Lack of appropriate seating was a frequent factor – parents regularly stationed the SWR in the 'best' chair and themselves some distance away, opposite, flanked by family members. Theoretically, side by side seating existed for work done in the SWR's car but in practice this was negated by adolescents demanding to sit in the front passenger seat for reasons of nausea, control of stereo or avoidance of family members consigned to the rear seats.

A high degree of effective participation in the recording process (point 10 and above on the scale of user involvement) required parents to be able to observe the SWR writing particular words agreed in discussion. Few home visits offered this facility as even the advantages of any favourable seating were often negated by interruptions, boisterous animals, visiting neighbours, small children or extended family dominating the session with their own concerns. Attempts to 'hold' parents to involvement in recording at the end of the home visit often collapsed in competition with television, ostensibly turned on to quieten children, or the noise and rumbustious behaviour of family pets, especially caged birds and big dogs. Young children frequently wished to write or draw on the record which the SWR was attempting to compile with their parents; the SWR's ability to concentrate upon negotiating the content of the record was considerably reduced by animals and toddlers climbing over her, tearing up the 'record in progress' and, in extremis, snatching her pen.

The impact of the needs and behaviour of the index child patient, his siblings and other children in the household often resulted in the SWR abbreviating or omitting the recording in order to focus on other interaction. Three examples will illustrate the low priority which she had to afford shared recording in the face of the behaviour and needs of these children. The session in her office with the Godfrey family proved chaotic with two very young, homeless parents shouting at each other and at their three pre-school children who whined, cried and demanded attention continuously. The middle child repeatedly bit the youngest one whose piercing screams punctuated the SWR's attempts to help the parents explain their situation and decide upon priorities. Neither SWR nor overwhelmed parents could have given attention to recording when other concerns were paramount. The Tarzan-like antics of Jim E have previously been described and graphically exemplify a situation in which it was impossible to envisage writing anything, with or without parental participation. At the point where future plans were to be written down, joint recording of a first assessment summary with the parents of the epileptic Graham S had to be abandoned due to Graham returning home unexpectedly. His mother became distraught and tearful as Graham's bizarre behaviour dominated the interview: swearing, hitting his head, talking non-stop, muttering and stuttering. The boy's exhibition of inappropriate behaviour eventually became too painful and the SWR suggested he leave them for a while. Graham refused to comply and his continued shouting made it impossible to carry on the interview, let alone compile case notes.

Securing sufficient time for recording within the session proved difficult. Time often ran out and the SWR had then to make another visit in order to complete the paperwork, as in history taking with Leon's parents. Parents themselves often limited the time available by having other appointments and, by being in and out of the interview accompanied by a shifting attendance of family members and relatives, prevented a coherent approach being taken to recording. In the two cases where mothers had secured involvement of the agency against the fathers' wishes, the SWR felt under pressure to complete the tasks before their return. This was especially so with Molly's mother whose fear that Mr C would return caused the SWR to rush the joint recording in an atmosphere of 'now or never'.

Lack of time compounded the difficulties which out of clinic locations imposed upon participative recording. Tiring and emotional car journeys to schools and adolescent units left the participants with little or no capacity to embark upon paperwork. Recording parental feelings about a child present in a moving car was clearly a delicate task and one which required the child's direct involvement. The practice adopted in the case of Ronald P provides one possible way of working in such circumstances where the SWR was able to talk but not write while driving. After a successful visit to the special boarding school it had seemed important to record mother's fear that Ronald was 'too bad' for the school to handle and after discussing this, the SWR handed her pocket tape recorder round the car for all to record their views. It was particularly useful to record Ronald's agreement to attend the school and interesting that the SWR' s recorded statement of praise for his good behaviour during the day provoked a uniquely positive response from his mother.

On the whole, the SWR did not record at the end of these long car journeys but attempted to involve clients in compiling a 'recap' of the occasion during their next meeting. However, the particularly arduous 12-hour day spent by the SWR in taking Steven H, his parents and their three-week-old twins to visit an independent boarding school 200 miles away was apparently never recorded, despite the valuable information and observations it afforded. The needs of the tiny babies dominated the day and the SWR concentrated upon driving and giving attention to the fearful Steven and the incredulous head-master. Overwhelming situational factors obliterated any possibility of record-ing within this 'session' and it would seem from the research notes that subsequent pressure of work resulted in no record being made for the clinic file.

Ownership of information, third parties and participation

The problem of defining 'the client' was discussed in an earlier chapter but the dilemma is central to consideration of the extent to which clients could participate in record keeping when third parties had to be accorded protection. In the sample cases, information provided by other professionals, by or about the 'other' parent, by or about other clients, siblings and relatives, or by members of the community, was given in confidence and not revealed to the child or his parent(s). Such third party information, if recorded, could not be shared, and this reduced the level of client participation.

Vigilance was needed to avoid 'giving away' information in the absence of specific permission to do so. In the course of day to day conversations with professionals the SWR found herself under a barrage of verbal requests for information about her work with the sample cases. Sometimes the cases were closed and it was impossible for the SWR to obtain clients' permission. Such discussions with other professionals were often of no direct benefit to the clients, being of a political or training nature and, if recorded at all, were not shared with the latter.

Correspondence and reports made of discussions, telephone calls and practical arrangements quite frequently referred to subjects of more than one case and needed thoughtful decisions about access, third parties and appropriate filing. In recording her encounter with Mrs W at the home of another client, the SWR later realised that she had included the names of both clients in each other's file. The cross-referencing between the two files did not respect the commitment to maintain a confidential record on either. Work done with the boarding placement of Daniel B became substantially entangled with that of another boy, Sam, in which arrangements for transport to the distant private boarding school, progress reviews and child guidance input were identical. The SWR sent a long letter to the education authority setting out the arguments for provision of private transport, which were based upon sensitive information and opinion about weaknesses in both boys and their home circumstances. The entire letter could not be shown to either family, although the half relating to their own case was fully discussed.

Verbal information and opinion flowed freely between SWR and child psychiatrist, and reference has previously been made to the way the SWR conveyed sensitive recommendations by coded messages. Parents appeared to give personal information to the SWR on the understanding that it would be 'passed' to the consultant before their first clinic appointment. They frequently alluded to these prior conversations during conjoint sessions by deflecting the psychiatrist's questions with remarks to the SWR such as 'I told you how upset I was, didn't I?' The research interviews with ex-clients in Chapter Four provided clear evidence that parents expected, and relied upon, the SWR to report competently and comprehensively on all the information they had given to her during the initial home visit. Generally the SWR's experience in the action research fully supported that finding but an interesting exception arose in the case of Steven H which illustrates the delicacy required in handling issues of confidentiality in multi-disciplinary settings.

Steven and his parents met with both SWR and psychiatrist in various constellations; separately, together, in the clinic, at home, parents alone, Steven alone, all the family. There was therefore much scope for choice as to who told what to whom, and parents chose to reveal two major secrets, one to the consultant and one to the SWR. Mrs H told the SWR that she was pregnant and had concealed this from everyone for some months, including other family members. Father told the consultant 'in confidence' that he had recently been in prison and that this was the reason why the family had moved house on his release. It emerged that while father was in prison Steven adopted the position of parental child, became over-involved with his mother's emotional life, assumed power at home and thus became unable to cope with the normal pressures of school life. Until very near the end of her pregnancy the mother never discussed her own condition with the consultant, and the couple never referred to father's sentence in the presence of the SWR. A state of partial truth pervaded the case, mutual trust developed only slowly and parents and professionals were both wary. It was never clear whether parents expected the information given to one member of the team to be shared with the other(s). In practice the SWR and consultant shared the items about imprisonment and pregnancy during their verbal discussions, but neither recorded the items selectively revealed to them.

Because the SWR was unable to identify a single client for each case file, she appeared to be caught up in the conflicting interests of family members whose lives, attributes and influence upon the consultant's index patient she was consistently committing to paper. It seems that the SWR regarded these 'others' as the 'real' subjects of her social work records and the invitation to participate in recording was extended in practice to the adult others who initially presented themselves as custodial parents. Only two cases in the sample involved index patients who were over 14 years of age at the time of referral (Alex W and John M). With neither boy did the SWR discuss the record she was making about them and their family, nor did she seek their views or agreement to notes about them being read by their parents. This was particularly significant in the case of Alex who was in fact over 16 years of age. The research notes illustrate the rapid decision making process requiring the SWR to decide what to record and to whom it could, or should, be shown.

> The task of recording a full social history was very congenial to Mrs W. Unfortunately she had no insight into the extent to which her own life-style had affected her son. Therefore the SWR felt unable to share her assessment of mother's contribution to the problem. The eldest son then burst into the room, disrupting the home based interview, and in a very infantile way, dominated his mother and was extremely offensive and threatening to the SWR when she refused his demand to 'get his brother dealt with' in the way he thought necessary. Mother smilingly accepted this appalling behaviour in her 20-year-old son and partly because of her attitude, and partly because this young man was not the subject of the file, his 'contribution' was not recorded in any form.

The breach of confidentiality in the SWR's clandestine approach to the school in this case has already been mentioned. However three other important issues arose in this piece of work: protection of third parties, the eldest son recognised as not the client; the extent to which assessment could be shared, taking into account mother's lack of insight; and the exclusion of a 16-year-old from participation in compiling a file labelled with his name.

Other material supports the need to weigh carefully the interests of index patient and his siblings when recording about the latter in the file of the former. One approach (as with the uncouth brother of Alex) is a decision not to record third party material relating to siblings but in practice this may prejudice appropriately informed decision making about the welfare, needs and treatment of the index patient. The case of Daniel B provided the SWR with a typical dilemma. Making an unplanned visit to the home, the SWR met Daniel's 15-year-old brother, Harold, who presented as enormously fat, depressed, over-attached to his mother whose handbag he carried perpetually and overtly jealous of the boarding school arrangements being offered to Daniel. The SWR felt that her recorded observations on Harold were important not only for the team's work with Daniel but also in preparing a strongly argued case for expensive boarding provision by painting a picture of the likely future for Daniel. In the SWR's opinion the clinic team were dealing with the less disturbed boy but neither the record nor this thinking was shared with the mother, Daniel or Harold, the third party.

Thinking about protecting third parties in shared recording brought to light conflicts of interests between parenting figures. Where parents were separated or divorced, information given by the main carer about the other was usually recorded by the SWR and accessed by the parent giving the information. Strictly, such unsubstantiated, often pejorative material, was given on the tacit understanding that it would be 'confidential', that is, not shown to anyone other than the donor parent and certainly not to the ex-spouse or child subject of the file. Thus descriptions of absent parents figured in the child's file – each parent being, technically a third party not only in relation to the subject of the file but also to material given by each about the other. If both parents lived together, were aware of and agreeable to referral of their child and could be seen together the SWR found little difficulty in reaching agreement as to what should be recorded about the parents, individually and as a couple. However it was not always easy to decide how far parents could be considered a 'couple'. The parents of Jim E were officially separated, mother having custody but with father living almost next door he saw the boy every day and joined the interviews when in the house. Justin W's parents had divorced after much acrimony following father's desertion to live with another woman. This relationship having broken down, he spent much of his time returning to the family home on the pretext of seeing Justin. It was difficult to establish how far Justin's parents functioned as a couple and who was actually taking responsibility for training and supervising the boy. Given that they were neither together nor apart it was hard to deal with third party issues in the records containing their criticisms of each other.

Cases where fathers refused to give consent to their daughters attending the child guidance clinic posed different problems. Mother and fathers have equal rights to give consent for the necessary help, but Mr C and Mr J disagreed with their wives over the need for referral. The SWR never met Lily J's father but as Mrs J stated that he did not agree with her asking for help the SWR decided to omit all reference to the father, took no detailed family history and recorded only her work with the mother. Nevertheless, the file was labelled with the child's name. The father of Molly C felt disgraced by the involvement of outsiders and welfare people. The mother had deliberately kept him in ignorance of her request for referral and concealed the resulting appointment for the SWR to visit them at home. When confronted he agreed to his dissension being recorded and to his wife receiving one further visit from the SWR but not to any direct involvement with his daughter. Again the file subject was the girl but the contents reflected the mother's painful emotional life as she struggled to cope with the stillbirth of twins, cultural isolation and guilt about her inability to feel close to Molly.

A concern not to prejudice work in the future influenced the SWR's handling of acute third party problems in the recording on Ronald P. Ronald's parents had lived together in an unstable and often violent cohabitation throughout his life. The mother constantly threatened to leave, made intermittent allegations to the SWR about father's unreasonable behaviour and inadequacy as a parent and always engineered interviews so that Mr P was excluded. The SWR felt it prudent not to record mother's complaints against the father for fear of jeopardising any future work with him during times of reconciliation when he might he expected to become more involved not only in the work but also in the recording.

Sometimes one parent contacted the SWR 'in confidence'. The mentally ill father of Graham S telephoned the SWR giving important messages but specifically requested that the long calls not be made known to his wife. The substance of the calls was recorded but put in the confidential section of the clinic file so that both Graham and his mother were denied access to it, thus protecting the father's interests as a third party. It was more usually mothers who sought the SWR's complicity in keeping distressing news a secret from the other parent. If the SWR complied with this it was then never possible to show reports relating to the secret incidents: confronting the mother with the disadvantages of recording secrets substantially reduced the manipulation and infantilising of fathers by mothers.

Notwithstanding high levels of confusion about the custodial parent's right of access to a file not labelled with their name, the research material illustrates conflicts of interest between parents and their (file subject) children. The SWR found it very difficult to weigh the several interests involved in order to decide whether to record sensitive material about a parent on the child's file and if so, whether to share all or part of it in the course of open participative recording. Although very little work was undertaken individually by the SWR with the 18 index patients of the sample, material provided by the case of Daniel B illustrates the difficulty in sharing the child's recorded perceptions with parents who may be unable to put his needs before their own.

Daniel was pleased to learn from the SWR that he had been offered a place at a boarding school and had found the introductory visit a positive experience. He told the SWR 'I cannot wait to get out of here'. This significant remark was recorded verbatim in the social work record. His frankness in wanting to get away from home was treated as a confidential communication between himself and the SWR: it would certainly have upset his over-protective mother and the record of it was not disclosed to her. In this case the needs of the boy (independence) and the mother (dependence and emotional support) were frequently in conflict and this caused substantial third party difficulties with sharing information and assessment between parent and child. Two weeks into the boarding placement, the SWR visited the school, spent time alone with Daniel and recorded the following perception of his progress on an incident sheet:

> I felt that Daniel viewed the boarding school as a necessary evil…he was making little effort to invest anything of himself in it. His bedroom area was quite bare and he had few clothes or possessions, telling me he chose to leave them all at home. This contrasted with other boys. Daniel complained about many aspects of his life at the school. I felt that his apparent compliance reported by the staff may be a strategy to avoid the structured activity at weekends by going home from Friday to Sunday. He seemed ignored by the other boys and his silly overtures did not result in acceptance. He told me he had not yet made a friend and 'didn't want to anyway' but denied being lonely.

Such a report conveys the unhappiness of an immature, obese boy trying to find his feet in the early weeks at a special boarding school without the over-protection of his mother. Daniel himself denied the problems and the SWR felt he would not therefore have benefited from seeing such opinion in writing. The record could not be shown to Mrs B as such a stark picture of her son's life might cause her to remove him to the comfort of home. If neither mother nor son could see this record one might ask why the SWR felt she should write it. In fact she felt more than usually responsible for reporting on Daniel's welfare in an independent private school as it seemed unlikely that the mother would be able to identify or protect her son's real interests. She therefore felt obliged to record Daniel's complaints, his isolation, lack of investment and constant desire to escape from the demands of group life, together with her own interpretation and opinion of the significance of these observations. Essentially then this part of the record served as a baseline against which Daniels's future progress could be measured: a therapeutic yardstick of use to the clinic team but not to be shared at that time with either file subject or his mother.

The SWR made very few contacts with the wider community on behalf of the 18 families in the sample, and consequently the records referred to few third parties who were not professionals or members of family networks. One exception was Mrs G's landlord who, unknown to her, made three separate allegations to social services that she left Carol alone in the flat. Each incident was investigated and Mrs G told the SWR about the complaints and, ironically, praised the landlord as someone who was most helpful and supportive to her. The allegations of neglect were of course very important and needed to be recorded to inform the clinic team. The SWR could not, though, let Mrs G see this item of recording as there was a need to protect the landlord, as a third party; the social services department who gave the SWR the information, as another third party; and lastly the mother herself whose sense of security would have been further eroded.

Less than half (48%) of the items recorded by the SWR were available for clients to read: complex factors influenced decisions not to record or not to share social work material

Throughout the action research the SWR noted details of all occasions on which she had felt unable to share the whole or parts of recorded material and where she had decided not to record the material in any form. Personal or covert notes were not made in the 18 sample cases so all items of social work recording under consideration were contained within the multi-disciplinary 'clinic' file. By using contact sheets alongside research notes of items unshared or unrecorded, it was possible to obtain empirical evidence of the extent to which records of social work were 'open' to clients.

A total of 232 items of social work took place. Of these, 36 were not recorded by the social worker, 15 were only available in part to the client and 69 were considered unshareable with their subject. Thus only 112 items were judged fully available to the client – slightly less than half. However not all items were of the same length or significance: they ranged from a three-page social history report to two lines about a telephone call, and included reports on discussions with other professionals, closing summaries and letters. In the sample cases some nine types of social work 'writing' were being aggregated by the SWR into the social work record and the items on contact sheets were therefore collected under these same headings. Table 7.1 summarises the findings which merit further explanation of their pattern and significance.

Eighty-eight (38%) of the items recorded on contact sheets were letters or reports written to or by the SWR. It is notable that of these, 42 (48%) were not shared with the clients they concerned, but it has to be recognised that 36 (41%) of such letters related to the process of notification between SWR and social services department that the subject had become, or ceased to be, a clinic client. As families were unaware of this contact, the letters could not be shown retrospectively.

**Table 7.1 The extent and type of social work records
shared with the sample of clinic clients**

Type of Social Work	Number of Items (n = 232)			
Being Recorded	Fully Shared	Not Shared	Partly Shared	Not Recorded
Letter/report by SWR	34 (58%)	1	23	1
Letter/report to SWR	9 (31%)	1	19	0
Telephone call by SWR	16 (76%)	1	3	1
Telephone call to SWR	14 (58%)	1	7	2
SW sessions with family	33 (72%)	9	2	2
SW sessions with child	1 (33%)	1	1	0
Clinic team session	4 (14%)	1	2	22
Discuss with professionals	1 (10%)	0	4	5
Clinical communication	0 (0%)	0	8	3

Forty-five of the contacts were telephone calls from and to the SWR. Records were open for clients to see in 30 of these calls, with material in 12 calls being considered unshareable. Work between SWR and family was recorded in 46 reports of which 33 (72%) were wholly available to clients and a further nine (20%) had parts which could be shared. This high percentage is interesting and suggests that reports of therapeutic work undertaken directly with clients are more easily shared than those concerning multi-disciplinary negotiating processes, of which only ten per cent were shared.

Thirty-six items noted on contact sheets were not otherwise recorded by the SWR. The SWR had chosen either not to record the item (14 occasions) or had allowed the consultant's clinic notes to reflect her own social work contribution to their joint sessions (22 occasions). Eleven items concerned communication between clinical personnel and, if recorded at all, were rendered inaccessible to the client. These last categories of record illustrate the difficulty in deciding whose work is being reflected by the writer. The psychiatrist's notes contained the social work contribution to their joint session but in this way buried part of the social work record within clinical writings. The SW's involvement in multi-disciplinary discussion and decision making resulted in her reporting upon matters which were not confined to the social work arena, as for example, discussion between child psychiatrist and clinical medical officer in securing early school entry and day care. The material of such discussion was not social work per se, yet her presence and contribution led the SWR to add a written account of it in the social work notes, largely to inform the process of her own decision making. Clients remained unaware that their social work records gave accounts of discussion of their needs and circumstances by professionals other than the SWR. In fact 50 of the 232 items on the contact sheets (22%) fell into this category, with the SWR feeling able fully to share only five.

It is important to examine in more detail the SWR's thinking behind her decisions not to share, or make, social work records in the sample cases.

Decisions not to share an item placed in the social work file

Some records conveyed a high level of 'unprofessional wrangling' and the SWR felt that clients' anxiety would be raised by such evidence of inter-disciplinary discord. In the case of Daniel B, records of angry ward meetings described in-house fighting for resources as adolescent unit staff and education officers 'traded' admissions to the unit for scarce boarding places. Similarly the SWR did not recount to parents her tense conversations with the headmaster of Steven H's public school over the matter of Steven's suspension for alleged pot smoking, the 'grass' concerned turning out to be lawn grass.

A desire to protect the client from further anxiety frequently underlay decisions not to share certain records. In the case of the epileptic boy and his ill parents the SWR judged that showing frank school reports of his disturbed behaviour would cause unmanageable levels of distress, for no therapeutic gain. In the case of Lily J the SWR did not share her thinking about the prevention of school phobia lest the already high levels of maternal anxiety be increased.

Sharing letters to and from other agencies was often considered inadvisable because the contents and opinion seemed likely to sabotage the relationship between SWR and client. This might be because parents denied the problem (Graham S), disagreed with the diagnosis (Steven H) or because of discrepancy between the problem as stated by the referrer and that written by the SWR (Carol G). In some instances the material 'belonged' to agencies who requested confidentiality as third parties, for example many doctors' letters and reports from schools. Information given by the social services department about Carol G fell into this category and thus could not be disclosed.

A fear of jeopardising the best interests of the child influenced many decisions not to share items of recorded material. This was frequently connected with the risk of increasing parental low self image by communicating strongly negative assessment before confidence in the SWR had developed to a point which allowed the possibility of resolution of the problem. A quotation from the research notes on Daniel B illustrates this point.

> Mother's capacity to participate was constantly being evaluated by the SWR whose main concern was always how to help the boy mature, attend school and accept control despite maternal over-protection. Material in almost half the recorded items was judged likely to prejudice this aim if in seeing or participating in its recording the mother became more

defensive and added the SWR to the list of people whose help and advice she rejected. Therefore all decisions concerning the sharing of opinion with mother were taken so as to minimise this risk to the best interests of Daniel.

Although most decisions not to share records focused upon relationships, three other specific situations were identified by the research. It is surprising that shortage of time was rarely the reason for not sharing records but time was short when Mrs B arrived late for a session to plan for Daniel's review and the SWR felt unable to give the time to shared recording. Tension between the need to write opinion to secure resources and the SWR's feeling that it was premature to share her thinking also resulted in records not being shared with parents (as, for example, the application for Jim E's play school fees). The filing of press cuttings is interesting evidence of scrutiny and surveillance of personal lives. A cutting from the local newspaper 'recorded' the birth of twins to the parents of Steven H and was filed in the social work case notes without comment, constituting the only record of a very significant event. The SWR did not inform the family that this cutting was included in the file and their reaction remains unknown. The SWR clearly felt uncomfortable about the practice of including press cuttings in personal files and, being unable to predict parental feelings on the matter, decided not to 'rock the boat'.

Decisions not to record certain items of material

The thinking in such decisions appeared to fall roughly into seven categories and can best be described by reference to the material in which it arises.

1. Discussions with other professionals on closed cases were not recorded in detail but were referred to on the contact sheet, as for example when abuse to Carol G was being investigated by another local authority.

2. In several cases material arose outside the boundary of 'professional work' which the SWR decided not to record in any form. One example concerned discussions with referring health visitors in which the SWR fed back her assessment and resulting change in some detail (the cases of Molly and Lily). The purpose was professional development of the health visitors rather than direct benefit to the subjects of the files and the discussions were not recorded. In another example, considerable time was spent by the SWR in helping the mother of Lawrence W with her anger and distrust when she failed to obtain the job of secretary to the clinic of which she had recently become a client. The SWR decided not to record this material considering the matter lay within an area of Mrs

W's life which had overlapped professional involvement only by chance. In a somewhat similar coincidence Mrs B eventually revealed that the clinic secretary was in fact her sister and again the SWR did not record the extent to which this secretary/sister counselled and comforted Mrs B before and after sessions in her office. The SWR decided such events were 'outside' of her work (even though they occurred in her clinic!) and turning a blind eye, made no reports of them.

3. In several cases the SWR judged that 'clandestine negotiation' was the most effective way to secure the best 'deal' for her clients but considered they would not be helped by sight of material which recorded such communications. Equally, records made of such delicate 'wheeling and dealing' attract a high level of responsibility to protect multiple third parties and thus can be more trouble than they are worth. For such reasons the SWR decided not to record the transactions between two headmasters, both manipulated by Mrs B into admitting her delinquent son on the basis of inaccurate information. A less experienced worker might have recorded such involvement but would then have had to protect the interests of two head teachers and an education welfare officer as third parties in an open records system. The tense negotiations between clinic, parents, school staff and Graham S himself could not be recorded in detail: they would have reflected no credit upon the headmaster as he attempted to manipulate the SWR into 'getting Graham away'. As has been noted before, the clinic/education boundary provides particularly difficult issues concerning recorded information.

4. Feelings of unsubstantiated concern and uncertainty are commonplace in social workers' thinking. It as therefore to be expected that the SWR should have carefully considered her recording of nebulous, yet potentially important, aspects of her thinking which often accompanied negotiations. Her decision to record neither her doubts about Steven's ability to fit into a middle class public school nor her hard work to 'sell' the boy to a sceptical, questioning headmaster was a typical example. The SWR wondered if this was a rare opportunity for a talented boy or an imposition of middle class values and social training which would further reduce Steven's sense of security. Being unable to decide, she discussed with the educational psychologist but made no record of her sales work, doubts or discussion.

5. To commit material to memory after initial sessions was a decision
    sometimes taken by the SWR when subsequent meetings would offer
    the possibility of compiling a history with the participation of
    parents. For example, the SWR's initial session with the H family
    was never recorded: the SWR 'kept it in her head' until she visited
    five days later to 'take the history'.

6. Some particularly sensitive material was never recorded if the client
    requested it remain unshared and the SWR was satisfied that by
    doing so there were no implications of a child protection nature. For
    example, Mrs H chose to tell only the SW that she was pregnant,
    having concealed this from everyone for some months. The SWR
    decided not to record this selective revelation.

7. Omitting her professional opinion from assessments was a decision
    taken where the level of trust between client and SWR was very low.
    Good illustrations are provided in the case of Justin W whose mother
    projected her own feelings of disgust about soiling onto the boy
    himself. After an emotional first interview the SWR recorded only
    information and opinion offered by Justin and his tearful mother. A
    final plan was stated and agreed: '(a) clinic appointment with child
    psychiatrist late pm 4/6 (b) school nurse to devise plan with bell and
    buzzer (c) no contact with school as mother does not want teachers
    to know that Justin is seeing a psychiatrist'. Such jointly recorded
    practical plans, in the tradition of contract practice (Hutten 1977,
    Mullender 1979, Corden and Preston-Shoot 1987) gave the mother
    reassurance over confidentiality, made explicit the voluntary nature of
    the contract and indicated in black and white that it was possible for
    her to re-negotiate the terms on which it was offered. The 'price' of
    such empowerment might be the loss of the SWR's opinion at the
    end of the initial assessment. (It could no doubt be argued that
    assessment without interpretation or opinion is not assessment at all
    – hence the use of the term 'social history' in child guidance clinics.)
    The SWR continued to omit her own view of the situation from the
    records of work with Justin and his mother. Summarising 'where
    they had got to' on meeting Mrs W in another client's house, the
    SWR decided not to record important areas of doubt, difficulty and
    dissent. Thus this record constitutes a view of the situation according
    to the mother – the SWR's thinking was not recorded as it had not
    been shared with the mother in conversation. The SWR felt Mrs W
    completely lacked insight into the idea of retention as a more serious
    stage of soiling than defecating into pants. Although the damaging
    effects of long-term retention had been explained many times to Mrs

W, she clung to her own construction of the problem, and feeling that a further explanation would be rejected, the SWR decided not to record her own 'professional' thinking.

Empowerment and enhanced therapy were positive outcomes for clients

Despite the SWR's experience of participative recording as personally demanding and professionally complex, the research material demonstrates that in some cases the changed practice brought benefits which enhanced therapeutic processes whilst simultaneously addressing inequalities of power, between worker and client. Mindful of the idea of words themselves (Entrago 1969) and the language of social work (Rojek, Peacock and Collins 1988) as hidden negative methods of social control it is not surprising that 'giving' clients the opportunity to share words with the therapist would be an empowering experience, improving self image and building trust. It is possible to identify some six benefits arising from the record keeping and to view them as an inter-related system in which empowerment and therapeutic gain continuously feed each other. The six benefits are best described under headings and illustrated with case material.

Negotiated words

The struggle to establish common ground through common vocabulary seemed to enhance the quality of communication between the SWR and her clients. Agreeing alternatives to 'encopresis' and the implications of 'bullying' and 'over-protection' are typical examples. The long discussions about what words to write on these matters clearly led to clients having a much greater understanding of the SWR's view of the situation. A frank discussion arose from the stated intention to offer 'on-going social work' as a 'resource' to Daniel's mother. Mrs B agreed that she would need support to set and enforce appropriate limits for Daniel. However she felt guilty having this need stated in writing as she 'ought to be able to manage her children'. This led to considering why she could not, as she said sadly, 'This day and age, why can't our generation cope when our parents could?' It seemed that Mrs B actually wanted social work support but felt ashamed to see it written down as a plan and this required increased frankness by the SWR about the nature of social 'work' – what exactly it was that the SWR was offering and why.

Particular words appeared to require such discussion that clients' understanding of their situation increased and they became able to consider different perspectives to their problems. This process seems akin to that of 'reframing', as used in structural family therapy (for example, Carpenter and Treacher 1984), and 'reformulation' in cognitive-analytic therapy where shaping the original accounts with written statements by the therapists to the patients 'guided them towards helpful forms of introspection' (Ryle 1991). It was surprising what flowed from the SWR's efforts to explain the word 'ambivalent' to the parents of Jim E when she wrote that 'Mother is ambivalent about disciplining in a clear and positive way'. Using the phrase 'blowing hot and cold' helpfully enlarged their understanding but also provoked an emotive argument between parents about each other's capacity to tolerate conflict without 'giving in'. Mrs E admitted that she had rejected similar ideas put to her at another clinic. The SWR acknowledged that the mother felt attacked by the observations she had made and written down. Mrs E wept and the pain attached to undergoing change was able to be described and weighed against possible benefit in taking the risk to do things differently.

Such examples illustrate not only the advantages of discussing the words to be used as they are written down, dynamically, as part of the ever-changing relationship of client and worker, but also indicate that negotiating words is in fact negotiating therapeutic work.

Structured recording addresses chaos

The BASW/BIOSS (1986) format proved helpful in providing a baseline recording for both SWR and client to measure how far their aims were being achieved. This extract from the research notes about an interview with the parents of Steven H shows recording acting as a container for powerful feelings:

> Steven's language and behaviour toward both parents were becoming progressively more offensive. The SWR therefore recorded her advice in some detail – what she felt Steven actually needed, and then challenged parents to say if they could provide that. Their 'no' was recorded, as was their statement that they really did need help from the clinic. Father accepted the SWR writing 'father feels unable to bear his own feelings about Steven's distress and he needs the SWR to help him make and keep to decisions'. The anxiety and vacillation of the parents made the SWR feel she was also being overwhelmed and could see no clear way forward which would meet the boy's needs. By insisting that her own advice about Steven's needs be recorded in an authoritative manner it became possible to 'fix' on the paper something of the parental indecisiveness and to agree the writing of their own need for support. The SWR felt the shared recording of the session had helpfully provided a structure to contain and process the paralysing level of anxiety.

The SWR was bombarded by Mrs C's feelings of grief, frustration, anger and sadness: the structure provided by joint recording effectively 'gathered things together' for her. Mrs C seemed relieved that her difficulties could be condensed and written down. This process of giving words to describe painful problems felt helpful: it seemed to bring them 'down to size' in a way which enabled the mother to feel hopeful about the possibility of managing to deal with them. The act of writing seemed to close the tense interview with the impression that something had been offered, promised, accepted – something which was made more concrete by writing.

Drawing the client into identifying content and process of the interview assisted not only towards internalising the reality of the boundary to the service offered but also with closure of that particular session. Hutten (1977 p35) recommends reviewing with clients the 'what, why and how' so as to establish a shared conceptual map or 'snap' of their situation which can be adjusted at each meeting. She stresses the importance of personal and institutional boundaries in containing the joint struggle to perceive themselves and the situation accurately. It seemed that participative recording using the BASW/BIOSS format provided a concrete container for such reality testing. Research notes made of recording Carol G helpfully illustrate this point:

> The structure imposed by the BASW form was helpful in writing a plan. The chaotic situation was making both mother and SWR feel overwhelmed and there seemed a real need to agree tasks before the SWR left. Thus the plan was formulated and written together.

Extending therapeutic parameters

Aspects of participative record keeping augmented the therapeutic intervention usually provided by the social worker at the child guidance clinic. Clients seemed to perceive the extra time as extra attention. Although the SWR did not always adhere to hourly appointments, clients were aware of the need to make, and keep, appointments and viewed the social worker's time as a valuable resource to be 'shared out'. The changed recording method resulted in more time being given to each client as interviews lengthened to accommodate the considerable negotiation about content and vocabulary. It seemed that the SWR had shifted her previously office-based recording time into longer interviews – causing the secretary to comment that the SWR was 'never in the office nowadays'. The mother of Justin W, a very deprived and needy woman said 'The extra time is alright...it's good to have time to talk'. It seemed that she welcomed attention being given to solving her boy's problems but the extra time needed to discuss reports was more valuable because it increased the availability of the SWR's attention for herself.

Joint recording of aims and action led to careful consideration of what might happen in the future and how individuals would then respond. This became, in effect, a rehearsing of difficult tasks: literally a script for future action arising from jointly recording difficult times ahead. Such scripts are commonly used in systemic family therapy.

Seeing painful aspects of one's life written down and reading them over with a social worker cannot be easy. In fact much of the work with parents of difficult children involves acceptance of unpalatable truths and the research indicated that joint recording was often an extra intervention which assisted parents towards a deeper and more concentrated consideration of their difficulties and the insights being offered by the SWR. Research notes on the work with the defensive Mrs B illustrate the way record keeping added to the therapeutic input and are worth quoting verbatim:

> Despite the difficulties, the jointly recorded conclusions at the end of the social history seemed to help the mother face some of the reality although she could not accept the full extent of her own part in Daniel's problems. She agreed she had been over-protective, in the past, and after much mutual searching for the right words, agreed to the SWR writing that 'Daniel expects her to sort out the world for him'.

The part played by pictures, models, charts and diaries cannot be underestimated as an aspect of record keeping which is central to therapy. The views of both social workers and clients have been obtained about children's drawings but it remains difficult to decide the status of such records: are they evidence? diagnostic tools? play materials? In many cases that which was compiled jointly with the SWR (or as part of a regular reviewable session) stands as the work done, but the doing was itself integral to the process of therapy. Steven H repeatedly produced examples of traditional clinic artwork in which the expression of fear and anger using paint and paper is considered therapeutic. Behaviour modification charts, especially with young children, constitute another dimension as a 'record' of therapy occurring at 'arms length', outside of the session. Children completing charts can be asked to draw smiling faces for success at the task: big smiles on boldly drawn faces give an indication of self confidence and high self esteem (Appendix 8).

Reduced secrecy

Sharing records appeared to reduce the phantasy (so often expressed in the research interviews with clients) that only negative opinion would be recorded, that unshared diagnoses and prognoses were withheld during conversation but written in the record. The feeling that secret professional insights lay in the records was prevalent and it was clear that conjoint compilation of the notes clarified what was in fact within the record and to some extent encouraged both client and worker to be more frank about what was 'knowable'.

The value of sharing observations of parenting skills seemed reinforced by joint recording of the points noticed, followed by the parent re-reading them. There were many times with the 18 cases when the SWR felt the relationship and level of her work was enhanced by this more thorough sharing of her opinion. The multiple instructions and inconsistencies of Mrs W and Mrs E in their handling of Lawrence and Jim were obvious examples.

Information given by one parent was sometimes recorded on the understanding that it would not be shared with other family members. Such recorded 'secrets' increase the volume of third party material and also decrease the 'openness' of the record as a working tool. However, in the case of Steven H, discussion of how and what to record actually secured better practice. Mrs H discussed her husband's distress with the SWR in some detail – it seemed that he had not been made aware of the SWR's visit, nor that his ineptitude in failing to 'capture' Steven was now known to her. Mrs H was confronted with the difficulty of recording such 'secrets' in case her husband read the file. She then agreed that the SWR needed to discuss with both parents and that it was not helpful for her to protect her husband from his own distress.

Work with the same case showed a way to deal with secrecy in referral letters. A joint meeting in which the referring education welfare officer and the whole family explained to the SWR their several understandings of the problem allowed notes to be made which recorded the different perspectives in parallel. Open discussion and open recording reduced secrecy, conferred equal value upon all contributions and left no secret letter of referral upon the file.

Transfer of control to clients

Participative recording appeared also to shift the assumption that professionals know best. In presenting the task in the mode of partnership clients were offered, and exercised, more control over the service they received. Greater involvement thus led to greater control and greater resource power. Case material illustrates such empowering when plans of action were discussed and written by client and worker together. Work is then located in areas of actual concern to the client, as shown by the research notes made when recording for Jim E:

> PLAN: CLIENT'S AIMS: The SWR suggested nothing and a long silence was broken when the mother said 'I've got to decide, haven't I...not you?' She then suggested using the word 'strategy' instead of 'plan' and dictated 'Sort out for herself a strategy for managing Jim in difficult places like cafes and shops as well as at home'. Given such evidence that the mother was actively engaged in the task of learning to control Jim, it felt helpful to write down what the SWR was offering to contribute to the process. The parallel lists of proposed actions then flowed easily in the form of a bargain or informal contract. The SWR felt the two lists communicated concrete intentions, which, unwritten, would have carried less conviction.

An important aspect of participative recording was the extent to which it allowed clients' priorities to emerge, be articulated, recognised and validated as a component of the written record. Studies of client opinion on the value of social work help (e.g. Mayer and Timms 1970, Sainsbury 1975) indicate frequent misunderstanding about the function of worker and agency. Involvement in recording provided an opportunity to check out expectations as to what needed to be done and who should do it. The SWR was often surprised by clients' priorities. Having given parents permission to decide the agenda, the SWR often found herself having to facilitate a lengthy list of aims which did not accord with her own priorities. This was so with Steven's mother. Steven had been recently admitted to the adolescent unit and there was much anxiety about arrangements for his first leave and the emotional issues surrounding his return to the unit. When discussing what to record as 'clients' aims' Mrs H amazed the SWR by stating that what she most wanted were exact details of Steven's weight and academic progress. This seemed a strange request in the circumstances and one which the SWR would never have thought to address. The SWR continued to wonder at its significance and felt obliged to go to considerable trouble to obtain the requested information.

In exposing factual errors in the notes, participative recording also exposed the fallibility of the SWR. Inaccuracies in case records are extremely prevalent. Giving client joint responsibility for the level of accuracy not only increases their control over the file contents but also avoids treatment programs being damaged by error. Such an example occurred when clinic attendance was jeopardised by a wrong address for Justin W being perpetuated in his file.

Positive reinforcement

Finally, the SWR considered that her jointly written reports often reinforced the positive actions, changes and capacities which were being discussed and described. Reflecting back positive assessment raised self confidence and improved self image as was demonstrated by showing the school's report to Joanie and her mother. The SWR emphasised the more positive comments, Joanie flushed and looked animated while her mother hugged her and said 'You see, you do really well, it says so here'. Similarly, positive effects arose from recording the good behaviour of Daniel B on his visit to the adolescent unit. The SWR felt that seeing this written down supported him and his mother in making and acting upon the difficult decision to agree to admission. Later in the same case it felt relaxed and easy for the SWR to record with the mother a very satisfactory state of affairs and to share pleasure in this improvement.

Identification of such progress seems to be reinforced and its value made more explicit by a concrete record of the client's achievements in taking control of difficulties. Shared recording supported parents' capacities to wrestle with painful changes, as the research notes on Daniel B illustrate:

> The statement 'Mother impressed me as seeking guidance on what would now really be in Daniel's best interests' was written overtly and confidently in an attempt to support this mother's limited capacity to deal with conflict and take action to regain control of her son. The act of writing this in the notes seemed to add something to the work being done to 'stiffen' her resolve that she could actually change things for the better.

Using writing to praise, reduce secrecy and chaos, to identify strengths, to give confidence, to take pleasure in progress and to encourage efforts to change or make difficult decisions appears to powerfully reinforce positive messages given in conversation. Most of the 18 clients indicated that they felt powerless, trapped and 'at the end of their tether'. Raising self esteem was an important aspect of the therapeutic process which simultaneously reduced this sense of powerlessness. Participative case recording appeared to be an effective vehicle for such sensitive communication.

Conclusion

Some discussion of the findings

The research examined one routine task carried out by social workers in high status multi-disciplinary teams which were undergoing considerable organisational change. The findings expose 'taken for granted' thinking about record keeping: what it is, what it means, what it is for and what it does. Such challenge to assumptions about its ordinariness is in the tradition of Garfinkel's experiments in which students forced members of the public to respond to unusual situations and answer questions about 'ordinary' things in such a way as to disclose the underlying assumptions (Garfinkel 1967 pp42–44). Clinic social workers, other professionals and clients take for granted that case records are about writing, written by the social worker, the property of the social worker or her agency, an adjunct to 'real' work, and comprise a boring task holding little of interest for professionals to be concerned with. Social workers and clients initially responded with astonishment, irritation and even amusement when asked to spend time discussing recording. The accepted belief that record keeping was an insignificant boring chore was challenged by varying its definition and forcing clients and workers to consider the meaning it held for them personally. Stripping away views which were taken for granted unleashed intense reactions about communication, information and the role of social work records in client/professional/agency networks.

Records actually occupied a 'hot seat' in the power relations between social workers, their managers and consultants, and functioned not only as an index of power but also as a bearer of meanings, codes, resources and emotions. This is a very important finding. Taken for granted recording practice provides a way to understand the negotiated activities and relationships which comprise a complex clinic system largely closed to non-members.

Challenging the status quo was painful. Experienced social workers wept as they recounted their fear of managerial dictates with which, in their specialised settings, they could not comply. Clients were anxious about the contents of records which they had never had the courage to ask to read. The social worker-researcher herself felt de-skilled as she tried to establish a practice routine which empowered clients to participate meaningfully in compiling records. Asking 'What is a record?' widened the field to encompass children's drawings, charts and diaries, and exposed a range of issues about ownership and purpose. Other items of clinical practice (genograms on wall boards, attendance registers, messages from secretaries) conveyed 'accounts' and 'monitored' in ways of which neither social workers nor researcher had previously been aware.

It is interesting to consider why the clinic social workers initially felt recording to be 'boring', and why clients said they would have 'nothing to say about it'. Perhaps 'boring' actually masks feelings of discomfort and fear which neither social workers nor clients had ever had a safe opportunity to explore. Certainly their perceptions of accounts, and the process of accounting, reflects important conflicts and negotiated practice surrounding social work to child-clients of a multi-disciplinary team.

The material exposes a network of power relations in which social work activity (including recording) is suspended. As an agent of the local authority the clinic social worker was herself subject to the 'discipline' of local government. She was required to keep and produce for her manager records and statistics about her work, and her duty to protect children from physical, sexual, neglectful and emotional abuse was paramount. Her records dealt almost entirely with parents' histories and abilities in parenting the referred child-file-subjects, and in that respect, provided detailed surveillance about 'how they were getting on'. Such 'policing of families' (Donzelot 1979) was feared by clients; properly recorded evidence was acknowledged by social workers to be part of their role in promoting the interests of their child-clients.

Such 'supervisors, perpetually supervised' (Foucault 1975 p176) were also functioning as therapists in the child psychiatry team. This encouraged clients to view the clinic social worker as 'other' than the local authority social services department and many clients were completely confused about her professional identity. As part of what she had to offer therapeutically the social worker-researcher considered how she could best share records with parents so as to benefit the child. The action research demonstrated that changing to a participatory method of case recording brings both benefits and difficulties. Sharing records and assisting clients to think about what should be recorded provides a therapeutic space where ideas, language and meaning can be exchanged, shared and fixed as text, a process which enhances trust and self esteem. Yet this space (opportunity) can only be provided to adults if it does not adversely affect the welfare of the child(ren); part of the social worker's therapeutic responsibility is to identify information which is 'damaging' to clients and to devise ways of making it bland or inaccessible. As with the generality of practice in social work, shared recording involves a delicate balancing of care (therapy) with control (supervision of parenting), a balance frequently tipped by situational factors surrounding the recording.

However, the social worker-therapists were often constrained by the expectations of their own social services departments which required details of clients worked with, copies of reports for supervision, and data for computerisation. Such active management of the social workers' work was usually unacceptable to the psychiatric consultants who feared their patients might not attend a clinic where their colleagues were so strongly identified as agents of the local authority. Thus clinic social workers were caught in the conflict between social services managers and the medical consultants. The demands of the Access to Personal Files Act (HMSO 1987) were not appreciated by consultants already alarmed over the separation of psychiatric and social work records, a separation which mirrored the division of their work into 'clinic cases' and 'social cases'. This appeared to lessen the control which high status clinicians wished to exercise over clinic social workers: in some clinics where issues of open records and computerisation could not be resolved, social workers were withdrawn and redeployed. Social services managers found records of structural family therapy uninformative and frustrating, and displayed no interest in records which were not reports – pictures, charts, models and genograms were generally felt to be 'clinical' material stored in the clinic.

It is difficult to be sure how far the sharing of recording was integral to the therapeutic process. Part of the difficulty is that the social worker-researcher only compiled accounts of the record keeping itself. There are no separate *research* notes of therapy. Communication between social worker-researcher and client must have involved unconscious as well as conscious messages, but, in retrospect, little material revealed such unconscious processes. The social worker-researcher's state of mind was documented in practical and descriptive terms (tired, overwhelmed, guilty, embarrassed, unsure etc.) but the accounts say little about the effect of her own internal processes upon the interpretations which she made of clients' behaviour, communication and affective state. She is shown processing information so as to make it 'tolerable' and managing interpretation in ways usual in psychotherapy. The social worker-researcher carefully considered the timing of interpretations. Clients failed to 'hear' unpalatable interpretation; both worried about distortion in their communication. It does seem likely that what could be said and not said, written and not written, must depend partly upon the states of mind of both client and worker, but a detailed examination of such unconscious factors is clearly beyond the scope of this book.

Reduced secrecy was identified as one benefit of participative recording. Client involvement in recording exposed the social worker's thinking, forced discussion of parental differences and avoided secrets being recorded and filed so as to be inaccessible to the subject. By allowing clients access to the recording process the power of the information was reduced. However it is also suggested (Rustin 1991 pp87–113) that psychotherapeutic practice depends upon a high level of confidentiality and care in the management of information. Rustin compares the attributes of psychoanalytic institutions with those of Simmel's 'secret society' and stresses that for psychotherapy, strict confidentiality, work in the oral mode and 'structural inequality' within the client/worker relationship are very important. In the child guidance setting clients knew that information given to the social worker would be shared with others and in that sense it was not 'secret' to their relationship. The recording method relied upon an understanding that the information was potentially damaging and both client and worker had to agree forms of words in order to record it in the least toxic manner. Where possible the social worker tried to record secrets arising in the session in ways which would preserve her therapeutic relationship with the client, but her responsibility to children and the wider public interest sometimes prevented this.

Implications of the research for social work with families

Whilst it is recognised that practice changes have occurred to child guidance clinics in which this research took place, the context for social work is increasingly multi-agency, multi-professional or multi-disciplinary. The findings are therefore also of interest to social work practitioners working with adults under the provisions of the NHS and Community Care Act 1990 (HMSO 1990) where traditional professional boundaries are being eroded within a contract culture. Communication between professionals concerned with child protection work and with identifying children in need has to be of a high order, and it is clear from enquiries into cases which have gone badly wrong that communication failures were largely to blame. Emotive accounts contained in this book emphasise the intricate negotiation which underpins oral and written communication between professionals, as well as between workers and clients.

Currently communication in child care social work seems to be subject to opposing influences. On the one hand social workers are specially trained to relate to children and to communicate in ways which will not 'lead the witness' so as to contaminate evidence needed by their police colleagues (*Memorandum of Good Practice on video-recorded interviews with child witnesses for Criminal Proceedings*, Home Office and Department of Health 1992). On the other hand they are equipped with procedures and check lists to regulate and support the communication which they have with parents and children. Their reporting arrangements are a similar mixture of blank sheets and prescribed formats. Whatever they write, their ability to communicate effectively with parents and children needs to be of the highest order, and there should be recognition of the difficulties inherent in this task. The material in this research makes clear the complexity and trickiness of conversations between social workers and their clients and stresses the extent to which the subsequent records are 'doing things' as well as 'meaning things'.

Professional work in this decade is governed by written procedures, consumerist models and the contract culture. The provision of, for example, counselling for an abused child, may become the subject of a series of written communications detailing many aspects of a contract in which human need has to be estimated, costed and serviced. Well meaning attempts to 'share' or 'work in partnership' with distressed people who may, or may not, have asked for help are frequently only partly successful, and serve (like the research) to emphasise the difficulties involved in true participation. The research therefore has implications for the goals of 'participation' and 'partnership' which underpin, for example, client attendance at case conferences, and complaints procedures.

Clients attend child protection case conferences but the discussion is frequently based upon written reports. It is as if no one would be able to 'trust' the oral report. A written report, even if given to the client to read beforehand, does, in a curious way, set the agenda, and chairs of case conferences seen powerless to prevent the social worker's written report dominating the proceedings. Clients reading or re-reading reports in the company of professionals are often at a disadvantage and not just because they may read more slowly or be unfamiliar with the language used. One social worker quoted the case of a woman apparently struggling to read a report who threw it despondently on the table and sobbed, 'I can't read it and cry at the same time'.

Complaints procedures entail written communication backwards and forwards to those involved in giving a service. A complaints officer, sometimes re-named the 'representations officer' or the 'customer liaison officer', is given only a spurious independence by being organisationally at one remove from the service givers yet has the task of deciding whether the client has a case to complain about. Clearly the client who can put the facts articulately, especially with the aid of a solicitor, is more likely to have their complaint upheld. The research interviews with clients contained vivid material about the way many people felt unable to communicate clearly on important matters. They worried about the effects of any misunderstandings, and considered it their responsibility to 'get it across' to the professionals. They expected not only to be judged but also to be misunderstood. These findings resonate with the work of Sennett and Cobb (1972) who conducted intensive interviews with 'ordinary' American workmen in order to uncover and define the emotionally hurtful forms of class difference in American society. Such 'hidden injuries' included the way workers felt uneasy in the company of the 'educated' interviewers, felt 'shamed' but also considered that professional people had the 'right' to judge them. The following quotation illustrates the force of this felt difference:

Rissarro talked to the interviewer in a peculiar way. He treated him as an emissary from a different way of life, as a representative of a higher, more educated class, before whom he spread a justification of his entire life...a class of people who could do what they wanted and make him feel inadequate. (Sennett and Cobb 1972 p24)

Case material presented in *Boring Records?* has implications for areas of social work practice which are trying to redress such inequalities, and suggests that relying upon written communication may aggravate the problem rather than be a successful attempt at simplifying communication.

Why do we put our trust in written communication? From the standpoint of records as texts it may be helpful for social workers to be aware of the 'turn' to text, information and language within the professions. It is as if the preoccupation with radical social work and its emphases upon organisational roles and oppositional discourses of class has left major questions unanswered. This shift to text (the linguistic turn) has perhaps arisen as a consequence of a 'pluralism' of points of view, trying one solution after another within a general loss of confidence in any one 'right' way. It does certainly seem to be the case that the welfare and educational professions are specialists in symbolic production and the transformation of human subjects through symbols and language. Social work records (including artwork and electronic writing on computers) might be thought to portray the communication which actually took place with clients. This research demonstrates the need for workers to be more aware of the complexity and loadedness of their communication with clients and to view more critically the written accounts of past and present contacts which comprise such vast child care files.

In the period around the launch of the Client Access to Personal Files Act local authorities widely adopted the BASW/BIOSS format for social services records, instructed social workers that 'open' recording was to be the 'norm' and devised systems for clients to apply to read their files. Such systems were 'low key', the leaflets advising clients of their rights being placed unobtrusively in reception areas. Some local authorities toyed with the idea of charging an administration fee to make the file available and provide a social worker to support the applicant's reading of his file. Little has been heard of the outcome of such arrangements but it seems that local authority social workers do not routinely share records with clients unless forced to do so by a formal application. The latter allows some 28 days for removal of items thought damaging to the client and third parties. Allowing clients to 'view their records' in such a context seems nonsense. This study suggests that access to recorded material is not a simple matter, and is not synonymous with participation, as clients have no part in the compilation of their files.

Clients interviewed in the research valued the opportunity to be effectively informed about record keeping practice and subsequently to decide the content of records in a way which ensures their own version of events is encapsulated. This increased level of participation is achieved by agencies such as insurance companies, police and solicitors whose versions of events are constructed with their clients who subsequently receive copies. Thus it would seem that agencies who provide a contracted service or whose function is social control find no difficulty in sharing written statements with their clients. The complex problems experienced by social services departments appear to reflect the confusion about what it is that social workers are actually doing – offering services, being agents of social control or acting as therapists.

Division of local authority social work into children and adult sections is resulting in different styles of record and filing systems. Files now kept on adults comprise a plethora of forms to assess, contract and review the services required. Files kept about children and families are also changing as fewer children are looked after for life, courts intervene at an early stage and a higher degree of multi-agency work occurs. The findings are therefore relevant to decisions about changes to recording practice within local authority social work teams, and stress the importance, not of complex *systems* for clients to access files, but of increasing their knowledge and understanding of the purpose and content of records.

The findings from interviews with clinic social workers are surprising in that they attached so much importance to their record keeping practice. Records occupy a central role in negotiated systems within the clinic team, and between clinic professionals and outside others. This work, particularly case examples and practice descriptions, should indicate to multi-disciplinary teams that they ignore frank discussion about record keeping at their peril. Newly forming teams need to pay careful attention to the role records will play in their organisation, and to the initial involvement of team members' managers in such discussions. Decisions about ownership of material and the status of clients' work and family therapy notes need agreement by team members and their managers if they are not to become pawns in multi-agency power games.

The research questions whether sharing records with clients is actually helpful and how far it is compatible with the aims of a therapeutic relationship between worker and client. A focus upon the purpose of record keeping shows clearly that clients and social workers do not always share common thinking about the reasons for such large volumes of writing. It is surprising that so many clients feel records are to track hereditary conditions. Many views are incompatible and the research depicts clinic social workers spending one fifth of their time on a task misunderstood by clients, managers and colleagues alike. Therefore more sophisticated thinking is needed about the purposes of these records. It seems that the concept of 'open' records empowering clients is an over-simplification of very complex degrees of participation and that for clients, the talking is all important.

The intention of *Boring Records?* was to explore and present issues surrounding social work case recording in child guidance clinics and to do so largely by allowing the often conflicting opinions of ex-clients and professional workers to emerge by direct quotation from the research material. The action style research aimed to examine process rather than quantitatively to measure the success or failure of any particular recording method or format used with the eighteen cases. Nevertheless, it is possible to identify particular findings which emerge uncontradicted from the copious qualitative material and which not only inform our thinking about the value of open participative recording but also emphasise what has been learnt from changing the method of case recording:

- ° Clients preferred the social worker to take responsibility for writing.
- ° Parents' wish or ability to participate was very variable.
- ° Situational factors often prevented client recording.
- ° Less than half the items in the social work file were available to clients.
- ° Issues of confidentiality were crystallised by the difficulty in identifying one file subject.
- ° Rendering material sufficiently bland required constant assessment of clients' capacities and the balance of child/parent interests.
- ° Negotiating words to write enhanced communication.
- ° Jointly compiled records exposed the fallibility of the social worker, reduced secrecy and increased levels of client self esteem.
- ° Drawings, charts and diaries made by children are recorded accounts of the work of both child and therapist.

From these points and earlier discussion of the difficulties experienced by the social worker-researcher, it should be admitted that the gains to clients must be considerable if social workers are to be persuaded to invite clients to participate actively in case recording. This material should help social workers to become aware of the circumstances in which client recording is likely to be possible, successful and to meet the need not only of the individual client for greater investment in the help giving process, but also that of the agency for information, accountability and legal record. There continue to be calls for clear concise accurate records to be made of all client contacts and for these records to be 'open' to their subjects as laid down by the Access to Personal Files Act

(HMSO 1987). This study illustrates the need to be less concerned with the record and to pay more attention to the quality of the communication which it seeks to represent, and for social workers to become more aware of the complexity of their linguistically grounded enterprise.

Autonomous clinic professionals and their more bureaucratic 'contract culture' managers appear to be seriously divided in their approach to communication. Speech is valued by the professionals whose practice and supervision is suspended within the speech activities of their peer group. However, standardised written records are usually preferred by managers – hence the particular challenge posed to their control by specialised writings of family therapists.

'Opening a can of worms' was a phrase often used by those with whom the research material was discussed. There is indeed a sense that detailed examination of spoken and written communication in social work allows uncomfortable opinion to emerge and reveals conflicts previously unacknowledged. Personally, I prefer the metaphor 'peeling an onion' to describe the layers of complex thinking about speaking and writing which *Boring Records?* has been able to illustrate through the perceptions of clients and social workers. But there are many layers of the onion yet to be peeled and I hope that future work will aim to clarify the purpose of child care social work recording, study further the process by which clients' words are turned into workers' writings and, above all, develop a more substantive focus upon the complexity of communication in social work practice.

Schedule of Semi-Structured Interview with Clinic Social Workers

1. The social work recording task

(a) *How* do you keep social work records in your clinic? Other than written, video, tape, computer, charts? Records of groups, family therapy? How much time each week do you spend recording and writing?

(b) What is *required*? Have you been instructed, trained or given documents about recording practice? Are you free to decide yourself on the form and extent of records? What influences your decisions as to how and when to record? Who do you feel you are writing it for – the audience?

(c) Do you *discuss* records with the *client*? What do you tell them? In your experience, what views do clients have about records?

2. The purpose of recording – why keep bulky files?

(a) What do you consider the most important reason for recording social work practice in this clinic?

(b) Are there any other purposes?

(c) In the past many reasons have been given for recording; here is a list of purposes [see Appendix 4]. Please indicate how important each is to you.

(d) Should social work records never be made for any of these purposes?

(e) For whose benefit is the record – agency? client? worker?

(f) Practice teaching – what do you require of students with respect to recording?

3. Records and communication

(a) Should the record reflect the flavour of the interview?

(b) Do you feel your records accurately convey the communication which actually occurred? Are they true records? How do you attempt to achieve this?

(c) Are they distorted? Do you choose or avoid certain words or expressions? Do you use codified words or expressions for colleagues? Clients' own words? What about jargon? What material might you decide not to record and why?

(d) What are the cultural, intellectual, language issues?

(e) Do you record direct work with children? What are your thoughts about this material? What are your thoughts about social work records?

4. Power and social control

(a) What effect do you think the file of records has on your relationship with the client and on the client's feelings about the worker and the agency? To whom does the file belong?

(b)   Do parents think records stigmatise their child? Have they ever complained to you about that? What would you do if they did? Do clients expect a record?

(c)   Do you feel the standard of your work can be judged from your case records? Why/why not? How does your agency evaluate your work?

5. Confidentiality, open records and client participation

(a)   Is confidentiality of the record discussed with clients?

(b)   Have the Data Protection Act and open records systems affected your agency? In what ways do you envisage it changing your recording practice?

(c)   What arrangements would you make over third party information with respect to other agencies? Other family members? Parent/child/sibling?

(d)   What sort of material would you feel unable to let clients see if your social work records were all open? What would you decide to do with that material?

(e)   Have you ever involved a client in compiling his own record? Reports for special purposes such as court? Multi-disciplinary assessment? What were the positive and negative aspects of doing this?

APPENDIX 2

Number of Interviews According to Premises and Style

	Rural/Shire County	Urban/Metropolitan
Premises		
Education	11	4
Health centre	2	7
Hospital based	1	3
Main Orientation		
Psychodynamic/behaviourist	5	7
Family therapy	5	3
Adolescents/group	2	2
Diagnosis/crisis	1	1
Psychotherapy/art therapy	1	1

APPENDIX 3

Description of the Sample of Clinic Social Workers

Over one third of the sample (9 out of 28) were male and this probably represents a higher proportion of male practitioners than is usually found in social work teams dedicated to child and family work.

Nine out of twenty-eight had trained as psychiatric social workers (PSWs), one as a probation officer and some as child care officers, although the majority possessed the more generic training offered by the certificate of qualification in social work (CQSW). The sample had undertaken a high level of additional specialist training in psychotherapy, family therapy, play and art therapy, and counselling. One clinic social worker also practised as a qualified hypnotist.

Four of the sample held part time posts which enabled them to, variously: meet domestic commitments, practise privately as a counsellor, undertake family therapy training, hold two half-time posts one of which allowed autonomous practice using her psychotherapy skills.

The sample were in general very experienced in child guidance work. Twenty out of twenty-eight had more than five years in the setting and many, especially the PSWs had chosen the setting as the focus of their careers. Seven out of twenty-eight were senior social workers whose task often included staff supervision and team management of practitioners on different sites many miles away.

APPENDIX 4

The Importance of Purposes for which Social Workers Kept Records on Child Guidance Cases

Purpose	Number of sws rating importance as			
	Very	Fairly	Not	Inappropriate
Evaluation of agency's work	7	13	4	2
Evaluation of the worker	7	11	7	1
Continuity of casework	18	8	0	0
Financial control	0	5	9	12
Information	15	11	0	0
Legal record	15	6	5	0
Planning by agency	6	11	3	5
Research	3	12	5	6
Staff supervision	5	15	6	0
Practice teaching	8	12	3	3
Support worker's own practice	17	7	1	1
Self justification of worker	5	11	6	3

APPENDIX 5

Profile of Sample of Child Guidance Clinic Ex-Clients

Spread of sample

The sample of 20 children reflected experience of record keeping by seven social workers (two male, five female) working in five clinics with four consultants in child psychiatry (three male, one female). All seven social workers were professionally qualified, two were senior social workers, two had worked in child guidance for less than two years – the remaining three had lengthy experience ranging from 4 to 18 years. Cases had received help in the range of 6 to 36 months (mean 13.5).

Details of the child clients

Twelve were boys, age range 6–13 years (mean 9 years).

Eight were girls, age range 10–15 years (mean 13 years).

Problems as referred were considered typical for local clinics:

Behaviour – seven cases (temper, stealing, delinquency)

Anxiety – five cases (fears, enuresis, headaches, withdrawal, crying)

Education – four cases (including school phobia and leaning problems)

Other – four cases (soiling, anorexia, hyperactivity, hair pulling).

Details of the parents

Six of the 20 families had lone parents (three divorced, one separated, two where death of father was a factor in referral). Despite 14 being two parent families, in only three did both mother and father participate in the interviews.

The sample was 'balanced' for social class, parental occupation being used to assign families to working or middle class groups. Random selection of the first 18 cases produced a ratio of ten working class to eight middle class. Cases 19 and 20 were therefore sought using the alphabetical system but being allocated to the sample only if they fell into the middle class group.

APPENDIX 6

Interview Schedule – The Client's Perception

Contact

How long since child went? Who did you see? How much contact was there with clinic SW? What was the child's problem? How has child progressed? When was case closed? What sort of records did you think were kept by SW? Who could have seen these records? In your case who do you think did see them? How long do you think they are kept for, and where?

Purpose

Why do you think SW does keep this record? Are there any disadvantages ? Who do you think gains most from the record? Why? Who does it belong to?

Task and social control

When you first went to the clinic did the SW discuss her records with you? What did you feel about the idea of her making a record? Did it make any difference to what you said or did? Have you had any thoughts since about the SW keeping written notes?

Communication

Did you ever ask the SW not to write something? Can you remember what it was? Do you think there are things SWs should not write down about people who come to the CGC? How 'true' do you think the record would be? Was a lot left out? Were the details not accurate? Why would mistakes be made? How well did you and the SW understand each other? Did you speak 'the same language' when talking about your child? Did you ever misunderstand each other? Did the SW use words you didn't understand about your child's problem? Technical words? What was it that made it easy/difficult to understand each other?

Confidentiality and access

Did the SW talk about who could see the SW record? What did she say? Did you ever ask to see the record? Did you ever want to see the notes? Why/why not? Did your child ever ask about what the SW wrote about him? Did he do any drawings? Charts, diaries? What happened to them? Who do you think such things belong to?

Participation

Did the SW discuss with you what should be written? Or show it to you afterwards? What about the statement of special educational needs… Did your child have one? Did the SW invite you to write that with her? What would you feel about writing the case notes together? Do you think it's different, saying it or writing it down on paper? What makes it different?

Do you have any other ideas about child guidance?

APPENDIX 7

Example of Conventional Star Chart Record

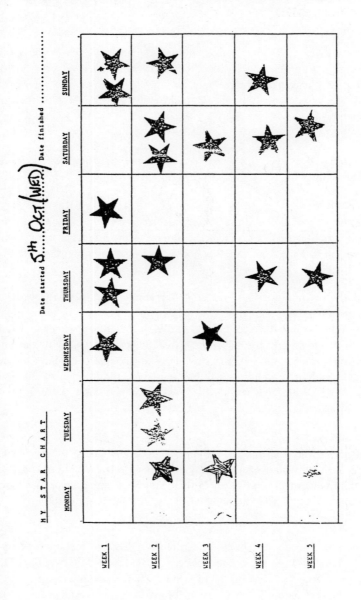

Example of Record of Progress by Young Child – Child Draws a Smiley Face for Success

APPENDIX 9

Scale of User Involvement in Social Work Recording

1. Client informed of his/her right to see all or part of the record under the provisions of the Access to Personal Files Act.

2. Client supplied with details of how he/she can actually do this, such as a leaflet.

3. Client informed of what has been written and social worker offers to show it if client wishes.

4. Explaining to client what social worker intends to write.

5. Explaining to client what will be written and offering to show it.

6. Explaining what will be written and showing it as part of the next session.

7. Discussing with the client what should be written.

8. Discussing what to write and offering to show it.

9. Discussing what should be written and sharing it during the next session.

10. Writing the file version in the client's presence – revealing the content as the notes are written.

11. Seeking client's agreement to each point being written in his/her presence.

12. Seeking client's opinion on what he/she feels should be recorded, and writing that verbatim in his/her presence.

13. Client writes a separate contribution to be placed alongside the social worker's recording.

14. The client's record, such as a diary, is the sole record of events for the file.

Access: levels 1– 14 Partnership: levels 4 – 14 Participation: levels 8 – 14

APPENDIX 10

Confidentiality and 'A Code of Ethics for Social Workers' British Association of Social Workers 1986

Members of the British Association of Social Workers are bound by the Code of Ethics and thus accept section XI of the Principles of Practice (p3):

> They will recognise that information clearly entrusted for one purpose should not be used for another purpose without sanction. They will respect the privacy of clients and others with whom they come into contact and confidential information gained in their relationships with them. They will divulge such information only with the consent of the client (or informant) except where there is clear evidence of serious danger to the client, worker, other persons or the community or in other circumstances judged exceptional on the basis of professional consideration and consultation.

References

Arnstein, S. (1969) 'The ladder of participation in the USA.' *Journal of the American Institute of Planners 1969,* cited by J. Kelsall and B. McCullough (1988) *Family Work in Residential Care* 94–95. Cheadle: Boys' and Girls' Welfare Society.

Badding, N. (1989) 'Client involvement in case recording.' *Social Casework: The Journal of Contemporary Social Work.* November 1989 539–540.

Baker, P. (1989) 'Talking the client's language.' *Social Work Today* March 1989, 24.

Barclay, P. (1982) *Social Workers: Their Role and Tasks.* London: National Institute for Social Work, Bedford Square Press.

Barrett, M. (1991) *The Politics of Truth: From Marx to Foucault.* Cambridge: Polity Press.

Barthes, R. (1967) *Elements of Semiology.* Trans. Larers and Smith. London: Jonathon Cape.

Becker, H. (1970) *Sociological Work: Methods and Substance.* Chicago: Aldine Publishing Company.

Bennathon, M. (1989) 'Inaugural address.' *Young Minds Newsletter 1.*

Bergmann, G. Quoted by R. Rorty (1967) In *The Linguistic Turn* 1–39. Chicago: University of Chicago Press.

Bernstein, B. (1959) 'A public language: some sociological implications of a linguistic form.' *British Journal of Sociology 10,* 311–326.

Bion, W. (1965) *Transformations.* London: Karnac.

Bion, W. (1967) *Second Thoughts.* London: Karnac.

Blom-Cooper, L. (1987) *A Child in Mind – Protection of Children in a Responsible Society: The report of the Commission of Inquiry into the Circumstances Surrounding the Death of Kimberley Carlile.* London Borough of Greenwich.

Blumer, H. (1969) *Symbolic Interactionism: Perspective and Method.* Englewood Cliffs, New Jersey: Prentice-Hall.

Braye, S., Corby, B. and Mills, C. (1988) 'Progress on file.' *Insight 22,* April 1988.

BASW (1972) *Confidentiality.* Birmingham: BASW Publications.

BASW (1980) *Clients are Fellow Citizens.* Birmingham: BASW Publications.

BASW (1983) *Effective and Ethical Recording.* Birmingham: BASW Publications.

BASW (1986) *A Code of Ethics for Social Workers.* Birmingham: BASW Publications.

BASW/BIOSS (1986) *Improving Social Work Records and Practice – Report of the BASW/BIOSS Action Research Project into Social Work Recording and Client Participation.* Birmingham: BASW Publications.

Bristol, M. (1936) *Handbook on Social Case Recording.* Chicago: University of Chicago Press.

Bulmer, M. (1982) *The Uses of Social Research: Social Investigations in Public Policy Making.* London: George Allen and Unwin.

Burgess, E. (1928) 'What social case records should contain to be useful for sociological interpretation.' *Social Forces 6,* 4, 524–532.

Burke, N. and Miller, E. (1929) 'Child mental hygiene – its history, methods and problems.' *British Journal of Medical Psychology 9,* 3, 218–242.

Burke, P. (1988) 'Consultation and the use of policy guidelines in case recording.' *Social Work Education 7,* 3.

Burns, T. (1992) *Erving Goffman.* London: Routledge.

Burrill, G. (1976) 'The problem orientated log in social casework.' *Social Work 21,* 1, 67–68.

Butler, B. (1962) 'Casework jargon.' *Case Conference 8,* 7.

Bywaters, P. (1981) 'A new look for records.' *Social Work Today 25,* 14–15.

Carpenter, J. and Treacher, A. (eds) (1984) *Using Family Therapy: A Guide for Practitioners in Different Professional Settings.* Oxford. Blackwell.

Case, C. and Dalley, T. (eds) (1990) *Working with Children in Art Therapy*. London: Routledge/Tavistock.

Cohen, P. (1989) 'Doctors' code on health files.' *Social Work Today 25.5.89*, 10.

Cohen, P. (1992) 'Rights to reply.' *Social Work Today 6.8.92*, 11.

Cohen, R. (1974) *Whose File is it Anyway?* London: National Council for Civil Liberties.

Corden, R. and Preston-Shoot, M. (1987) *Contracts in Social Work*. Aldershot: Gower.

Cornwall, N. (1990) 'On record and open to question.' *Social Work Today 18.1.90*, 28–29.

Coventry, J. (1971) 'A cold look at jargon.' *Social work Today 3.6.71*, 9–10.

Cox, B. (1985) *The Law of Special Educational Needs: A Guide to the Education Act 1981*. London: Croom Helm.

Cypher, J. (1984) Progress report 1984. In *Effective and Ethical Recording. Report of the BASW Case Recording Project Group*. Birmingham: BASW Publications.

Davies, M. (1981) *The Essential Social Worker*. London: Heinemann.

Davies, M. (1991) *The Sociology of Social Work*. London: Routledge.

De Man, P. (1979) *Allegories of Reading: Figural Language in Rousseau, Nietzsche, Rilke and Proust*. New Haven: Yale University Press.

DES/DHSS/Welsh Office (1974) 'Child guidance.' *Local Authority Circular 3/74*.

DHSS (1983) 'Disclosure of information.' *Local Authority Circular 83/14*.

DHSS (1985) *Social Work Decisions in Child Care: Recent Research Findings and their Implications*. London: HMSO.

DHSS (1988) *Working Together*. London: HMSO.

Department of Health (1988) 'Personal social services: confidentiality of personal information.' *Local Authority Circular 88/17*.

Derrida, J. (1977) *Of Grammatology*. Trans. Gayatri and Spivak. Baltimore: John Hopkins University Press.

Derrida, J. (1978) *Writing and Differance*. Trans. Alan Bass. London: Routledge Kegan Paul.

Devereux, G. (1967) *From Anxiety to Method in the Behavioural Sciences*. The Hague: Mouton.

Doel, M. (1989) 'The Norse approach to open records.' *Social Work Today 12.10.89*, 14–15.

Doel, M. and Lawson, B. (1986) 'Open records: the client's right to partnership.' *British Journal of Social Work 16*, 407–430.

Doel, M. and Lawson, B. (1989) 'A Paper Dialogue.' *Community Care 8.5.89*, 26–27

Dolan, P. (1989) 'Access to personal files: a practical guide to the Act.' *Social Work Today 30.3.89*, 22–23.

Dourado, P. (1991) 'Good cause for complaint.' *Community Care 13.6.91* 16–17.

Donzelot, J. (1979) *The Policing of Families*. London: Hutchinson.

Dubowski, J. (1990) 'Art versus language.' In C. Case and T. Dalley (eds) *Working with Children in Art Therapy*. London: Routledge/Tavistock.

Dworkin, R. (1972) 'Paternalism.' *The Monist 56*, 54–84.

Elliott, D. and Walton, R. (1978) 'Recording in the residential setting.' *Social Work Today 9*, 14–16.

Entrago, P. (1969) *Doctor and Patient*. London: Weidenfield and Nicholson.

Family Rights Group. (1990) *Using Written Agreements with Children and Families*. London: Family Rights Group.

Fielding, N. (1989) 'Laying our cards on the table.' *Community Care 4.5.89*.

Fisher, B. and Strauss, A. (1979) 'George Herbert Mead and the Chicago tradition of sociology.' *Symbolic Interaction 2*, 1, 9–26.

Flanagan, R. (1986) 'When a family shares your records.' *Social Work Today 20.1.86*, 13–14.

Foucault, M. (1975) *Discipline and Punish: The Birth of the Prison*. Translated by Alan Sheridan. London: Allen Lane.

Foucault, M. (1980) *Power/Knowledge*. Ed. C. Gibson. Brighton: Harvester.

Freed, A. (1978) 'Clients' rights and casework records.' *Social casework 59*, 8, 458–464.

Friel, J. (1995) *Children with Special Needs: Caught in the Acts*. London: Jessica Kingsley Publishers.

Frings, J., Kratovil, R. and Polemis, B. (1958) *An Assessment of Social Case Recording*. New York: Family Service Association of America.

Froggatt, A. and Shuttleworth, J. (1984) 'Opening up the files: opening up ourselves.' *Social Work Today 16*, 16, 16–17.

Garfinkel, H. (1967) *Studies in Ethnomethodology*. Englewood Cliffs, New Jersey: Prentice Hall.

Garfinkel, H. (1967) 'Good organisational reasons for bad clinic records.' In R. Turner (ed) *Ethnomethodology*. Harmondsworth: Penguin Books.

Giglioli, P. (ed) (1990) *Language and Social Context*. Harmondsworth: Penguin Books.

Glastonbury, B., Bradley, R. and Orme, J. (1987) *Managing People in the Personal Social Services*. Chichester: Wiley.

Goacher, B., Evans, J., Welton, J., Wedsell, K. and Glaser, A. (1986) *The 1981 Education Act: Policy and Provision for Special Educational Needs*. London: Institute of Education.

Goffman, E. (1961) *Encounters: Two Studies in the Sociology of Interaction*. New York: Bobbs-Merrill.

Goffman, E. (1963) *Behaviour in Public Places: Notes on the Social Organisation of Gatherings*. New York: Free Press.

Goffman, E. (1968) *Stigma*. Harmondsworth: Penguin.

Goffman, E. (1975) *Frame Analysis, An Essay on the Organisation of Experience*. Harmondsworth: Penguin.

Goldberg, E. (1970) *Helping the Aged*. London: Allen and Unwin.

Hamilton, G. (1946) *Principles of Social Case Recording*. New York: Columbia University Press.

Harre, R. and Secord, P. (1972) *The Explanation of Social Behaviour*. Oxford: Blackwell.

Harris, T. (1984) 'Open secrets.' *Community Care* 27.9.84.

Herbert, S. (1989) 'Regina v. Norfolk County Council, ex parte M.' *Law report, Guardian Newspaper* 28.2.89.

HMSO (1984) *The Data Protection Act*. London: HMSO.

HMSO (1987) *Access to Personal Files Act*. London: HMSO.

HMSO (1987) *The Cleveland Report*. London: HMSO.

HMSO (1989) *The Children Act*. London: HMSO.

HMSO (1990) *The NHS and Community Care Act*. London: HMSO.

HMSO (1992) *The Criminal Justice Act*. London: HMSO.

Heritage, J. (1984) *Garfinkel and Ethnomethodology*. Cambridge: Polity Press.

Hiller, E. (1933) *Principles of Sociology*. New York: Harper.

Hillyard, P. and Percy-Smith, J. (1988) *The Coercive State*. London: Pinter.

Home Office and Department of Health (1992) *Memorandum of Good Practice on Video-recorded interviews with Child Witnesses for Criminal Proceedings*. London: HMSO.

Horovitz, A. (1982) *Social Control of Madness*. New York: Academic Press.

Horton, M. and Robson, K. (1992) 'Open secrets – involving families in child protection case conferences.' *Social Work Today* 17.9.92, 24–25.

Howard, L. (1968) 'Social work recording in the medical notes.' *Medical Social Work 21*, 299–307.

Howe, D. (1989) *The Consumer's View of Family Therapy*. Aldershot: Gower.

Hughes, E. (1958) *Men and their Work*. Illinois: Free Press.

Hughes, E. (1962) 'What other?' In A. Rose *Human Behaviour and Social Processes*. London: Routledge and Kegan Paul.

Hurley, M. (1992) 'Punishment of the innocent.' *Social Work Today*, 28.8.92.

Hutten, J. (1977) *Short Term Contracts in Social Work*. London: Routledge and Kegan Paul.

James, P.D. (1984) *A Mind to Murder*. London: Faber and Faber.

Kadushin, A. (1976) *Supervision in Social Work*. New York: Columbia University Press.

Kahan, B. (1979) *Growing up in Care*. Oxford: Blackwell.

Kagle, J. (1990) *Social Work Records*. California: Wadsworth.

Kroll, B. (1994) *Chasing Rainbows: Children, Divorce and Loss*. Lyme Regis: Russell House Publishing.

Kogan, L. and Brown, B. (1954) 'A two year study of case record users.' *Social Casework 35*, 6, 252–257.

Lees, R. and Smith, G. (1975) *Action Research in Community Development*. London: Routledge and Kegan Paul.

Lennon, P. (1992) 'The guru and the gall.' *The Guardian 30.3.92.*

Leslie, A. (1989) 'A challenge to the system.' *Social Work Today* 9.2.89, 22–23.

Levi-Strauss, C. (1961) *The Writing Lesson; Tristes Topiques.* Trans. John Russell. London: Hutchinson.

Loveday, S. (1985) *Reflections on Care.* Bath: The Childrens Society.

Mann, P. (1984) *Children in Care Revisited.* London: Batsford.

Martens, W. and Holmstrup, E. (1974) 'Problem orientated recording.' *Social Casework 55,* 9, 554–561.

May, P. (1991) 'Caseload of key words.' *The Guardian 15.6.91.*

Mayer, J. and Timms, N. (1970) *The Client Speaks.* London: Routledge and Kegan Paul.

McKay, A., Goldberg, E. and Fruin, D. (1973) 'Consumers and a social service department.' *Social Work Today 4,* 16, 486–491.

Mittler, H., Wolstenholme, F., Greener, P., Gleisner, S., Clifford, D., Levinson, M. and Cohen, A. (1986) 'A report shared.' *Community Care,* 7.8.86, 21–22.

Mullender, A. (1979) 'Drawing up a more democratic contract.' *Social Work Today 11,* 11, 17–19.

Murray, N. (1984) 'A relationship of trust.' *Community Care* 22.11.84, 26–28.

Naidoo, S. (1972) 'Record keeping.' *Concern 10,* 26–28.

National Foster Care Association (1990) *Put it in Writing.* London: N.F.C.A.

Neville, D. and Beak, D. (1990) 'Solving the case history mystery.' *Social Work Today* 28.6.90, 15–17.

Norris, C. (1982) *Deconstruction; Theory and Practice.* London: Routledge.

Norris, C. (1987) *Derrida.* London: Fontana.

Ogden, J. (1992) 'Councillors win right to see ritual files.' *Social Work Today* 27.8.92.

Ovretveit, J. (1986) *Client Access and Social Work Recording.* Birmingham: BASW Publications.

Parry, A. (1985) 'Just good practice.' *Community Care* 24.10.85.

Parsloe, P. (1992) 'One and all.' *Social Work Today* 6.8.92 18–19.

Payne, M. and Petersen, A. (1985) 'Putting the record straight with clients.' *Social Work Today,* 22.4.85, 19–21.

Pinker, R. (1971) *Social Theory and Social Policy.* London: Heinemann.

Pithouse, A. (1987) *Social Work; The Social Organisation of an Invisible Trade.* Aldershot: Avebury.

Poster, M. (1990) *The Mode of Information; Post Structuralism and Social Context.* Cambridge: Polity Press and Blackwell.

Rapoport, R. (1987) *New Interventions for Children and Youth: Action Research Approaches.* Cambridge University Press.

Raymond, Y. (1989) 'Empowerment in practice. Clients views on seeing records: themes emerging from twelve interviews with clients.' *Practice 1,* 5–23.

Rees, S. (1973) 'Patronage and participation, problem and paradox: a case study in community work.' *British Journal of Social Work 3,* 3–18.

Rojek, C., Peacock, G. and Collins, S. (1988) *Social Work and Received Ideas.* London: Routledge.

Rorty, R. (ed) (1967) *The Linguistic Turn; Recent Essays in Philosophical Method.* Chicago and London: University of Chicago Press.

Roth, J. (1962) 'The treatment of tuberculosis as a bargaining process.' In A. Rose *Human Behaviour and Social Processes.* London: Routledge and Kegan Paul.

Rousseau, J. (1967) *Essay on the Origin of Languages.* Trans. J. Moran. New York: F. Ungar.

Rowe, J. (1990) *The Use of Written Agreements in Child Care Placements.* Barnado's Publications.

Rustin, M. (1991) *The Good Society and the Inner World.* London: Verso.

Ryle, A. (1991) *Cognitive Analytic Theory: Active Participation in Change.* Chichester: Wiley.

Sacks, H. (1974) 'On the analysibility of stories by children.' In R. Turner (ed) *Ethnomethodology.* Harmondsworth: Penguin.

Sainsbury, E. (1975) *Social Work with Families.* London: Routledge and Kegan Paul.

Sampson, O. (1980) *Child Guidance; Its History, Provenance and Future.* Manchester: British Psychological Society.

Satyamurti, C. (1981) *Occupational Survival.* Oxford: Blackwell.

Saussure, F. (1974, first published 1916) *Course in General Linguistics.* London: Fontana.

Schegloff, E. (1968) 'Sequencing in conversational openings.' *American Anthropologist 70*, (6), 1075–1095.

Schegloff, E. (1972) 'Notes on a conversational practice: formulating place.' In D.Sudnow (ed) *Studies in Social Interaction*. New York: Free Press.

Schleiermacher, F. (1977) *Hermeneutics: The Handwritten Manuscripts* (ed H. Kimmerle, Trans. J. Duke and J. Forstman). Atlanta: Scholars Press.

Seaberg, J. (1965) 'Case recording by code.' *Social Work 10*, 5, 92–98.

Searle, J. (1971) *The Philosophy of Language*. Oxford: Oxford University Press.

Seebohm, F. (Chairman) (1968) *Report of the Committee on Local Authority and Allied Personal Services*. London: HMSO.

Selden, R. (1991) 'Does literary studies need literary theory?' *Critical Survey 3*, 1, 96–103.

Sennett, R. and Cobb, J. (1972) *The Hidden Injuries of Class*. Cambridge: Cambridge University Press.

Sheffield, A. (1920) *The Social Case History – its Content and Construction*. New York: Russell Sage.

Shemmings, D. (1991) *Client Access to Records: Participation in Social Work*. Aldershot: Avebury.

Shemmings, D. and Thoburn, J. (1990) *Parental Participation in Child Protection Case Conferences*. Norwich: University of East Anglia.

Shepherd, J. (1991) 'Every day I write the book.' *Community Care* 20.6.91.

Schutz, A. (1976) *Collected Papers II: Studies in Social Theory*. The Hague: Nijhoff.

Smith, J. and Schumm, S. (1992) 'Dare to believe.' *Social Work Today* 1.10.92, 29.

Stein, M. and Carey, K. (1986) *Leaving Care*. Oxford: Blackwell.

Stein, T., Gambrill, E. and Wiltse, K. (1978) *Children in Foster Homes: Achieving Continuity of Care*. New York: Praegar Publications.

Stockbridge, M. (1968) 'Social case recording.' *Case Conference 1968*, 15, 307–311.

Strauss, A., Schatzman, L., Erlich, D., Bucher, R. and Sabshin, M. (1963) 'The hospital and its negotiated order.' In E. Friedson (ed) *The Hospital in Modern Society*. New York: Macmillan.

Strauss, A. (1978) *Negotiations. Varieties, Contexts, Processes and Social Order*. California and London: Jossey Bass.

Susman, G. and Evered, R. (1978) 'An assessment of the scientific merits of action research.' *Administrative Science Quarterly 23*, 582–603.

Swift, L. (1928) 'Can the sociologist and social worker agree on the content of case records?' *Social Forces 6*, 4, 535–538.

Thoburn, J. (1988) 'Implementation of a shared recording policy – an example of co-operation between social work educators, managers and practitioners.' *Issues in Social Work Education 8*, 136–148.

Thomas, W. (1928) *The Child in America*. New York: A. Knopf.

Thomas, W. (1966) *On Social Organisation and Social Personality. Selected Papers*. Ed. M. Janowitz. Chicago: University of Chicago Press.

Timms, N. (1968) *Language of Social Casework*. London: Routledge and Kegan Paul.

Timms, N. (1972) *Recording in Social Work*. Boston: Routledge and Kegan Paul.

Timms, N. (1973) *The Receiving End*. London: Routledge and Kegan Paul.

Turner, R. (ed) (1974) *Ethnomethodology*. Harmondsworth: Penguin.

Underwood, J. (Chairman) (1955) *Ministry of Education Report of the Committee on Maladjusted Children*. London: HMSO.

Walczak, Y. and Burns, S. (1984) *Divorce: The Child's Point of View*. London: Harper and Row.

Warnock, M. (Chairman) (1978) *Special Educational Needs: Report of the Committee of Enquiry into the Education of Handicapped Children and Young People*. London: HMSO.

Weed, L. (1968) 'Medical records that guide and teach.' *New England Journal of Medicine 278*, 593–600.

Whitaker, D. and Archer, L. (1989) 'Engaging practitioners in formulating research purposes.' *Social Work Education 8*, 2, 29–37.

Wilczynski, B. (1981) 'New life for recording: involving the client.' *Social Work 26*, 4, 313–317.

Subject Index

References in italic indicate tables or figures.

Author
Index